GENESIS

AN INTRODUCTION AND COMMENTARY

by

THE REV. DEREK KIDNER, M.A., A.R.C.M.

formerly Warden of Tyndale House, Cambridge

INTER-VARSITY PRESS
LEICESTER, ENGLAND
DOWNERS GROVE, ILLINOIS, U.S.A.

Genesis
Inter-Varsity Press
38 De Montfort Street, Leicester LE1 7GP, England
P.O. Box 1400, Downers Grove, Illinois 60515 U.S.A.

© *The Tyndale Press 1967*

Inter-Varsity Press, England, is the publishing division of the Universities and Colleges Christian Fellowship (formerly the Inter-Varsity Fellowship), a student movement linking Christian Unions in universities and colleges throughout the United Kingdom and the Republic of Ireland, and a member movement of the International Fellowship of Evangelical Students. For information about local and national activities in Great Britain write to UCCF, 38 De Montfort Street, Leicester LE1 7GP.

InterVarsity Press®, U.S.A., is the book-publishing division of InterVarsity Christian Fellowship®, a student movement active on campus at hundreds of universities, colleges and schools of nursing in the United States of America, and a member movement of the International Fellowship of Evangelical Students. For information about local and regional activities, write Public Relations Dept., InterVarsity Christian Fellowship, 6400 Schroeder Rd., P.O. Box 7895, Madison, WI 53707-7895.

Text set in Great Britain
Printed in the United States of America

UK ISBN 0-85111-823-2 (paperback)
Library of Congress Catalog Card Number: 75-23851
USA ISBN 0-87784-881-5 (hardback)
USA ISBN 0-87784-251-5 (paperback)
USA ISBN 0-87784-880-7 (set of Tyndale Old Testament Commentaries, hardback)
USA ISBN 0-87784-280-9 (set of Tyndale Old Testament Commentaries, paperback)

31   30   29   28   27   26   25   24   23   22   21
06   05   04   03   02   01   00   99   98   97

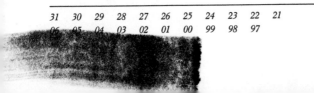

The Tyndale Old Testament Commentaries

General Editor:
PROFESSOR D. J. WISEMAN, O.B.E., M.A., D.LIT., F.B.A., F.S.A.

GENESIS

GENERAL PREFACE

THE aim of this series of *Tyndale Old Testament Commentaries*, as it was with the companion New Testament volumes, is to provide the student of the Bible with a handy, up-to-date commentary on each book, with the primary emphasis on exegesis. Major critical questions will be discussed in the introductions and additional notes, but as far as possible undue technicality will be avoided in the commentary itself.

While all are united in their belief in the divine inspiration, essential trustworthiness and practical relevance of the sacred writings, individual authors are free to express their own point of view on all controversial issues. Within the limits of the space available they frequently draw attention to interpretations which they themselves do not hold but which represent the conclusions of equally sincere and loyal Christians. In Genesis, a book which has been the subject of so much debate, it would be easy to devote a disproportionate amount of space to such discussions. But the aim throughout has been to draw the reader as close as possible to the meaning of the text rather than to speculations about it.

In the Old Testament in particular no single English translation is adequate to reflect the original text. The authors of these commentaries freely quote various versions, therefore, or give their own translation, in the endeavour to make the more difficult passages or words meaningful today. Where necessary, words from the Hebrew (and Aramaic) Massoretic Text underlying their studies are transliterated. This will help the reader who may be unfamiliar with the Semitic languages to identify the word under discussion and thus to follow the argument. It is assumed throughout that the reader will have ready access to one, or more, reliable rendering of the Bible in English.

There are signs of a renewed interest in the meaning and message of the Old Testament and it is hoped that this series will thus further the systematic study of the revelation of God and His will and ways as seen in these records. It is the prayer of the editor and publisher, as of the authors, that these books will help many to understand, and to respond to, the Word of God today.

D. J. WISEMAN

CONTENTS

AUTHOR'S PREFACE

A music critic once demolished a certain descant to a great hymn tune, with the remark that it impoverished the immaculate harmony and sure-footed rhythm of its companion, 'like a Mini round a Rolls-Royce'. Any book on Genesis is bound to invite some such comparison (even if theological reviewers usually resist the impulse to put things quite as pungently), and particularly a commentary as slim, in more ways than one, as this.

What is almost equally unavoidable is the offence which any writer on this subject is likely to give to many of his readers at one point or another, in discussing the immense issues that are raised by Genesis at every turn. There can scarcely be another part of Scripture over which so many battles, theological, scientific, historical and literary, have been fought, or so many strong opinions cherished. This very fact is a sign of the greatness and power of the book, and of the narrow limits of both our factual knowledge and our spiritual grasp. If the interpretations and discussions offered here are found far from infallible or complete, no-one is more aware of it than the author; but they are put forward in the hope that even where they are unpalatable they will provoke all the closer study of the inspired text itself.

A preface gives an opportunity of making some acknowledgments, and I am glad to express gratitude first to those who have drawn my attention to a number of archaeological and linguistic matters, especially Professor D. J. Wiseman, the General Editor of the series, and Mr. A. R. Millard, the Librarian of Tyndale House; also to the Rev. J. A. Motyer, whose theological insight has at several points made him 'eyes to the blind'. Dr. R. E. D. Clark was kind enough to read part of the manuscript where it touched on cosmology, and to make valuable criticisms and suggestions. The help of all these has reduced, but naturally not eliminated, my errors and omissions. Unfortunately Mr. K. A. Kitchen's *Ancient*

AUTHOR'S PREFACE

Orient and Old Testament (Tyndale Press, 1966) was published too late to be consulted for this commentary, but it is good to know that its wealth of information on the world in which Genesis has its setting is now available to fill out (and no doubt to correct) the picture which is only lightly sketched in the present book.

Finally it is a pleasure to thank the publishers for their encouragement and expertise, and Miss J. M. Plumbridge who deciphered and typed a far from easy manuscript with extraordinary accuracy and cheerfulness.

May this commentary be found as faithful and straightforward a servant of the text as was Abraham's steward to his master.

DEREK KIDNER

CHIEF ABBREVIATIONS

AASOR	*Annual of the American Schools of Oriental Research.*
AN	*Abr Nahrain.*
ANET	*Ancient Near Eastern Texts*[2] by J. B. Pritchard, 1955.
ARI	*Archaeology and the Religion of Israel*[3] by W. F. Albright, 1953.
AV	English Authorized Version (King James).
BA	*Biblical Archaeologist.*
BASOR	*Bulletin of the American Schools of Oriental Research.*
BDB	*Hebrew-English Lexicon of the Old Testament* by Brown, Driver and Briggs, 1907.
Bennett	*Genesis* (Century Bible) by W. H. Bennett, *c.* 1900.
Bib.	*Biblica.*
Calvin	*Commentaries on the Five Books of Moses, Genesis* by J. Calvin.
Cassuto	*Commentary on Genesis*, I, II, by U. Cassuto, 1961, 1964.
CBQ	*Catholic Biblical Quarterly.*
Delitzsch	*New Commentary on Genesis*, I, II, by F. Delitzsch, 1888, 1889.
DOTT	*Documents from Old Testament Times* edited by D. W. Thomas, 1958.
Driver	*The Book of Genesis*[15] by S. R. Driver, 1948.
ET	*Expository Times.*
FSAC	*From the Stone Age to Christianity*[2] by W. F. Albright, 1957.
G–K	*Hebrew Grammar*[2] by W. Gesenius, E. Kautzsch and A. E. Cowley, 1910.
HDB	*Hastings' Dictionary of the Bible.*
Hooke	*In the Beginning* (Clarendon Bible, VI) by S. H. Hooke, 1947.
HUCA	*Hebrew Union College Annual.*
IB	*The Interpreter's Bible*, I, 1952.
IBD	*The Interpreter's Bible Dictionary*, 1962.
ISBE	*International Standard Bible Encyclopaedia*, 1939.

CHIEF ABBREVIATIONS

JASA	*Journal of the American Scientific Affiliation.*
JBL	*Journal of Biblical Literature.*
JCS	*Journal of Cuneiform Studies.*
JIAS	*Journal of the Institute of Asian Studies.*
JNES	*Journal of Near Eastern Studies.*
JSS	*Journal of Semitic Studies.*
JTS	*Journal of Theological Studies.*
JTVI	*Journal of the Transactions of the Victoria Institute.*
K–B	*Lexicon in Veteris Testamenti Libros* by L. Koehler and W. Baumgartner, 1953.
LXX	The Septuagint (pre-Christian Greek version of the Old Testament).
mg	margin
Moffatt	*A New Translation of the Bible* by James Moffatt, 1935.
MT	Massoretic Text.
NBC	*The New Bible Commentary* edited by F. Davidson, A. M. Stibbs, E. F. Kevan, 1953.
NBD	*The New Bible Dictionary* edited by J. D. Douglas *et al.*, 1962.
RSV	American Revised Standard Version, 1952.
RV	English Revised Version, 1881.
Simpson	C. A. Simpson (see *IB*).
Skinner	*Genesis*[2] (International Critical Commentary) by J. Skinner, 1930.
Speiser	*Genesis* (The Anchor Bible) by E. A. Speiser, 1964.
UM	*Ugaritic Manual* by C. H. Gordon, 1955.
UT	*Ugaritic Textbook* by C. H. Gordon, 1965.
Vergote	*Joseph en Égypte* by J. Vergote, 1959.
von Rad	*Genesis* (Old Testament Library) by G. von Rad, Eng. tr. 1961.
VT	*Vetus Testamentum.*
Vulg.	The Vulgate (translation of the Bible into Latin, by Jerome).
WTJ	*Westminster Theological Journal.*
ZAW	*Zeitschrift für die alttestamentliche Wissenschaft.*

INTRODUCTION

I. THE PATTERN AND PLACE OF GENESIS

NO work that is known to us from the Ancient Near East is remotely comparable in scope, to say nothing of less measurable qualities, with the book of Genesis. Certain epics from Babylonia tell of Creation, others of a Deluge; the fullest extant version of the Epic of Atrahasis, more than 1,200 lines long, links the two events in a continuous story[1] which provides some sort of parallel to Genesis 1–8; but when these come to an end, Genesis has barely begun. Its story has started at an earlier point than theirs (since with them the waters, personified, are the beginning, and the gods who will overcome them are only their offspring) and it will not end until the church of the Old Testament has been firmly rooted and four generations of patriarchs have lived out eventful lives against the background of two different civilizations.

The book falls into two unequal parts, of which the second begins with the emergence of Abram at the junction of chapters 11 and 12. Chapters 1 to 11 describe two opposite progressions: first, God's orderly creation, to its climax in man as a responsible and blessed being, and then the disintegrating work of sin, to its first great anticlimax in the corrupt world of the Flood, and its second in the folly of Babel.

With this, the general history of man gives way in chapter 12 to the germinal story of 'Abraham and his seed', with God's covenant no longer a general pledge to all mankind as in chapter 9, but narrowed down to a single family through which 'all the families of the earth' will be blessed (12:3). Abram, landless and childless, is made to learn that the great promise,

[1] On this, see A. R. Millard, 'A New Babylonian "Genesis" Story', *Tyndale Bulletin*, 18, 1967. For the rest of the Babylonian Creation material see A. Heidel, *The Babylonian Genesis* (University of Chicago Press, Phoenix Edition, 1963), and for the Flood stories see A. Heidel, *The Gilgamesh Epic and Old Testament Parallels*[2] (University of Chicago Press, 1949).

the lodestar of his life, must be fulfilled divinely and miraculously or not at all. In this context his nephew's hard-headed choice of the cities of the plain, and his own desperate attempts at self-protection or the raising of a family, stand out in contrast to the fruitful way of faith. There is no future, the story makes plain, in Sodom or Egypt, or in Ishmael, as there is in the promised Canaan and Isaac. Such lessons persist in the remainder of the book as men accept or fight against the will of God over the choice of Jacob against Esau in the second generation, Joseph above his brethren in the third, and Ephraim above Manasseh in the fourth. By the end of Genesis the chosen people has begun to take shape, while its cousins and neighbours have settled into their territories and patterns of life. But it has migrated meanwhile from the promised land, and the story cannot end at such a point.

By its close, then, the book has lost nothing of its impetus. Its fifty chapters are the spring-board for the greater things of the exodus which its final events demand and its closing words anticipate. It is only the first of 'the five fifths of the law', as the law itself is the seed of a still bigger harvest. One of the impressive facts about the Old Testament, and about Genesis within it, is this forward thrust towards a consummation which is foretold yet, in detail, unforeseeable; which fulfils it without destroying it.

Genesis, in fact, is in various ways almost nearer the New Testament than the Old, and some of its topics are barely heard again till their implications can fully emerge in the gospel. The institution of marriage, the Fall of man, the jealousy of Cain, the judgment of the Flood, the imputed righteousness of the believer, the rival sons of promise and of the flesh, the profanity of Esau, the pilgrim status of God's people, are all predominantly New Testament themes. Finally there is the symmetry by which some of the very scenes and figures of the earliest chapters reappear in the book of Revelation, where Babel (Babylon) and 'that ancient serpent, . . . the deceiver of the whole world' come to their downfall, and the redeemed, though they are now veterans rather than untried innocents, walk again in Paradise by the river and tree of life.

II. THE DATE AND AUTHORSHIP OF THE BOOK

a. *Indications from Scripture*

While the New Testament speaks of the Pentateuch in general as 'Moses' or the 'book' or 'law' of Moses, it nowhere points specifically to Genesis by itself in these terms. The Pentateuch for its own part tells of Moses' decisive share in its making, from his first written records of the curse against Amalek (Ex. 17:14) and the book of the Sinai covenant (Ex. 24:3–7) to the writing and safe keeping of his final exposition of the law (Dt. 31:24–26). Under God, the core and substance of the books Exodus to Deuteronomy are his work, just as under God the events are his life-story.

Yet Moses is always 'he', never 'I', in these events. Even the 'log-book' of Numbers 33 is in the third person (*i.e.*, it has been written up from his record, not simply inserted), and when he does speak in the first person, as in Deuteronomy, an introduction and conclusion frame his words and make the final account history, not autobiography. There is nothing to correspond to the unintroduced memoirs of Nehemiah or the 'we'-passages in Acts.

The New Testament, in attributing the Pentateuch as a whole to Moses, seems to imply for Genesis a similar relation between substance and final shape as it implies for the rest of the books: that is, that the material is from Moses, whoever was his biographer and editor. It seems artificial, for instance, to exclude Genesis from our Lord's dictum, 'Moses . . . wrote of me' (Jn. 5:46) and from His Emmaus exposition 'beginning from Moses' (Lk. 24:27; *cf.* 44). Such a distinction would have occurred to none of the original readers of the Gospels.

This estimate of Moses' relation to the books that bear his name seems to agree with some of the small clues on the surface of Genesis, though it must be emphasized that they are inconclusive. On the one hand, for example, Genesis 47:11 uses the expression 'the land of Rameses' for the Israelite territory, a term which could have come especially easily to Moses if he was a contemporary of Rameses II. On the other hand 36:31ff., which tells of kings reigning in Edom 'before there reigned any king over . . . Israel', dates itself, on any normal understanding, in or after the time of Saul. This king-list however could be an addendum to bring an old book up to date, as easily as it could indicate the time of composition; there is no sure means of telling. Other minor phrases with a possible bearing on the date are 12:6 (*cf.* 13:7), 'the Canaanite was then in the land', and 14:14, 'as far as Dan' (*cf.* Jdg. 18:29). The former is inconclusive, since 'then' can mean 'then, as now' (*cf.* Jos. 14:11), while the latter, like 36:31ff. cited above, could indicate the period either of the author or of a scribe who substituted a current name for an archaic one.

The scriptural evidence, then, within and without the book itself, leaves it an open question whether the inclusion of Genesis among the writings of Moses implies simply that it is the foundation of the Pentateuch or that Moses himself wrote it. But it may be added perhaps at this point that the book shows a breadth of conception and a combination of erudition, artistry and both psychological and spiritual insight which make it outstanding, by common consent, even in the Old Testament. If its chief architect was not Moses, it was evidently a man of comparable stature.

b. *Pentateuchal criticism*

It is generally held that Genesis provides many more clues to its composition than the few that are mentioned above. The first of these to attract notice were the variations in the use of divine names and the apparent repetitions in the narratives. In 1753 J. Astruc attempted by these means to isolate different documents used by Moses, and by the close of the eighteenth century the figure of Moses was receding from the view of investigators, to be replaced by an unnamed redactor. Passages using the term God (Elohim) were ascribed to the 'Elohist', abbreviated to E; others which spoke of the Lord (Jahveh, Yahweh) were the work of the 'Yahwist', J. It was soon decided that there were more than one Elohist, and the initial P (Priestly source) was eventually added to E and J to distinguish the first Elohist from the second. A far-reaching revolution took place however in the 1860s and '70s when K. H. Graf, followed by J. Wellhausen, produced arguments for reversing the chronological sequence PEJ to JEP – an upheaval which was more radical for the rest of the Pentateuch than for Genesis, since it put the levitical law near the end instead of the outset of Israel's history. For Genesis it meant that P, thought of as an exilic or post-exilic writing, supplied the final framework, interweaving its own version of events with J in the earlier part of the book, and with J and E from chapter 15 onwards.

Once this method of study had established itself, other distinguishing marks of the documents were reported in great numbers, and in the latter half of the nineteenth century the Pentateuch was so rigorously dissected that it was not uncommon to find a single verse parcelled out between two or even three sources, since each of these was held to have its own vocabulary, character and theology. If there were two synonyms available for some noun, verb or pronoun, one of them might be virtually the fingerprint of J or E, the other of P. If there were genealogies or dates, these were mostly the special interest of P; if attention centred on the northern tribes it was likely to be the work of E. Theologically it appeared that, in J, God would speak with men directly, His personality strongly evident; in E, His messages would tend to come in dreams or by angels speaking from heaven; in P, He was majestic and remote, planning the progress of events towards the establishment of an ecclesiastical state.

The presence of duplicate and composite narratives continued to be pillars of the theory. Stories which professed to be distinct were taken to be variants of the same events, while single narratives were so meticulously sundered and so brilliantly reconstructed that it became a commonplace to find two accounts standing where only one had shown itself before. Under these miracles of surgery scarcely an Adam, so to speak, now lacked an Eve, fashioned from his bones, to contradict him. The classic examples of the technique are the analyses of the Flood and of the Joseph stories, which are discussed in the Additional Notes to chapters 8, 37 and 42.

Study of the Pentateuch has since branched out in various

directions, with a growing interest in recent years in Form Criticism, which looks for the literary units underlying a connected work, and tries to understand them as the products of various types of situation. The consequent emphasis on the life of the community in which the writings arose has modified the conception of JEP, which are no longer pictured as the straight products of, say, the ninth, eighth and sixth centuries respectively, but as bodies of tradition preserved and developed in different Israelite circles over the centuries, each containing its share of very ancient material.

While this approach, among others, has broken down some of the rigidity of the earlier criticism, so that A. Bentzen, for one, could declare (his italics) '*I think we must stop speaking of "documents*" ',[1] the initials JEP are still predominantly used and still signify for most purposes, in spite of Bentzen, the documents that are thought to embody their respective traditions. Even the suggested dates for these documents are broadly unchanged, and individual scholars continue to subdivide them as of old, or to discover sources hitherto unsuspected. So, *e.g.*, C. A. Simpson[2] follows E. Meyer and others in dividing J into J[1] and J[2]; R. H. Pfeiffer[3] adds to JEP his Edomite 'S'; and O. Eissfeldt[4] isolates an early 'lay' source, 'L', to arrive at a Pentateuchal documentary sequence LJEBDHP.

The old literary analysis of the Pentateuch is in fact still treated as substantially valid and is made the basis of most subsequent work, even if primary interest has now shifted to other areas. It therefore seems worth pointing out that much of it falls very far short of proof.

1. *The divine names* are not as safe a criterion of authorship, even (in practice) to the literary critic, as they seem to be at first sight. For example, it is very widely held that the E document begins, fragmentarily, in Genesis 15; yet with

---

[1] *Introduction to the Old Testament*[2] (Gad, Copenhagen, 1952), II, p. 31. See further C. R. North in H. H. Rowley (ed.), *The Old Testament and Modern Study* (O.U.P., 1951), pp. 48–83; E. J. Young, *An Introduction to the Old Testament* (Tyndale Press, 1964 edn), pp. 107–154.

[2] *IB*, I, pp. 192ff.

[3] *Introduction to the Old Testament*[2] (A. and C. Black, 1952), pp. 159ff.

[4] *The Old Testament. An Introduction* (Blackwell, 1965), p. 239.

'Elohim' quite absent from that chapter and 'Yahweh' occurring seven times, certain commentators are ready where
necessary to ascribe verses containing 'Yahweh' to the Elohist,
on the assumption that a later hand has marred the evidence
that once stood there. In 22:1–14, a stronger E passage, there
are three occurrences of 'Yahweh' to five of 'Elohim', which
have to be similarly explained. Again, in 17:1 and 21:1b, P
speaks of 'Yahweh'. To dismiss these and other anomalies
with such a remark as 'Originally '*el* . . . must have stood
here'[1] is to abandon the existing evidence simply because it is
inconvenient.

Such a situation cries out for a more flexible approach, so
that one allows not only for possible sources but for an author's
conscious and unconscious choice between the more personal
term 'Yahweh' and the more general 'Elohim' in certain
contexts, and for the aesthetic impulse, where the choice is
theologically open, to use a run of one expression or another,
or again a free alternation of the two.[2] The usage of other
ancient peoples amply supports this: *cf.*, *e.g.*, the interchangeable terms Baal and Hadad in the Ugaritic Hadad
tablet,[3] or the multiple designations of Osiris on the stele of
Ikhernofret,[4] to give no more examples.

Against this free variation, Exodus 3:13ff. and 6:3 are often
quoted as proof-texts to show that in Genesis E and P could
not have used the name Yahweh, since it was unheard of, in
their view, before the call of Moses. But this is to neglect the
context of those verses. In Exodus 3:14 the divine exposition,
'I AM . . .' introduces and illuminates the name given in
3:15, and this remains the context for 6:3 as well, in the book
as we have it. The name, in short, was first *known*, in any full
sense of the word, at its first expounding; but the name of

[1] C. A. Simpson, on 22:14.
[2] It is a modest but illuminating exercise to examine the distribution
of these terms in the book of Jonah. *Cf.* also the study of the use of the divine
names in the Pentateuch and in the rest of the Old Testament, in
U. Cassuto, *The Documentary Hypothesis* (Magnes Press, 1961), pp. 15–41.
This work is an abbreviation of *La Questione della Genesi* (Florence, 1934).
[3] G. R. Driver, *Canaanite Myths and Legends* (T. and T. Clark, 1956),
pp. 70–72.
[4] K. A. Kitchen, *NBD*, p. 349a. The text is in *ANET*, pp. 329f.

Moses' own mother Jochebed (Ex. 6:20), a name compounded with Yahweh,[1] is proof enough that it was already in common *use*, according to P itself. *Cf.* E. Jacob (who accepts the JEP analysis): '. . . we do not have in the Exodus narrative the revelation of a new name but the explanation of a name already known to Moses which in that solemn hour is discovered to be charged with a content the richness of which he was far from suspecting.'[2]

2. *Other linguistic criteria* are equally inconclusive. In the first place, as U. Cassuto[3] has pointed out, to treat alternative expressions for a given idea simply as hallmarks of different authors is often to miss the nuance of a word. For example, to 'cut'[4] a covenant highlights the historic moment and manner of its making; to 'give'[5] a covenant emphasizes the sovereignty and grace of its Initiator; and to 'establish'[6] it puts a stress on His faithfulness in giving it effect. (Incidentally the last two of these terms are allowed to co-exist in P; should they not be criteria for dividing it?) Again, to bring Israel 'forth' (J) from Egypt emphasizes the aspect of liberation, while to bring them 'up' (E) directs attention to their destination, the promised land. These are worth-while distinctions. Or the nuance may be one of rhythm and weight, observable in the principles which govern the choice of the long or short pronoun 'I' ('*ānōkî*, critically ascribed to JE, or '*anî*, the alleged mark of P). Incidentally the Ugaritic equivalents of these two forms can be found side by side: they occur, *e.g.*, within two lines in Aqhat III.vi.21,23,[7] where there is no question of dual authorship.

In the second place, examples of many of these uses are too few to be statistically significant or too minutely circumscribed to allow for an author's freedom. Eissfeldt's two

---

[1] *Cf.* H. Bauer in *ZAW*, LI, 1933, pp. 92f.
[2] *Theology of the Old Testament* (Hodder and Stoughton, 1958), pp. 49f. See also J. A. Motyer, *The Revelation of the Divine Name* (Tyndale Press, 1959), *passim*.
[3] *Op. cit.*, pp. 42–54.
[4] Allegedly the JE word, found at 15:18; 21:27,32; 26:28; 31:44.
[5] Attributed to P; found at 9:12; 17:2.
[6] Also attributed to P; found at 6:18; 9:9,11,17; 17:7,19,21.
[7] Text in G. R. Driver, *op. cit.*, p. 56.

instances of J and E words will illustrate the point. His first is E's use of the name 'Amorites', where J has 'Canaanites', for the natives of the promised land.[1] Only two E passages can be produced for this, while 15:21, which mentions *both* 'the Amorites, and the Canaanites', is ignored in spite of its proximity to 15:16 which is cited. Eissfeldt's other example is the pair of terms *šiphâ* and *'āmâ* for 'handmaid', attributed to J and E respectively. The reasoning however begins to look laboured when it makes Rachel offer her maid to Jacob in E (30:3) and carry out the offer in J (30:4). Confidence in the method is hardly restored by Eissfeldt's corollary that yet another source, a variant of J, betrays its presence in the third noun, *pîlegeš*, for these subordinate wives.[2]

3. *'Doublets'* tend to fall still further short of proof, for they are postulated almost as a matter of course when two stories resemble one another. If the events are closely similar, the matter is felt to need no arguing; if they are dissimilar, they only show how far the traditions diverge. These assumptions can be detected, for instance, in the standard analysis of Hagar's two departures from home. Treating chapters 16 and 21 as the J and E versions of a single event, with P insertions, G. von Rad, in company with most critical scholars, notes the contrasts between the two stories, in that Abraham is passive and pliable in 16, responsible in 21; Hagar is proud and impetuous in the first story, an innocent victim in the second; again, the angel seeks out Hagar in 16:7, but calls to her from heaven in 21:17; and so on.

These are true and fascinating distinctions. What is tacitly dismissed is any possibility that they reflect two different occasions, as they profess to do. Yet for Hagar to despise the barren Sarah in 16, and for her son to be caught bullying[3] the child who has now dispossessed him in chapter 21, are not mutually exclusive possibilities but an organic sequence, true to the tensions of fourteen years implied in the family history. The same can be said of Abraham's two attitudes to these

---

[1] Eissfeldt, *op. cit.*, p. 183.
[2] *Ibid.*
[3] See on 21:9.

crises, for on the second occasion he had a powerful precedent to give him pause, in that Hagar had been divinely ordered home the first time this had happened (16:9). (Similar marks of sequence can be noticed in the attempts of Abraham and Isaac to pass off their wives as sisters: see the opening comments on chapter 26.)

It is surely prejudice rather than reason which will leave Scripture's own and self-consistent version of events either undiscussed or, in the case of its explanatory comments (*e.g.* 26:1a), dismissed as artificial harmonizations.

4. The existence of *composite* narratives, intricately inter-woven, is particularly open to question. As an editorial method it would be unparalleled (it was first suggested in the days before our access to old Near Eastern literature offered a control to speculation), and the analysis which tries to unravel the design is based on the improbably rigid idea of literary style which has already been noticed in paragraphs 1 and 2 above. Extended examples and a critique of the method can be found in the Additional Notes to chapters 8, 37 and 42.[1]

c. Some conclusions

With the study of Genesis *on its own terms*, that is, as a living whole, not a body to be dissected, the impression becomes inescapable that its characters are people of flesh and blood, its events actual, and the book itself a unity. If this is right, the mechanics of composition are matters of small importance, since the parts of this whole are not competing for credence as rival traditions, and the author of the book does not draw attention, as do the writers of Kings and Chronicles, to the sources of his information.

No lack of such sources, oral and written, however, need be supposed for an author of the period indicated in section *a*. (pp. 15f.), since Abram had migrated from a country that was rich in traditions and genealogies,[2] and Joseph (like Moses after him) had lived many years in the intellectual climate of the Egyptian court on the one hand (with access to, *e.g.*, the

[1] See pp. 93ff., 184ff., 200ff.
[2] *Cf.* W. F. Albright, *FSAC*, p. 238.

detailed ethnography reflected in Genesis 10) and of the patriarchal society on the other, with ample opportunities of preserving these stores of information. Accordingly there have been some attempts to find traces of material compiled at earlier dates than those that are suggested for the completed J, E and P. Two of these ventures are now briefly described.

P. J. Wiseman, in *New Discoveries in Babylonia about Genesis*[1], examined the possibility that the recurring phrase 'These are the generations of . . .', which punctuate Genesis at eleven places,[2] give a clue to the keeping of family records by successive patriarchs. He interprets this refrain as a colophon,[3] to be translated 'These are the historical origins of . . .'. In other words, in his view it always marks the *conclusion* of a section, rounding off the archives written or possessed down the years by Adam (Gn. 5:6), Noah (6:9), Noah's sons (10:1), and so on: a growing series entrusted to successive heads of the family.

In support of his argument this author points out that no section overshoots the lifetime of the person so named; that the blocks of material reflect accurately (*e.g.*, in vocabulary and place-names) the different stages which they record; and that the art of writing, which was copiously practised for many centuries before Abraham, is of very high antiquity.[4] He also lists a number of duplicate expressions occurring in the vicinity of the 'colophons', which could be catch-phrases, a device commonly used to link successive tablets in their right sequence.[5]

But the case for referring the word 'generations' (*tôl⁴dôt*) only to the past has its weaknesses. It is clearly inapplicable, for example, to Ruth 4:18, where the phrase 'these are the generations of', exactly as in Genesis, can only point forward. In Genesis itself it can always refer as suitably (and often more so) to the future as to the past. From 2:4 onwards, every occurrence is followed by an account of what *issued* from the

[1] Marshall, Morgan and Scott, 1936.
[2] These are listed at 2:4.
[3] *Op. cit.*, pp. 47–60. A colophon is an identifying phrase at the end of a tablet.
[4] Some that survives is over 5,000 years old: *cf. NBD*, p. 1341.
[5] *Op. cit.*, p. 67.

point just named, whether this point is the bare world (2:5ff.) or Adam (5:3ff.) or Noah (6:9ff.), *etc.* So from Terah, for example, (11:27) spring not only Abraham, who will dominate the scene, but Abraham's kinsmen from whom eventually the bride of Isaac must be chosen; and from Jacob (37:2) arise the twelve tribes (whose fortunes are traced far ahead in chapter 49), not merely the hero Joseph. To make the phrase an ending instead of an opening gives us the anomaly, if it is strictly applied, of having the whole story of Abraham preserved by Ishmael (11:27b – 25:12), while Isaac keeps Ishmael's archives (25:13–19a), Esau those of Jacob (25:19b – 36:1) and Jacob those of Esau – a situation of almost operatic complexity, and a conclusion which the author rather arbitrarily avoids.[1]

Further, by insisting on a complete succession of named tablets the theory implies that writing is nearly if not quite as old as man. Genesis itself, read in any other way, does not require this: it leaves it perfectly tenable that while the genealogies were committed to writing at an early but unspecified stage[2] the rest of the family history may have been passed down by word of mouth, as its manner often suggests. Some of the characteristics of oral tradition listed by E. Nielsen bring Genesis to mind, *e.g.*: '. . . recurrent expressions, a fluent, paratactic style, a certain rhythm and euphony which are especially noticeable when one hears the account . . .'.[3] It is worth pointing out that this kind of transmission can be exceedingly accurate where it is in regular use.[4]

The second approach, from quite different presuppositions, is that of E. Robertson,[5] who drew attention to the unusual opportunities of Samuel to gather and record Israel's traditions as he visited Beth-el and other centres (1 Sa. 7:16) in regular

[1] *Op. cit.*, p. 80.
[2] See on chapter 5.
[3] *Oral Tradition* (Studies in Biblical Theology, No. 11, S.C.M. Press, 1954), p. 36.
[4] *Cf.* the examples cited from other peoples by Nielsen, *op. cit.*, pp. 23f., 31f.
[5] *The Old Testament Problem* (Manchester University Press, 1950), pp. 33–53.

rotation as judge. Robertson recalls the critical state of Israel at the time, with the old order crumbling, the sanctuary destroyed, and the demand for a king threatening to paganize the theocracy. A recall to the law of Moses must have been vital at such a moment. Pointing out in some detail the appropriateness of Deuteronomy to this whole situation, Robertson finds it specially significant that according to 1 Samuel 10:25 Samuel 'recited the constitution of the kingdom (*mišpaṭ hammamlākâ*) to the people, wrote it in a book, and deposited it before the Lord'.[1] This, in his view, was the crown of Samuel's labours, which had amounted to the editing of the whole Pentateuch, possibly with the help of 'scholarly scribes working . . . under the direction of Samuel's ecclesiastical councils'. To Robertson, then, 'the different writers, or rather compilers, of the Torah all lived in the same age and all were occupied with their great tasks at the same time'.[2]

Robertson's thesis gives Samuel and the sanctuaries a more creative part in the making of the Pentateuch than Scripture itself seems to allow (*cf.* section *a.* above), but it may point in the right direction. Certainly the spiritual stature of Samuel, and his experience of the realms of government, priesthood and prophecy, make him as likely a final architect of the Pentateuch as any of whom we know before Ezra; and if he was the narrator who told of Moses and edited his writings, the occasional references to post-Mosaic names and situations referred to in section *a.* would be fully in keeping with the fact.

But all these attempts are, in their different degrees, speculative and of only secondary importance. One has the feeling that Paul, if he were inveigled into such a discussion, would say sooner or later 'I speak as a fool'; though he might add, 'you forced me to it' – for the debate, once started, has to continue. Perhaps the last word, again from the New Testament, would be more appropriately the gentle reminder to Simon Peter when he was too fascinated by Moses and Elijah, on the mount, to remember their *raison d'être*. Whether we are tempted, in our pentateuchal studies, to erect many

[1] Robertson, *op. cit.*, p. 45.
[2] *Op. cit.*, pp. 42f.

tabernacles or few, for Moses or a multitude, the answer of heaven is, 'This is my beloved Son: hear him.'

III. HUMAN BEGINNINGS

In the main, two outlines of man's infancy confront the modern Christian. The book of Genesis portrays, in a few strokes of the pen, a creature fashioned from earthly matter, God-breathed and God-like, whose spiritual history runs from innocence to disobedience and on into a moral decline which the beginnings of civilization can do nothing to arrest.

The second picture, that of palaeontology, a mosaic of many fragments, depicts a species fashioned over perhaps a million years or more into the present human form, showing the outward characteristics of modern man upwards of twenty thousand years ago, not only in his bodily structure but in his practice of making tools, using fire, burying his dead, and, not least, creating works of art comparable with those of any period. Even at this remote time the apparent forerunners of our chief racial groups seem to be distinguishable,[1] and the species had already spread widely over the world, displacing another type of hominid, 'Neanderthal Man', whose own relics, rough as they are, indicate that tools, fire and burial had been in use for long ages before this. On the other hand, the first known signs of pastoral and agricultural life and, later, of metal working (*e.g.* by hammering copper or meteoric iron; *cf.* on 4:19–24) are much more recent, appearing in the Near East, on present evidence, somewhere between the eighth and fifth millennia BC at earliest.

How the two pictures, biblical and scientific, are related to each other is not immediately clear, and one should allow for the provisional nature both of scientific estimates (without making this a refuge from all unwelcome ideas) and of traditional interpretations of Scripture. One must also recognize the different aims and styles of the two approaches: one probing the observable world, the other revealing chiefly the unobservable, the relation of God and man. The style of

[1] *Cf.* M. Boule and H. V. Vallois, *Fossil Men* (Thames and Hudson, 1957), p. 325; C. S. Coon, *The Origin of Races* (J. Cape, 1963), p. 5.

reporting will be drily factual for the former, but the latter may need the whole range of literary *genres* to do it justice, and it is therefore important not to prejudge the method and intention of these chapters.

Other scriptures, however, offer certain fixed points to the interpreter. For example, the human race is of a single stock ('from one', Acts 17:26); again, the offence of one man made sinners of the many, and subjected them to death (Rom. 5:12–19): and this man was as distinct an individual as were Moses and Jesus Christ (Rom. 5:14).[1] Others too are counted as individuals in the New Testament: *e.g.*, Cain, Abel, Enoch, Noah. These guidelines exclude the idea of myth (which dramatizes the natural order, to 'explain and maintain' it[2]), and assure us that we are reading of actual, pivotal events.

It could be that the events are presented here in simplified pictorial form (*cf.* the opening comments on chapter 3), or are landmarks punctuating an immense tract of time. Even so there are difficulties. If Genesis is abbreviating a long history, the sheer vastness of the ages it spans, on this view, is not so sharp a problem as the fact that almost the whole of this immensity lies, for the palaeontologist, between the first man and the first farmer – that is, in terms of Genesis, between Adam and Cain, or even between Adam inside and outside Eden. Yet the birth of Seth, or of his ancestor, sets an upper limit of a mere 130 years to this (4:25; 5:3). Even if the figures in Genesis 5 are non-literal, the proportions raise the same difficulty. Some other approach therefore seems necessary.[3]

[1] Any attempt to argue that in Rom. 5 Paul was reinforcing his exposition of imputed righteousness by an analogy drawn only from the *wording* of Gn. 3, somewhat as Heb. 7:3 uses the wording of Gn. 14, seems to be precluded by the distinction between Adam's and other men's sins in Rom. 5:14. No room is left there for a collective Adam or for 'every man his own Adam'.

[2] *Cf.* B. S. Childs, *Myth and Reality in the Old Testament* (Studies in Biblical Theology, No. 27, S.C.M. Press, 1960), pp. 29, 66.

[3] Various answers to the problem are discussed in B. Ramm, *The Christian View of Science and Scripture* (Paternoster, 1955), pp. 119–156. Two that have had a wide influence in some Christian circles are (a) the 'Gap' theory, which postulates a catastrophic period between Gn. 1:1 and 1:3, long enough to produce the main phenomena of geology, after which the world was reconstituted in six days (see especially G. H. Pember, *Earth's*

To the present author various converging lines point to an Adam much nearer our own times than the early tool-makers and artists, let alone their remote forbears. On the face of it, the ways of life described in Genesis 4 are those of the neolithic and first metal-working cultures alluded to above, *i.e.*, of perhaps eight or ten thousand years ago, less or more. The memory of names and genealogical details also suggests a fairly compact period between Adam and Noah[1] rather than a span of tens or hundreds of millennia, an almost unimaginable stretch of time to chronicle. Yet this seems to widen the gap still further between Genesis and current chronologies.

The answer may lie in our definition of man.

Man in Scripture is much more than *homo faber*, the maker of tools: he is constituted man by God's image and breath, nothing less. It follows that Scripture and science may well differ in the boundaries they would draw round early humanity: the intelligent beings of a remote past, whose bodily and cultural remains give them the clear status of 'modern man' to the anthropologist, may yet have been decisively below the plane of life which was established in the creation of Adam. If, as the text of Genesis would by no means disallow,[2] God initially shaped man by a process of evolution, it would follow that a considerable stock of near-humans preceded the first true man, and it would be arbitrary to picture these as mindless brutes. Nothing requires that the creature into which God breathed human life should not have been of a species prepared in every way for humanity, with already a long history of practical intelligence, artistic sensibility and the capacity for awe and reflection.

On this view, Adam, the first true man, will have had as

Earliest Ages[13] (Pickering and Inglis, 1921). On this, see the comment and first footnote at Gn. 1:2. (b) 'Flood Geology', which makes the single year of Noah's Flood the period in which were deposited the sediments and fossils usually considered to have been laid down over many millions of years. This view is expounded in detail in J. C. Whitcomb and H. M. Morris, *The Genesis Flood* (The Presbyterian and Reformed Publishing Co., 1961); it has not won support amongst professional geologists.

[1] On this period, see Additional Note to chapter 5, p. 82.

[2] *Cf., e.g.*, Jb. 10:8ff., Ps. 119:73, where God's use of natural processes is described in terms of the potter's art as in Gn. 2:7.

contemporaries many creatures of comparable intelligence, widely distributed over the world. One might conjecture that these were destined to die out, like the Neanderthalers (if indeed these did), or to perish in the Flood, leaving Adam's lineal descendants, through Noah, in sole possession.[1] Against this, however, there must be borne in mind the apparent continuity between the main races of the present and those of the distant past, already mentioned, which seems to suggest either a stupendous antiquity for Adam (unless the whole accepted dating of prehistory is radically mistaken, as some have tried to show – *e.g.*, Whitcomb and Morris, *op. cit.*) or the continued existence of 'pre-Adamites' alongside 'Adamites'.

If this second alternative implied any doubt of the unity of mankind it would be of course quite untenable. God, as we have seen, has made all nations 'from one' (Acts 17:26). Genetically indeed, on this view, these two groups would be of a single stock; but by itself that would avail nothing, as Adam's fruitless search for a helpmeet makes abundantly clear. Yet it is at least conceivable that after the special creation of Eve, which established the first human pair as God's viceregents (Gn. 1:27,28) and clinched the fact that there is no natural bridge from animal to man, God may have now conferred His image on Adam's collaterals, to bring them into the same realm of being. Adam's 'federal' headship of humanity extended, if that was the case, outwards to his contemporaries as well as onwards to his offspring, and his disobedience disinherited both alike.

There may be a biblical hint of such a situation in the surprising impression of an already populous earth given by the words and deeds of Cain in 4:14,17.[2] Even Augustine had to devote a chapter to answering those who 'find this a difficulty',[3] and although the traditional answer is valid

---

[1] *Cf.* A. Rendle Short, *Modern Discovery and the Bible* (I.V.F., 1942), p. 81, in a discussion of various views.

[2] *Cf.* Rendle Short's tentative suggestion (*op. cit.*, p. 81) that the dwellers in Cain's city 'may conceivably have been members of a more primitive type of man' – a suggestion, however, which did not envisage them as fully human.

[3] *The City of God*, XV, viii.

enough (see commentary on 4:13,14, below), the persistence of this old objection could be a sign that our presuppositions have been inadequate. Again, it may be significant that, with one possible exception,[1] the unity of mankind 'in Adam' and our common status as sinners through his offence are expressed in Scripture in terms not of heredity[2] but simply of solidarity. We nowhere find applied to us any argument from physical descent such as that of Hebrews 7:9,10 (where Levi shares in Abraham's act through being 'still in the loins of his ancestor'). Rather, Adam's sin is shown to have implicated all men because he was the federal head of humanity, somewhat as in Christ's death 'one died for all, therefore all died' (2 Cor. 5:14). Paternity plays no part in making Adam 'the figure of him that was to come' (Rom. 5:14).[3]

Three final comments may be made. First, the exploratory suggestion above is only tentative, as it must be, and it is a personal view. It invites correction and a better synthesis; meanwhile it may serve as a reminder that when the revealed and the observed seem hard to combine, it is because we know too little, not too much – as our Lord impressed on the Sadducees about their conundrum on the resurrection. What is quite clear from these chapters in the light of other scriptures is their doctrine that mankind is a unity, created in God's image, and fallen in Adam by the one act of disobedience; and these things are as strongly asserted on this understanding of God's word as on any other.

Secondly, it may be thought that this whole discussion allows science too much control over exegesis. This would be a serious

---

[1] If Gn. 3:20, naming Eve 'mother of all living', is intended as an anthropological definition, with the sense 'ancestress of all humans', the question is settled. This may be its purpose. But the meaning of her name, 'life', and the attention drawn to it by the term 'living', suggest that the concern of the verse is to reiterate in this context of death the promise of salvation through 'her seed' (3:15).

[2] Is. 43:27, which may spring to mind against this, is asserting Israel's long history of sin (whether back to Jacob, Abraham or Adam), not Adam's fatherhood of man.

[3] *Cf.*, *e.g.*, C. K. Barrett, *A Commentary on the Epistle to the Romans* (A. and C. Black, 1957), p. 111; F. F. Bruce, *Romans* (Tyndale Press, 1963), p. 130.

charge. But to try to correlate the data of Scripture and nature is not to dishonour biblical authority, but to honour God as Creator and to grapple with our proper task of interpreting His ways of speaking. In Scripture He leaves us to find out for ourselves such details as whether 'the wings of the wind' and 'the windows of heaven' are literal or metaphorical, and in what sense 'the world cannot be moved' (Ps. 96:10) or the sun daily 'runs its course' (Ps. 19:5,6). Some of these questions are answered as soon as they are asked; others only by the general advance of knowledge;[1] most of them are doctrinally neutral. We are asserting our own infallibility, not that of Scripture, when we refuse to collate our factual answers with those of independent enquiry.[2]

Thirdly, however, the interests and methods of Scripture and science differ so widely that they are best studied, in any detail, apart. Their accounts of the world are as distinct (and each as legitimate) as an artist's portrait and an anatomist's diagram, of which no composite picture will be satisfactory, for their common ground is only in the total reality to which they both attend. It cannot be said too strongly that Scripture is the perfect vehicle for God's revelation, which is what concerns us here; and its bold selectiveness, like that of a great painting, is its power. To read it with one eye on any other account is to blur its image and miss its wisdom. To have God's own presentation of human beginnings as they most deeply concern us, we need look no further than these chapters and their New Testament interpretation.

---

[1] It was Galileo's telescope, not his church, that conclusively refuted the interpretation of Ps. 96:10 as a proof-text against the earth's rotation. Galileo incidentally realized that the new astronomy discredited only the expositors, not the Bible. See, *e.g.*, G. Salmon, *The Infallibility of the Church*[4] (John Murray, 1914), pp. 230ff.; A. Koestler, *The Sleepwalkers* (Penguin, 1964), pp. 440ff.

[2] 'It is tempting ... to deny the problem, either by discounting one or other set of facts, or by locking them into separate compartments in our minds. ... The truth is that the facts of nature yield positive help in many ways for interpreting Scripture statements correctly, and the discipline of wrestling with the problem of relating the two sets of facts, natural and biblical, leads to a greatly enriched understanding of both.' J. I. Packer, *'Fundamentalism' and the Word of God* (I.V.F., 1958), p. 135.

IV. THE THEOLOGY OF GENESIS

There is material in Genesis for a substantial book under this title. Here we shall briefly consider only three of its themes, namely God, man, and salvation.

a. God

From the outset, Genesis confronts us with the Living God, unmistakably personal. The verbs of the opening chapter express an energy of mind, will and judgment which excludes all question of our conceiving God 'in the category of the "it" instead of the "Thou" ' (to borrow E. Brunner's phrase[1]); and the book continues to make this emphasis in its account of man's constitution in God's image, and of God's persistent concern for a personal relationship with His servants.

Secondly, He is the only God, the Creator and Sovereign of all that is. If the later chapters of Isaiah, the *locus classicus* of explicit monotheism, affirm this vehemently, in Genesis the question of other deities simply does not arise – except in the single episode of Jacob's flight from Laban, where, to an attentive ear, Laban can be heard invoking a separate god on his side of the covenant (see on 31:53), and where images make a brief and ignominious appearance, successively stolen, sat on and buried (31:19,30,34; 35:4). The creation story has settled the matter, and subsequent history confirms that God is as much the master of events in the rise and fall of nations (15:14,16; 25:23) as in the conception of a child or the call of a follower. Time and space, sin and even death (5:24) are no match for Him, whether He is working through obvious miracles or hidden providence. And this is the faith not only of the narrator but of the chief characters, who declare Him the Maker and Judge of all (14:19,22; 18:25) and the Disposer of the most intractable of situations (45:5–8).

Thirdly, His ways are perfect. The series of expulsions and cataclysms in Genesis declares that heaven can make no truce with sin, whether it is the Godward sin of unbelief and presumption (as at Eden and Babel) or the manward wrongs

[1] *Revelation and Reason* (S.C.M. Press, 1947), p. 401.

of violence, lust and treachery. Yet His righteous wrath is also grief (*cf.* 6:6). His judgments are sweetened with mercy (3:21; 4:15; 6:8; 18:32; 19:16,21; *etc.*) and are slow to fall (15:16). (His concern for the sinner's reclaiming is discussed below, in section *c*.3.) Equally, if His justice has love in it, His love contains moral demand. There is a trace of challenge in it even in the earthly paradise (*cf.* on 2:8–17), and Abraham was to find, over a long period, and supremely at mount Moriah (chapter 22), that to be the friend of God demanded, even if it repaid, everything he had.

Fourthly, He is self-revealed. Commanding, conversing and, above all, entering into covenant, He is always in some degree self-giving, never the aloof object of human groping. He is known in this book by many names, over and above the general term *God* and the personal name *Yahweh*.[1] Some are titles expressing facets of His being (*Most High*, 14:18–22, a frequent title in the Psalms; *Almighty*, 17:1 (see note) and elsewhere, also often in Job; *Everlasting*, 21:33; *cf.* Is. 40:28). Others commemorate a special moment of encounter (*God of seeing*, 16:13, when He revealed Himself to Hagar; *God, the God of Israel*, 33:20, recording the re-naming of Jacob, *cf.* 32:28; *God of Beth-el*, 35:7, in memory of Jacob's dream). Again others declare a pledged relationship (*God of Abraham*, 28:13, *etc.*; *Fear of Isaac*, 31:42,53; *Mighty One of Jacob*, 49:24). These three classes of title correspond to three main elements – propositional, historical and personal – in all revelation.

Finally we may note the occasional indications, in the terms 'the Angel of the Lord' or 'of God'[2] and 'the Spirit of God',[3] that God's unity is not monolithic. A study of 'the Angel of the Lord' passages (listed in the footnote) leaves no room for doubt that the term denotes God Himself as seen in human form; what should be added is that 'Angel', by its meaning 'messenger', implies that God, made visible, is at the same time

---

[1] See on 4:26.
[2] *Cf.* 16:7–11, with verse 13; 18:1, with verses 2,33 and with 19:1; 31:11, with verse 13; 32:24,30, with Ho. 12:3–6; 48:15, with verse 16.
[3] 1:2; *cf.* 6:3; 41:38.

God *sent*. In the Old Testament nothing is made of this paradox, but it should not surprise us that the apparent absurdity disappears in the New Testament. Just as 'the Spirit of God' was an Old Testament expression awaiting its full disclosure at Pentecost, so 'the Angel of the Lord', as a term for the Lord Himself, becomes meaningful only in the light of 'him whom the Father ... sent into the world', the pre-existent Son.[1]

b. Man

1. *Man before God.* Since this subject is discussed as its various aspects arise in the commentary on chapters 1–3, it is enough to mention the places where this is done.

(*i*) *Man's constitution:* see on 1:26 and 2:7.

(*ii*) *Man's calling:* see chiefly on 2:8–17, but álso the last paragraph on 1:26, and 3:22.

(*iii*) *Man's fall:* see chapter 3, chiefly the introductory remarks to the chapter, and the comments on verses 6 and 7.

(*iv*) *Man's plight:* see on 3:16ff., and the Additional Note to the chapter (on sin and suffering).

2. *Man in society.* For all the emphasis which Genesis lays on the individual, with God calling men by name and seeking the outcasts, its model for human life is not that of the solitary mystic or the freelance, but of a social being who lives within a certain pattern of responsibilities.

Already in Eden the beginning of this pattern is discernible, with its three dimensions of things, persons and authority, in relation to which a man must normally fulfil his calling and glorify God. As the book continues, the pattern is both developed and distorted; developed as time and increasing population enrich its content, but distorted as sin brings its disturbance into every part.

(*i*) *Things.* A large element of man's original calling was to 'cultivate and keep' (2:15) his immediate environment, and to 'subdue' as well as to fill the earth (1:28). From these terms, their vigour matching that of the earth's teeming fertility

---

[1] See also the discussion of the plural pronouns, *us ... our ... our*, towards the end of the comment on 1:26.

described in 1:11f. and its wealth of mineral resources glimpsed in 2:11f., it was obvious that man was blessed with an immense creative task from the first. If this was an inviting prospect, sin and the curse of God changed it largely to a burden, with poverty as the taskmaster and death as the final word (3:17–19). Work itself was not the legacy of the Fall; only its new character as toil.

The subsequent picture is of chequered progress, such as we still experience, and man's work and possessions are presented as tools that can be put to good or evil use, not as ends in themselves. The civilized arts and crafts are not hailed as a panacea, nor shunned because the Cainites invented them; yet we are shown which one of them caught the fancy of Lamech the tyrant (4:22-24), and what new terrors it consequently held for the race. As the story develops, skill is now a blessing, now a curse, as it serves God in the building of the ark or challenges Him at Babel. As for possessions, they are seen in the same light, to be enjoyed from God's hand and tithed in His honour (14:18–20, RSV; 28:22), but not accepted unconditionally ('lest you', the king of Sodom, 'should say, "I have made Abram rich" ', 14:23). Above all, these things must not become one's goal, as they became Lot's to his ruin, or one's obsession, as they became Laban's to his utter corruption.

It may be added that in the patriarchal stories some of the sting has gone out of the ancient curse on the ground, just as for Cain something was added to it (4:11,12). There were famines, true enough, and for Jacob at least, bitter hardships (31:40). But there were also exceptional blessings which attracted the notice of their contemporaries in each generation, whether of Abraham (21:22), Isaac (26:12–16,28), Jacob (30:27,30) or Joseph (39:5). Perhaps we are meant to see in this a fleeting foretaste of the general blessing which was promised to come through them in the end: nothing less than the lifting of the curse and the undoing of the Fall.

(*ii*) *Persons.* Companionship is presented in Eden as a primary human need, which God proceeded to meet by creating not Adam's duplicate but his opposite and complement, and by uniting the two, male and female, in perfect personal harmony. We shall confine the present study to this fundamental human relationship.

The shattering of the harmony of man and wife, not by any mutual disagreement but by their agreeing together against God, proved at once how dependent it had been on His unseen participation. Without Him, love would henceforth be imperfect, and marriage would gravitate towards the subpersonal relationship foreshadowed in the terms 'desire' and 'rule' (3:16, where see commentary).

While the rest of the book confirms this tendency, it shows at the same time God's restraining grace; for throughout Genesis marriage is strong and enduring, and the very fact that the verb 'to know' (4:1, *etc.*) is used of sexual intercourse suggests a view of it that was originally personal rather than purely sensual, even if the term degenerated (19:5,8) into a mere euphemism. Against this stability, however, must be set the fact that there is scarcely a family, of those that are described in any detail, which is not torn with murderous jealousies, most of which reflect parental conflicts.

Polygamy is partly to blame for this, but polygamy is itself the symptom of an unbalanced view of marriage, which regards it as an institution in which the wife's ultimate *raison d'être* is the production of children. Where God had created the woman first and foremost for partnership, society made her in effect a means to an end, even if a noble end, and wrote its view into its marriage contracts. It was admittedly a view which the wives seem to have shared (16:2; 30:3,9), and an arrangement which God did not rebuke. But its cost in human relationships, as chapter 30 among others demonstrates, could be very high. Similarly, levirate marriage, which was to become an obligation under the Mosaic law, illustrates in chapter 38 the tensions that were set up in any form of union that was a mere procreative mechanism, even when due weight is given to the unscrupulous characters involved in that particular story. Whatever the value of these institutions in their day – and some value is undeniable – they only confirm the wisdom of God's foundation ordinance in 2:24.

(*iii*) *Authority*. The responsibility of government (apart from man's dominion over the animals) seems at first sight to emerge only after the Fall; but germinally it goes back to the founding of human society, as 1 Corinthians 11:3,8–10 points out, in the priority of Adam over Eve.

A harsher note, as we have seen above in discussing marriage, intruded into the relationship at the Fall (3:16b), and it is the Cainite Lamech who is the first to be heard expressing it (4:19,23). His bombast draws attention to the element of brute force which is the dark side of all authority in a fallen world; for while God is the source of human rule, and has ordained it for the ends of order and fair dealing (Rom. 13:1–7; 1 Pet. 2:13,14), the powers that are in the saddle in a given situation usually owe their position, from another angle, largely to the aggressiveness of ambitious men. For a purer example of authority we have to turn to the patriarchs, whose headship of their little community owed everything to the divine ordinance. This was in part their prerogative simply as parents, a fact which is very evident in the incidents of 9:20ff. where Ham, the son of Noah, brought a curse on his own progeny by the dishonour he showed his father, while Shem and Japheth took elaborate care to avoid such an impiety. Noah's honour at this moment resided in the dignity of his office as father; all other dignity had deserted him. Yet God upheld his authority. The patriarchs from Abraham onwards, however, had the additional power of transmitting the divine promises to one or other of their sons before their death. The story of Isaac's blessing of Jacob and Esau illustrates both the power attaching to his office (for he could not revoke the blessing he had given, 27:33) and its independence of his personal merit.

But in the world outside, the patriarchs wielded no authority. Not even full citizens, they had to make what arrangements they could by private treaties (*e.g.* over disputed watering rights, 21:30; 26:15ff.) or alliances (as Abram's with Aner, *etc.*, 14:13) or purchases (23:4ff.; 33:19). While they disapproved of marrying into Canaanite families (24:3; 26:34) and dissociated themselves from flagrant immorality (14:23; 34:7), they conformed with local laws and customs, aware of no call to be social critics or to seek office. It was only Lot who set himself to rise in the world, and attained a seat 'in the gate' (19:1), which was all too ineffective when the test came (19:9).

The one apparent exception to this rule is Joseph. His promotion came unsought and was so clearly the work of God that he had no hesitation over accepting it and proving himself equally God's servant and Pharaoh's. Where Moses became his people's saviour by renouncing Egypt, Joseph did so, in his quite different context, precisely by giving all his energy and wisdom to promoting that country's interests.

The attitude of Genesis to government emerges, in fact, as substantially that of the New Testament, where human rule is upheld as a divine ordinance, and its officers as God's servants, while the people of God are required to live not only as 'strangers and pilgrims' (1 Pet. 2:11) but as co-operative citizens whose 'well doing' (1 Pet. 2:15) puts criticism to silence.

c. Salvation

1. *Grace* must be the beginning of this topic, and Genesis reveals that grace, so far from being a mere answer to sin, is fundamental to creation itself. It appears in the very decision to bring 'many sons to glory' which is implied by the making of man in God's image and by the preparing of a world in which sonship could be brought to maturity (see on 2:8–17), and immortality put within man's grasp (2:9; 3:22). The entry of sin brings other aspects of grace to the fore, in God's measures to preserve mankind at some level of decency and order, and to bring certain men into covenant with Himself, through whom He will ultimately bless the world (18:18). As 'Saviour' (*i.e.*, Preserver) 'of all men'[1] He is shown in Genesis restraining the corruption and anarchy of sin through the discipline of hardship and mortality (3:17ff., 22ff.), the constructive use of natural resources (3:21), the sanctions of law (9:4–6), and the power to recognize moral obligations (*cf.* Abimelech's use of moral terms in 20:5,9), as well as through the direct influence of His servants (*e.g.* 50:20). As Saviour 'especially

[1] 1 Tim. 4:10.

38

of those who believe', He reveals His grace in choosing and calling them, justifying them, bringing them into covenant and educating them in His ways. These activities are summarized under the remaining two headings.

2. *Election.* Romans 9:6–13 points out that Genesis makes God's sovereignty of choice indubitable by its birth-stories of Isaac and Jacob. Jacob, in particular, was marked out from his brother Esau 'though they were not yet born, and had done nothing either good or bad'. So far from being random volunteers, such men owed their very existence to God's intervention (for Rebekah as well as Sarah had been childless, 25:21), and His choice was maintained against a long history of parental wavering and scheming. The same divine initiative raised up all the deliverers, from Seth, the 'appointed' successor for Abel (4:25), through Noah (whose role was prophesied at birth, 5:29) and Abram (called out from his country and kindred) to Joseph, who was 'sent', against all human intentions, 'to preserve . . . a remnant' of the chosen family (45:7,8).

Yet it is important to notice, in passing, that the choice of Isaac and Jacob before birth, and the corresponding rejection of Ishmael and Esau, were related explicitly to their function, not to their own salvation or doom. This is especially clear in the case of Ishmael, who was rejected in the one capacity, accepted in the other. When Abraham prayed, 'O that Ishmael might live in thy sight!', God's answer was 'No' to the implied request that he should displace Isaac, but 'Yes' to the words at their face value. 'I have heard you; behold, I will bless him . . .' (17:18–21). Election, in Genesis, concerns a man's place in or outside the line of succession leading to Christ, the 'seed' for the blessing of the nations (Rom. 9:5; Gal. 3:16).

3. *The sinner's reclamation.* From the moment of the Fall, the mortal effects of sin are a major theme of Genesis, showing its immediate divisiveness manward and Godward, its increasing hold on man, which culminated in the general depravity evident at the Flood, and its various outbursts in presumption at Babel, decadence at Sodom, and, in the family circle, all the manward sins of the decalogue.

God's saving work is no less full and varied. His manner of
seeking the sinner may be through straight conviction of guilt
(whether by the personal questioning addressed to Adam and
to Cain, or by the enigmatic ordeal that broke down the
brothers of Joseph in 42:21; 44:16) or it may be through the
sheer grace that surprised Jacob into response at Beth-el.
But it is God, rather than man, who seeks. Lot is dragged to
safety, having 'found grace' (19:19) almost in spite of himself;
and it is grace, too, that begins the whole story of Noah (6:8).

On man's side, we might be tempted to suppose (but for the
clue of Noah just mentioned) that rectitude of worship and
life were his passport to acceptance, until we reach the statement that ends speculation, namely that Abram was justified by
faith (15:6; *cf.* Rom. 4:1–5,13–25) – a saying that illuminates
not only every subsequent age, but every previous one, by
making it clear that from the first, faith had been indispensable
for access to God (Heb. 11:4ff.).

But salvation in Genesis is much more than bare acceptance.
Full grown, it is an intimacy with heaven which is as varied
in tone as are the characters who enjoy it: men as diverse as
Enoch, for whom the barrier of death melted away; Abraham
'the friend of God', whose devotion was tested almost beyond
bearing; his servant Eliezer (chapter 24) with his straightforward, centurion-like faith; and Jacob, whose career was
virtually a 'taming of the shrew', epitomized in the wrestling
at Peniel. And this intimacy was not that of likemindedness
alone, but the pledged relationship of a covenant, in which God
promised, 'I will be their God' (17:8), and man responded,
'the Lord shall be my God' (28:21).

In the realm of character and manward conduct, salvation
similarly goes far beyond a merely imputed righteousness. In
a lawless age Noah stood alone in his integrity (6:9), and in
contact with Sodom Abram shunned even its wealth for
God's sake (14:22,23), while Lot himself rebuked its vice
(19:7–9; *cf.* 2 Pet. 2:7,8), even if his way of doing it revealed a
sadly lop-sided moral code. A similar moral insensitivity in
Abraham and Isaac could earn the contempt of the heathen
themselves on occasion; but if by nature these men were as

fallible as their contemporaries, by grace they could rise immeasurably higher. Abraham's intercession for Sodom, like Judah's for Benjamin, exhibits a selfless concern which is the mark of the saints from Moses to Paul, while Joseph's patience, purity, wisdom, and love for his enemies are little less than God-like.

On the ultimate aspect of salvation, deliverance from the last enemy, Genesis has only faint adumbrations. 'You are dust, and to dust you shall return' has a ring of finality; yet the context itself leaves a door ajar, for God had once breathed life into this very dust. Twice, too, there are more direct glimpses of His power over death: once when Enoch was taken (5:24), and once when Abraham realized that God could bring back Isaac from the dead ('we will . . . come again to you', 22:5; *cf.* Heb. 11:19).

These, however, were lessons for another time. Hope, at this stage, was God-directed towards the growth of the chosen family, the possession of the land and the blessing of the nations. If death was taken calmly meanwhile by the patriarchs, it was largely because burial in the family tomb anticipated that family's entry into its inheritance (*cf.* 47:29f.; 50:24f.); for the promise and mission were vested in the chosen 'seed', not in any of these individuals as such. 'God will surely visit you' (50:25): that was hope enough. From its fulfilment there would open out, in time, the fullness of salvation as the New Testament knows it. Genesis is content to see this from afar, and meanwhile to concern itself with the early flow of this river, rather than its distant estuary and ocean.

ANALYSIS

A. THE PRIMEVAL HISTORY (chapters 1–11)

I. THE STORY OF CREATION (1:1 – 2:3)

II. THE PROBATION AND FALL OF MAN (2:4 – 3:24)

III. MAN UNDER SIN AND DEATH (4:1 – 6:8)

IV. THE WORLD UNDER JUDGMENT (6:9 – 8:14)

V. RENEWAL AND REPEOPLING (8:15 – 10:32)

VI. END AND BEGINNING: BABEL AND CANAAN
   (11:1–32)

B. THE CHOSEN FAMILY (chapters 12–50)

I. ABRAM UNDER CALL AND PROMISE (chapters 12–20)

II. ISAAC AND THE FURTHER TESTS OF FAITH (chapters
   21–26)

III. JACOB AND THE EMERGENCE OF ISRAEL (chapters
   27–36)

IV. JOSEPH AND THE MIGRATION TO EGYPT (chapters
   37–50)

COMMENTARY

A. The Primeval History (chapters 1–11)

I. THE STORY OF CREATION (1:1 – 2:3)

1:1, 2. Prologue

1. It is no accident that *God* is the subject of the first sentence of the Bible, for this word dominates the whole chapter and catches the eye at every point of the page: it is used some thirty-five times in as many verses of the story. The passage, indeed the Book, is about Him first of all; to read it with any other primary interest (which is all too possible) is to misread it.

The opening expression, *In the beginning*, is more than a bare note of time. The variations on this theme in Isaiah 40ff. show that the beginning is pregnant with the end, and the whole process present to God who is First and Last (*e.g.*, Is. 46:10; 48:12). Proverbs 8:22f. reveals something of the Godward side of this beginning of creation; John 1:1–3 is more explicit; and the New Testament elsewhere at times reaches back behind it (*e.g.*, Jn. 17:5,24) into eternity.

Grammatically, this phrase could be translated as introducing a clause completed in verse 3 after a parenthetical verse 2: 'When God began to create . . . (the earth was without form . . .), God said, Let there be light . . . '. This would not be saying that the undeveloped earth was not of God's making; only that creation, in its full sense, still had far to go. But the familiar translation, 'In the beginning God . . . ', is equally grammatical, is supported by all the ancient versions, and affirms unequivocally the truth laid down elsewhere (*e.g.*, Heb. 11:3) that until God spoke, nothing existed.[1]

---

[1] *Cf.*, among recent discussions, von Rad, p. 46; B. S. Childs, *Myth and Reality in the Old Testament*, p. 31; W. Eichrodt, 'In the Beginning' in *Israel's Prophetic Heritage*, ed. Anderson and Harrelson (S.C.M. Press, 1962), pp. 1–10; P. Humbert, *ZAW*, LXXVI, 1964, pp. 121–131.

The meaning of *created* (*bārā'*; *cf.* 21,27; 2:3,4) is best determined from the Old Testament as a whole (including this chapter), where we find that its subject is invariably God, its product may be either things (*e.g.*, Is. 40:26) or situations (Is. 45:7,8, RSV), its companion verbs are chiefly 'to make' and 'to form' (Gn. 1:26,27; 2:7), and its precise sense varies with its context, which may emphasize either the initial moment of bringing into existence (Is. 48:3,7: 'suddenly', 'now') or the patient work of bringing something to perfection (Gn. 2:1–4; *cf.* Is. 65:18). In this opening statement it is possible either to see the whole span of the word, so that verse 1 summarizes the whole passage, or (as I prefer) to take it as stating the beginning of the process.

In verses 1,21,27 this impressive verb marks three great beginnings; but it does not define a particular way of creating, since in 2:3,4 it is parallel with *'āśâ* ('make') and covers the whole range of God's work.

2. *And the earth* would be better translated 'Now the earth . . . ', for the construction is exactly that of Jonah 3:3 ('Now Nineveh was an exceeding great city . . .'). By all normal usage the verse is an expansion of the statement just made, and its own two halves are concurrent.[1] It sets the scene, making *the earth* our vantage point; whatever the total pattern, this is our concern (*cf.* Ps. 115:16). The sombre terms of 2a throw into relief the mounting glory of the seven days; and if God alone brings form out of formlessness, He alone sustains it. In visions of judgment (Je. 4:23; Is. 34:11), chaos comes back, termed *tōhû* and *bōhû* as here. *Tōhû* (*without form*) is used elsewhere to mean, in physical terms, a trackless waste (*e.g.*, Dt. 32:10; Jb. 6:18), emptiness (Jb. 26:7), chaos (Is. 24:10; 34:11; 45:18); and metaphorically, what is baseless or futile (*e.g.*, 1 Sa. 12:21; Is. 29:21). The rhyming *bōhû*[2] (*void*)

---

[1] If verse 2 were intended to tell of a catastrophe ('And the earth *became* . . .'), as some have suggested, it would use the Hebrew narrative construction, not the circumstantial construction as here. See the debate between P. W. Heward and F. F. Bruce in *JTVI*, LXVIII, 1946, pp. 13–37. *Cf.* E. J. Young in *WTJ*, XXIII, 1960–1, pp. 151–178. For a broader critique of the 'gap' theory, see B. Ramm, *The Christian View of Science and Scripture*, pp. 135–144.

[2] Arabic *bhy*, 'be empty', gives a probable clue to its meaning.

is found only twice elsewhere (see above), each time paired with *tōhû*.

The deep (tᵉhôm) seems to be etymologically akin to (but not derived from) the word *tiamat*,[1] the personified ocean and rival of the gods in the Sumero-Accadian creation myth. But here it is the literal ocean, whatever poetic play is made elsewhere with the taming of its fury and its monsters (Ps. 74:13,14; 89:9,10; 104:6,7; Is. 51:9,10). See also on verse 21.

Not in conflict, then, but in evocative activity *the Spirit of God*[2] *was moving* (RSV rightly retains the participle). In the Old Testament the Spirit is a term for God's outgoing energy, creative and sustaining (*cf.* Jb. 33:4; Ps. 104:30). Any impression of Olympian detachment which the rest of the chapter might have conveyed is forestalled by the simile of the mother-bird 'hovering' (Moffatt) or fluttering over her brood. The verb reappears in Deuteronomy 32:11 to describe the eagle's movements in stirring its young into flight; this aspect of intimate contact must be kept in mind throughout.

This whole verse is sometimes felt to be out of key with the rest of the passage, its conjectured echoes of pagan myths (in which gods and monsters struggle for mastery) producing a calculated[3] or uncalculated[4] dissonance. But the knowledge of these myths has laid a false trail for us, diverting our attention from the familiar fact that God's *normal* method is to work from the formless to the formed. The whole process is creation. If Isaiah 45:18 forbids us to stop with this verse, all that we learn of God's ways from Scripture (*e.g.*, Ps. 139:13–16; Eph. 4:11–16) and experience, to say nothing of the natural sciences, insists that we start with something like it. Indeed the six days now to be described can be viewed as the positive counterpart of the twin negatives 'without form and void',

[1] See the well-documented discussion in D. F. Payne, *Genesis One Reconsidered* (Tyndale Press, 1964), pp. 10f.

[2] Some would translate this 'a mighty wind' (*e.g.* von Rad, p. 47). But Dn. 7:2, which glances at this passage, shows that a writer who meant to convey such a meaning could do so without requiring his readers to divine it from the familiar expression for the Spirit of God, construed in an unfamiliar way.

[3] *E.g.*, B. S. Childs, *Myth and Reality in the Old Testament*, pp. 30–42.

[4] *E.g.*, H. Gunkel, *Genesis*[4], pp. 104f., cited in B. S. Childs, *op. cit.*

matching them with form and fullness. They may be set out as follows:[1]

Form		*Fullness*
Day 1	Light and Dark	Day 4	Lights of Day and Night
Day 2	Sea and Sky	Day 5	Creatures of Water and Air
Day 3	Fertile Earth	Day 6	Creatures of the Land

For a discussion of this sequence, and of the word 'day', see Additional Note, pp. 54ff.

1:3-5. The first day

3. The simple phrase *And God said* precludes some far-reaching errors and stores up a wealth of meaning. These eight specific commands, calling all things into being, leave no room for notions of a universe that is self-existent, or struggled for, or random, or a divine emanation; and the absence of any intermediary implies an extremely rich content for the word 'said'. This may not be at once apparent, for we ourselves know what it is to order things to happen. But our commands, even at their most precise, are mere outlines: they rely on existing materials and agencies to embody them, and the craftsman himself works with what he finds, to produce what he only knows in part. The Creator, on the other hand, in willing an end willed every smallest means to it, His thought shaping itself exactly to the least cell and atom, and His creative word wholly meaningful. One might almost express this immediacy of knowledge by saying that He knows each mode of created existence by experience – only experience is too weak a word: 'Thou knowest it altogether' (Ps. 139:4; *cf.* Am. 4:13). This is not pantheism: it is taking creatorship seriously. So the New Testament reveals what is already latent here when it calls the Son and Word of God 'the first-born of all creation; for in him all things were created, . . . and in him all things hold together' (Col. 1:15–17, RSV; *cf.* Jn. 1:1–4; Heb. 1:2,3).

[1] This table is largely indebted to W. H. Griffith Thomas, *Genesis: A Devotional Commentary* (1946 edn., Eerdmans), p. 29. *Cf.* Driver, p. 2, using the terms 'preparation' and 'accomplishment'.

Let there be light: we may note in passing that the Vulgate's '*Fiat lux*' gives us the expression 'creation by fiat'. *Light*, which has lent its name to all that is life-giving (Jn. 1:4), truth-giving (2 Cor. 4:6), gladdening (Ec. 11:7) and pure (1 Jn. 1:5–7), appropriately marks the first step from chaos to order; and as it here precedes the sun,[1] so in the final vision it outlasts it (Rev. 22:5).[2]

4, 5. *God saw . . . divided . . . called.* To some of the ancients, day and night suggested warring powers; to modern man, merely a spinning world. Genesis knows nothing of either conflict or chance in this: only of the watchful Creator who assigns to everything its value (4a), place (4b) and meaning (5a). Darkness is part of the whole that is 'very good' (31a,b); it is not abolished, only subordinated. The idea of 'dividing' is specially prominent, both here (*cf.* 6,7,14,18) and in the law (*e.g.*, Lv. 20:25), since this way lies cosmos (*cf.* Eph. 4:16; Phil. 1:9,10) and the other way chaos (Is. 5:20,24).

The AV's *the evening and the morning were* gives the misleading impression that the reckoning starts with evening.[3] Rather translate it 'evening came and morning came' (Moffatt; *cf.* RV, RSV).

On *the first day* (AV), see the Additional Note on the days of creation, pp. 54ff.

1:6–8. The second day

The verb underlying *firmament* (*raqia'*) means to beat or stamp (*cf.* Ezk. 6:11a), often in connection with beaten metal. Job 37:18 shows that we are not meant to rarefy this word into 'expanse' or 'atmosphere': 'Can you, like him, spread out (*tarqia'*) the skies, hard as a molten (*i.e.* cast metal) mirror?' (RSV). It is pictorial language, like our expression 'the vault of heaven'. In another set of terms we should speak probably of the enveloping vapours being raised clear of the ocean-surface (*cf.* E. Bevan's reconstruction quoted on pp. 55f.), the two ways of speaking are complementary.

[1] See Additional Note, pp. 54ff.
[2] *Cf.* K. Barth, *Church Dogmatics*, III, 1 (T. and T. Clark, 1958), p. 167.
[3] For an extended discussion, see H. R. Stroes in *VT*, XVI, 1966, pp. 460–475.

On *divide, divided* (6,7), see the next paragraph.

1:9–13. The third day

God continues to give form to the world, by the process of differentiation (9,10; see on 4,5); but the emphasis begins to shift towards the theme of fullness (11,12) which will be prominent in the rest of the chapter.

11, 12. *The earth* is empowered to *bring forth* (AV) what is proper to it. Literally verse 11 runs: ' . . . Let the earth vegetate vegetation, herb seeding seed, fruit tree making fruit after its kind.' Comparably, in 20 the waters are to 'swarm with a swarm of living creatures', and in 24 the earth is to 'bring forth' the living creature. This emergence of life is no less 'creation' than was the first act. The two kinds of expression share the account in 21: 'And God *created* . . . every living creature . . . that the waters *swarmed with*'; and 25 says, of the beasts which the earth was to '*bring forth*' (24), God '*made*' them.

If this language seems well suited to the hypothesis of creation by evolution (as the present writer thinks), this is not the only scheme it would allow, and its purpose is not to drop a special clue for the present age. Rather it is to show that God has bound together all creatures in a common dependence on their native elements, while giving each the distinctive character of its kind. Each has an origin which is from one angle natural and from another supernatural; and the natural process is made self-perpetuating and, under God, autonomous. One implication of this is that it is part of godliness to respect the limitations within which we live as natural creatures, as from Him. Another is that fertility, so often deified in the ancient world, is a *created* capacity, from the hand of the one God.

1:14–19. The fourth day

Once more the description is unashamedly geocentric. On this, and on the appearing of the sun, *etc.*, so late on the scene, see the Additional Note, pp. 54ff. The view expressed there brings verse 14 into a simple relation with verse 4 by regarding the sun as the divider of day from night in each verse; veiled in 4, visible in 14. But again the dominant interest is theological. Sun, moon and stars are God's good gifts, producing the pattern of varied *seasons* (14) in which we thrive (*cf.* Acts 14:17) and by which Israel was to mark out the year for God (Lv. 23:4). As *signs* (14) they will speak for God, not for fate (Je. 10:2; *cf.* Mt. 2:9; Lk. 21:25,28), for they *rule* (16,18) only as lightbearers, not as powers. In these few simple sentences the lie is given to a superstition as old as Babylon[1] and as modern as a newspaper-horoscope.

1:20–23. The fifth day

20. The RVmg reproduces the Hebrew: ' . . . swarm with swarms of living creatures' (see note on 11,12). *Living creatures* (RSV) are the same expression as 'living soul' in 2:7, where see note. *Fowl* (AV, RV) or *birds* (RSV) are literally 'flying things', and can include insects (*cf.* Dt. 14:19,20). *The open firmament* (AV, RV) should be simply *across the firmament* (RSV): it is again the language of how things appear, as one looks up at the dome of the sky.

21, 22. The *sea monsters* (*tannînîm*) (RV, RSV; *whales*, AV) are specially noteworthy, since to the Canaanites this was an ominous word, standing for the powers of chaos confronting Baal in the beginning. Here they are just magnificent creatures (like Leviathan in Ps. 104:26; Jb. 41), enjoying God's blessing with the rest (22). Although in some scriptures these names will symbolize God's enemies (*e.g.* Is. 27:1), taunted in the very terms in which Baal exults over them,[2] no doubt is left by this chapter that the most fearsome of creatures were from God's good hand. There may be rebels in His kingdom, but no rivals. To the Canaanites, however, Baal's adversaries were gods like himself, or demons to be propitiated;[3] and to the Babylonians the chaos-monster Tiamat pre-existed the gods. Y. Kaufmann points out how deeply such a view affected

[1] *Cf. Enuma elish*, V:1,2: 'He constructed stations for the great gods, Fixing their astral likenesses as constellations' (*ANET*, p. 67). The belief is more ancient than the poem.

[2] See *DOTT*, p. 129, ll.24f., and notes 16,17, p. 132.

[3] *UM*, p. 333, *s.v. tnn*. Also *UT*, p. 498, ditto.

non-Israelite religion, for the worshipper could never be sure, as we can, that in serving God there is peace; there were always other unknown quantities in the background.[1]

1:24-31. The sixth day

24. *Let the earth bring forth:* see note on 11. *The living creature,* as in 20, is the same Hebrew expression as 'living soul' in 2:7 (where see note). The *creeping thing,* which suggests to us only the reptiles, is not a scientific classification but a description of the smooth or crawling motion of various kinds of creature. The Hebrew verb has already appeared in 21 ('moves'), evidently to denote the gliding of fish, as in Psalm 104:25. Probably the three kinds of animal in 24 are, broadly, what we should call domesticated animals, small creatures and game.

26. *Let us make man.* In both the opening chapters of Genesis man is portrayed as *in* nature and *over* it, continuous with it and discontinuous. He shares the sixth day with other creatures, is made of dust as they are (2:7,19), feeds as they feed (1:29,30) and reproduces with a blessing similar to theirs (1:22,28a); so he can well be studied partly through the study of them: they are half his context. But the stress falls on his distinctness. *Let us make* stands in tacit contrast with 'Let the earth bring forth' (24); the note of self-communing and the impressive plural proclaim it a momentous step; and this done, the whole creation is complete. *Vis-à-vis* the animals man is set apart by his office (1:26b,28b; 2:19; *cf.* Ps. 8:4-8; Jas. 3:7) and still more by his nature (2:20); but his crowning glory is his relation to God.

The terms, *in our image, after our likeness,* are characteristically bold. If *image* seems too pictorial a word, there is the rest of Scripture to control it; but at a single stroke it imprints on the mind the central truth about us. The words *image* and *likeness* reinforce one another: there is no 'and' between the phrases, and Scripture does not use them as technically distinct expressions, as some theologians have done, whereby

[1] *The Religion of Israel* (Allen and Unwin, 1961), chapter II, especially pp. 21-24.

the 'image' is man's indelible constitution as a rational and morally responsible being, and the 'likeness' is that spiritual accord with the will of God which was lost at the Fall. The distinction exists, but it does not coincide with these terms. After the Fall, man is still said to be in God's image (Gn. 9:6) and likeness (Jas. 3:9); nonetheless he requires to be 'renewed . . . after the image of him that created him' (Col. 3:10; *cf.* Eph. 4:24). See also 5:1,3.

When we try to define the image of God it is not enough to react against a crude literalism by isolating man's mind and spirit from his body. The Bible makes man a unity: acting, thinking and feeling with his whole being. This living creature, then, and not some distillation from him, is an expression or transcription of the eternal, incorporeal creator in terms of temporal, bodily, creaturely existence – as one might attempt a transcription of, say, an epic into a sculpture, or a symphony into a sonnet. Likeness in this sense survived the Fall, since it is structural. As long as we are human we are, by definition, in the image of God. But spiritual likeness – in a single word, love – can be present only where God and man are in fellowship; hence the Fall destroyed it, and our redemption recreates and perfects it. 'We are God's children now; . . . when he appears we shall be like him, for we shall see him as he is' (1 Jn. 3:2, RSV; *cf.* 4:12).

Among the implications of the doctrine we may note that on the Godward side it excludes the idea that our Maker is the 'wholly Other'. Manward, it requires us to take all human beings infinitely seriously (*cf.* Gn. 9:6; Jas. 3:9). And our Lord implies, further, that God's stamp on us constitutes a declaration of ownership (Mt. 22:20,21).

Us . . . our . . . our. The plural is interpreted by, *e.g.*, Delitzsch and von Rad as including the angels, whom the Old Testament calls at times 'sons of God', or, generically, 'god(s)' (*cf.* Jb. 1:6; Ps. 8:5 with Heb. 2:7; Ps. 82:1,6 with Jn. 10:34,35). This can claim some support from Genesis 3:22 ('as one of us'); but any implication that others had a hand in our creation is quite foreign to the chapter as a whole and to the challenge in Isaiah 40: 14: 'With whom took he counsel?' It is rather the plural of fullness, which is found in the regular word for God (*'elōhîm*) used with a singular verb; and this fullness, glimpsed in the Old Testament,[1] was to be unfolded as tri-unity, in the further 'we' and 'our' of John 14:23 (with 14:17).

The *dominion* over all creatures is 'not the content but the consequence' of the divine image (Delitzsch). James 3:7,8 points out that we still largely exercise it – with a fatal exception. Hebrews 2:6–10 and 1 Corinthians 15:27,28 (quoting Ps. 8:6) speak of its full reclamation by Jesus, and 1 Corinthians 6:3 promises the exalting of redeemed man above angels (*cf.* Rev. 4:4). In sad contrast, our human record of exploiting what is at our mercy proves the unfitness of fallen beings to govern, as ourselves ungoverned: *cf.* the ominous tone of 9:2.

27. The words *male and female*, coming at this juncture, have far-reaching implications, as Jesus made plain when He coupled them with 2:24 to make the two sayings the twin pillars of marriage (Mk. 10:6,7). To define humanity as bisexual is to make each partner the complement of the other, and to anticipate the New Testament doctrine of the sexes' spiritual equality ('all one', Gal. 3:28; 'heirs together', 1 Pet. 3:7b; see also Mk. 12:25). This is reaffirmed in Genesis 2:18–25, together with their temporal inequality (*cf.* 1 Pet. 3:5–7a; 1 Cor. 11:7–12; 1 Tim. 2:12,13), and again in 5:1,2.

28. *And God blessed them.* To bless is to bestow not only a gift but a function (*cf.* 1:22; 2:3; *cf.* also the parting blessings of Isaac, Jacob and Moses), and to do so with warm concern. At its highest, it is God turning full-face to the recipient (*cf.* Nu. 6:24–26) in self-giving (Acts 3:26). On the implications of *subdue*, see the Additional Note to chapter 3, p. 73.

29, 30. The assigning of *every green plant for food* (RSV) to all creatures must not be pressed to mean that all were once herbivorous, any more than to mean that all plants were equally edible to all. It is a generalization, that directly or indirectly all life depends on vegetation, and the concern of the verse is to show that all are fed from God's hand. See also on 9:3.

[1] See Introduction, pp. 33ff.

31. *God saw* . . . 'It is a part of the history of creation that God completed His work and confronted it as a completed totality' (K. Barth).[1] By His grace something other than Himself is granted not only existence but a measure of self-determination. And if the details of His work were pronounced 'good' (4,10,12,18,21,25), the whole is *very good*. Old and New Testament alike endorse this in their call to a thankful acceptance of things material (*e.g.,* Ps. 104:24; 1 Tim. 4:3–5) as both from and for God.

2:1–3. The seventh day

God's finished task is sealed in the words *he rested* (2,3; literally 'ceased'; from *šāḇaṯ*, the root of 'sabbath'). It is the rest of achievement, not inactivity, for He nurtures what He creates; we may compare the symbolism of Jesus 'seated' after His finished redemption (Heb. 8:1; 10:12), to dispense its benefits.

Our Lord based His own constructive use of the sabbath on this understanding of the divine rest ('My Father is working still', Jn. 5:17, RSV), and His double-edged saying in Mark 2:27, 28 preserves the pattern of gift (*God blessed*) and claim (*and hallowed*, RV, RSV) implicit in verse 3. Characteristically He went to 'the beginning' for His teaching; *cf.* Mark 10:6.

But God's rest was pregnant with more than the gift of the sabbath: it is still big with promise for the believer, who is summoned to share it (Heb. 3:7 – 4:11). As G. von Rad has well said: 'The declaration mounts, as it were, to the place of God himself and testifies that with the living God there is rest. . . . Even more, that God has "blessed", "sanctified" . . . this rest means that' the author 'does not consider it as something for God alone but as a concern of the world. The way is being prepared, therefore, for . . . the final, saving good.'[2] The formula that rounded off each of the six days with the onset of evening and morning is noticeably absent, as if to imply the 'infinite perspective' (Delitzsch) of God's sabbath.

[1] *Church Dogmatics*, III, 1, p. 222.
[2] *Genesis*, p. 60.

Additional Note on the days of creation

The symmetry of the scheme of Genesis 1 raises the question whether we are meant to understand the chapter chronologically or in some other way. The idea of 'form and fullness' could conceivably have imposed the present pattern on the material, some of which is displayed in a different order in chapter 2 in the interests of a different emphasis. Or again, as Karl Barth sees it, the mention of light before that of the sun and moon could be read as 'an open protest against all and every kind of sun-worship'[1] – in which case the polemical aim would need to be taken into account as contributing to the structure. Another theory makes the six days a sequence of days of instruction divinely given to the author, not days of the creation itself; but this largely rests on a misunderstanding of the word 'made', in Exodus 20:11.[2] Again, a liturgical interest could account for the scheme of days, if it could be substantiated that this 'hymn' of creation was composed for a seven-day New Year Festival in Israel akin to the *Akitu* Babylonian rite[3] – a hypothesis rather slenderly based. Yet again, it may be urged that the order belongs to the poetic form of the passage, and must not be overpressed, since the author's concern is to display before us the visible world as God's handiwork, not to inform us that this feature is older than that.[4] Just as it would be impossibly prosaic to cross-question the author of, *e.g.*, Job 38 on 'the waterskins of the heavens' or 'the cords of Orion', so it could be the wrong approach to this passage to expect its pattern of days to be informative rather than aesthetic.

It may be that one or other of these suggestions does justice to the intention of the chapter. Yet to the present writer the march of the days is too majestic a progress to carry no implication of ordered sequence; it also seems over-subtle to

[1] K. Barth, *Church Dogmatics*, III, 1, pp. 120f.
[2] P. J. Wiseman, *Creation Revealed in Six Days* (Marshall, Morgan and Scott, 1948), pp. 33f.
[3] Hooke, p. 36.
[4] J. A. Thompson, 'Creation' (article in *NBD*, p. 271); *cf.* D. F. Payne *Genesis One Reconsidered*, pp. 19–23.

adopt a view of the passage which discounts one of the primary impressions it makes on the ordinary reader. It is a story, not only a statement. As with all narrating, it demanded a choice of standpoint, of material to include, and of method in the telling. In each of these, simplicity has been a dominant concern. The language is that of every day, describing things by their appearance; the outlines of the story are bold, free of distracting exceptions and qualifications, free also to group together matters that belong together (so that trees, for example, anticipate their chronological place in order to be classified with vegetation), to achieve a grand design in which the demands now of time-sequence, now of subject-matter, control the presentation, and the whole reveals the Creator and His preparing a place for us.

The view that the chapter is intended to reveal the general sequence of creation as it affected this earth, is based on the apparent character of the writing. But it is reinforced, one may think, by the remarkable degree of correspondence that can be found between this sequence and the one implied by current science. This has often been pointed out, and not always by those who set any store on the factual accuracy of Scripture in passages of this sort, as the following extract from Edwyn Bevan's essay, 'The religious value of myths in the Old Testament', will show:

'The stages by which the earth comes to be what it is cannot indeed be precisely fitted to the account which modern science would give of the process, but in principle they seem to anticipate the modern scientific account by a remarkable flash of imagination, which a Christian may also call inspiration. Supposing we could be transported backward in time to different moments in the past of our planet, we should see it first in a condition in which there was no land distinguishable from the water and only a dim light coming from the invisible sun through the thick volumes of enveloping cloud: at a later moment, as the globe dried, land would have appeared; again at a later moment low forms of life, animal and vegetable, would have begun; sooner or later in the process the cloud-masses would have become so thin and broken that a creature standing on earth would see above him sun and moon and stars; at a still later moment we should see the earth of great primeval monsters; and lastly we should see the earth with its present fauna and flora, and the final product of animal evolution, Man.'[1]

The *days of creation* may be similarly understood: they give the reader a simple means of relating the work of God in creation to the work of God here and now in history. While a scientific account would have to speak of ages, not days, and would group them to mark the steps that are scientifically significant, the present account surveys the same scene for its theological significance. With this in view it speaks of days, not ages, and groups them into a week. The significance of the week is explicit in the sabbath-hallowing (2:3; *cf.* Ex. 20:11; 31:17) which makes man's proper rhythm of work and rest a reminder and miniature of the Creator's; and the division of the period into days may be meant to imply no more than this.[2] Yet days are not essential to the idea of the sabbath, for this can be expressed in longer units (Lv. 25:4,8), and an independent reason suggests itself for the term. It is simply the *brevity* of a day.

To a modern reader this at once raises the question of scientific accuracy. One may argue that 'day' can bear the sense of 'epoch' (*cf., e.g.,* Ps. 90:4; Is. 4:2), or that days of God have no human analogies (as Augustine,[3] and Origen[4] before him, urged); others will take the days literally and find proof of human fallibility in them: a husk of factual error concealing the good grains of theology in the chapter. The assumption common to these interpretations is that God would not have us picture the creation as compressed into a mere week. But this may be exactly what God does intend

[1] Edwyn Bevan, in Hooke, p. 161. Quoted by permission of the Clarendon Press, Oxford.
[2] *Cf.* D. F. Payne, *Genesis One Reconsidered*, pp. 17ff.
[3] *The City of God*, XI. vi.
[4] *De Principiis*, iv. 3, cited by E. Bevan, in Hooke, p. 155.

us to do. The creation story has stood as a bulwark against a succession of fashionable errors – polytheism, dualism, the eternity of matter, the evil of matter, astrology – and not least, against every tendency to empty human history of meaning. It resists this nihilism explicitly, in displaying man as God's image and regent; but also implicitly, in presenting the tremendous acts of creation as a mere curtain-raiser to the drama that slowly unfolds throughout the length of the Bible. The prologue is over in a page; there are a thousand to follow.

If every generation has needed this emphasis, perhaps none has had greater need of it than the age of scientific knowledge. The scientific account of the universe, realistic and indispensable as it is, overwhelms us with statistics that reduce our apparent significance to vanishing-point. Not the prologue, but the human story itself, is now the single page in a thousand, and the whole terrestrial volume is lost among uncatalogued millions. In face of these immensities we should not dare to set store on our own time and place, but for the divine word which orientates us and reveals the true proportion. Through the apparent naïvety of this earth-centred and history-centred account God says to each generation, whether it is burdened with the weight of factual knowledge which our own possesses, or with the misleading fantasies of the ancient religions, 'Stand here, on this earth and in this present, to get the meaning of the whole. See this world as My gift and charge to you, with the sun, moon and stars as its lamps and timekeepers, and its creatures under your care. See the present age as the time to which My creative work was moving, and the unconscious aeons before it as "but a few days", like the years which Jacob gave for Rachel.'

This interpretation may leave us dissatisfied on two counts. We may object, first, that the author shows no consciousness of speaking otherwise than literally, and secondly, that this reading of the chapter makes it guilty of saying one thing and meaning another.

The first point may well be true, but it is hardly an objection. We know that the full meaning of an inspired utterance was often hidden from the speaker: even Caiaphas exemplifies this, and the same is said of Daniel and of the prophets.[1] The latent truth does not make their words any less their own; nor do we have to shut our eyes to it, as though the full flower of meaning were less authentic than the bud.

The second point may seem more weighty. If the 'days' were not days at all, would God have countenanced the word? Does He trade in'inaccuracies, however edifying? The question hinges on the proper use of language. A God who made no concessions to our ways of seeing and speaking would communicate to us no meaning. Hence the phenomenological language of the chapter (like our own talk of 'sunrise', 'dewfall', *etc.*) and its geocentric standpoint; but hence also the heavy temporal foreshortening which turns ages into days. Both are instruments of truth, diagrams enabling us to construe and not misconstrue a totality too big for us. It is only pedantry that would quarrel with terms that simplify in order to clarify.

II. THE PROBATION AND FALL OF MAN
(2:4 – 3:24)

Man is now the pivot of the story, as in chapter 1 he was the climax. Everything is told in terms of him: even the primeval waste is shown awaiting him (2:5b), and the narrative works outwards from man himself to man's environment (garden, trees, river, beasts and birds) in logical as against chronological order, to reveal the world as we are meant to see it: a place expressly prepared for our delight and discipline. It is misleading to call this a second creation account, for it hastens to localize the scene, passing straight from the world at large to 'a garden . . . in the east'; all that follows is played out on this narrow stage.

Throughout the section, to the end of chapter 3, the rare, almost unique,[2] double name *the Lord God* (Yahweh Elohim)

---

[1] See Jn. 11:49–53; Dn. 12:8,9; 1 Pet. 1:10–12.
[2] But its rarity is not apparent in our versions, where the term *the Lord GOD* is used nearly 300 times to translate a different expression (lit. the Lord Yahweh). Only the capitals in the word '*GOD*' mark this difference.

adds its own impressiveness to the story and establishes the unity of the two terms,[1] the personal name and the title, which will dominate the Old Testament.

2:4-25. Man's felicity

4-6. Prologue. The refrain *These are the generations* (4a) divides Genesis into sections at 2:4; 5:1; 6:9; 10:1; 11:10,27; 25:12,19; 36:1,9; 37:2. The word *generations* (*tôlᵉḏōṯ*) properly means offspring, and here it corresponds to 'all the host of them' (verse 1). But it can have the wider sense of (family-) history, facing either the past (as in the family registrations of 1 Ch. 7:4,9, *etc.*) or the future (as in, *e.g.*, Ru. 4:18) according to context.

The view taken here, and defended in the Introduction (pp. 23f.), is that this phrase in Genesis always looks forward, introducing a new stage of the book.[2] P. J. Wiseman,[3] however, argued that it is always a conclusion (usually to a set of family records), and the documentary theory makes it a conclusion at this one point in Genesis, but anomalously an introduction everywhere else.

It is worth adding that the LXX somewhat inaccurately uses the noun which has given us the title of the book: *genesis*, 'origin'.

5, 6. These preliminary verses are saying from the special angle of this chapter what was declared in 1:2, namely that when God made the earth it was not initially (*no plant . . . yet . . . and no herb . . . yet*, 5, RV, RSV) the hospitable place that we know. Not even the wild growth (*plant*)[4] had appeared, still less the edible crops (*herb*, as 3:18b; *cf.* the phrase *to till the ground*, 5). Even the familiar sky with its clouds and rainfall was not yet in evidence: only a continual upsurging (6a; the verb is imperfective) of *mist* or (probably) *flood*,[5] so that the

[1] On these terms and their use, see Introduction, p. 33.

[2] *Cf.* the MT punctuation and the RV paragraphing. *Cf.* also D. Bonhoeffer, *Creation and Fall* (S.C.M. Press, 1959), p. 41.

[3] *New Discoveries in Babylonia about Genesis*, pp. 47-60. His view is discussed briefly in the Introduction, above, p. 23f.

[4] *Plant* (*śîaḥ*) is found elsewhere in the Old Testament only at 21:15 and Jb. 30:4,7, where it is the desert scrub, the refuge of the desperate.

[5] So RSVmg; K-B *Lexicon* calls attention to Akkadian *edû*, 'inundation'.

whole scene was a watery waste – for the meaning of *watered* (6) can range from a beneficial sense, as in 10, to that of complete inundation (*cf.* Ezk. 32:6, 'even to the mountains'); and the latter seems most consistent with the context, if 5b portrays the earth still shrouded in vapour. Scholars, curiously, have followed one another in reading dryness, of all things, into these verses, as though verse 6 marked a new development. The Hebrew does not allow this; it can only be read as expanding the description already given by an attendant circumstance.[1]

7. The making of man. This verse, with profound simplicity, matches and completes the classic 1:27. There it was the nouns ('image', 'likeness') that related man to God; here, the verbs, for revelation is as often given in story as in statement. The two verbs balance. *Formed* expresses the relation of craftsman to material, with implications of both skill (*e.g.* Ps. 94:9, 'He that formed the eye . . .'; *cf.* Ps. 139:14–16) and a sovereignty which man forgets at his peril (Is. 29:16: Je. 18:4); while *breathed* is warmly personal, with the face-to-face intimacy of a kiss and the significance that this was an act of giving as well as making; and self-giving at that. *Cf.* Job 32:8;[2] also John 20:22, where Jesus bestows the Holy Spirit as the animating breath of the new creation, the church. Even at our making, then, the pattern 'God so loved . . . that he gave . . .' is already visible.

The remaining expressions of the verse place man in his earthly setting, since he is as truly natural as supernatural: a creature of common chemicals, *from the ground* like the animals (*cf.* 19), and *a living being* (RSV) as they are (for this Hebrew expression is already found in 1:20,24, in spite of AV, RV; *cf.*

Cf. von Rad, p. 74: 'If the meaning is given from the Akkadian, it would mean "surging of waves".' See further E. A. Speiser, *BASOR*, 140, 1955, pp. 9–11.

[1] The present author discusses the passage more fully in *Tyndale Bulletin*, 17, 1966, pp. 109–114.

[2] It can be argued that *nᵉšāmâ*, breath, invariably denotes in the Old Testament this divine endowment which distinguishes man from beast. On this view, 7:22 refers to only the last two words of 7:21, which seems a little forced. See, however, T. C. Mitchell in *VT*, XI, 1961, pp. 177–187.

I Cor. 15:45). Note that man neither 'has' a soul nor 'has' a body, although for convenience he may be analysed into two or more constituents (*e.g.* I Thes. 5:23). The basic truth is here: he is a unity. *Nepeš*, translated *being* (RSV) or *soul* (AV, RV), is often the equivalent of 'life', and often of 'person' or 'self', according as one emphasizes the aliveness of the creature or the creature who is alive.

8-17. The earthly paradise. The Lord God's provision is a model of parental care. The fledgling is sheltered but not smothered: on all sides discoveries and encounters await him to draw out his powers of discernment and choice, and there is ample nourishment (as 9 alone displays) for his aesthetic, physical and spiritual appetites; further, there is a man's work before him for body and mind (15,19).

For his *spiritual* awakening, since he is made in God's image, he is given a divine word, double-edged, to live by: *thou mayest . . . thou shalt not* (16,17, AV, RV). The animals, with no such capacity and no such charge, are in contented bondage to their surroundings, their behaviour a product of inborn and incoming urges. Man is called to set a course and hold to it; and in deliberately allowing or rejecting the pressures on him he shows himself free. God furnished Adam with a better guiding-light than a policy, or even a moral principle, in giving him a bare word to steer by, for it meant that his Yes or No could be motivated by love, in naked filial loyalty, not by the pride of independence. If there is an element of cost in the solitary 'not' to Adam, Hebrews 5:8,9 makes it clear that growth to full stature demands it.

There is a hint of the *cultural* development intended for man when the narrative momentarily (10–14) breaks out of Eden to open up a vista into a world of diverse countries and resources. The digression, overstepping the bare details that locate the garden, discloses that there is more than primitive simplicity in store for the race: a complexity of unequally distributed skills and peoples, even if the reader knows the irony of it in the tragic connotations of the words 'gold', 'Assyria', 'Euphrates'.

Finally, to crown the chapter, man is seen as a *social* being (18–25, on which comment will be made in its place).

8. The phrase *a garden in Eden, in the east* (RSV) makes it clear that Eden is a locality here, not a symbol, although the same Hebrew form '*ēḏen* appropriately means 'delight'. The name seems to be related to the Sumerian *edin(na)* (plain, steppe), and verses 10–14 go to some lengths to present it as an actual, not an allegorical or mythical spot.[1] The *garden* (LXX *paradeisos*, 'parkland'; hence the term Paradise) formed only a part of it; how far the general area can be identified is discussed in the comments on 10–14 below.

9. On the many trees glimpsed in 9a, see the remarks introducing the section (verses 8–17), above. In 9b, it may be asked, are the trees two or one; and figurative or literal? The words could refer to a single tree, if translated as '*even* the tree of the knowledge . . .', as some have suggested. But while this suits Eve's expression 'in the midst of the garden' in 3:3 (*cf*. 2:9 on the tree of life), it only creates an insoluble problem at 3:22. The familiar translation is right: there are two trees.

The trees could be meant as metaphors for the respective means (such as wisdom, Pr. 3:18, or unbridled curiosity, Jude 8) of gaining either life or forbidden knowledge; see the further discussion of the knowledge of good and evil, below. Yet there is much to commend the literal sense, naïve though it may seem. It does not make the trees magical (for the Old Testament has no room for blind forces, only for the acts of God), but rather sacramental, in the broad sense of the word, in that they are the physical means of a spiritual transaction. The fruit, not in its own right, but as appointed to a function and carrying a word from God, confronts man with God's will, particular and explicit, and gives man a decisive Yes or No to say with his whole being.

---

[1] By contrast, Ezk. 28:11–19 presents a dazzling, celestial Eden in the taunt over the king of Tyre. It is depicting the earthly Eden of Gn. 2–3 in deliberately heightened form, either to match that king's pretensions (perhaps also his native version of the story – *cf*., *e.g.*, H. L. Ellison, *Ezekiel* (Paternoster, 1956), *in loc*.) or else, as tradition has it, to sing of the fall of Satan in terms that evoke the Fall of man.

The knowledge of good and evil is perhaps best understood in this living context. In isolation it could mean a number of things, many of them with biblical support. The phrase can stand for moral or aesthetic discernment (*e.g.* 1 Ki. 3:9; Is. 7:15); yet Adam and Eve are already treated as morally responsible (2:16,17) and generally percipient (3:6) before they touch the tree.[1] It could be a hebraism for 'everything'[2] (*i.e.*, man is not to covet omniscience); yet it can hardly mean this in 3:22. It has often been regarded as sexual awakening, in the light of 3:7; recently R. Gordis[3] suggested that this tree thereby offers a rival immortality to that of the tree of life, in the procreation of a family and a posterity. This too is open to several objections, including the fact that 3:22a is incompatible with it (heaven is sexless in the Old as in the New Testament), and that God instituted marriage after forbidding the use of the tree that is said to symbolize it.[4]

In the context, however, the emphasis falls on the prohibition rather than the properties of the tree. It is shown to us as forbidden. It is idle to ask what it might mean in itself; this was Eve's error. As it stood, prohibited, it presented the alternative to discipleship: to be self-made, wresting one's knowledge, satisfactions and values from the created world in defiance of the Creator (*cf.* 3:6). Even more instructive is the outcome of the experiment; see on 3:7. In all this the tree plays its part in the opportunity it offers, rather than the qualities it possesses; like a door whose name announces only what lies beyond it.

10–14. The *river*, fine symbol though it would be of the vitality that flows from holy ground (*cf.* Ps. 36:8,9; Ezk. 47:1–12; Rev. 22:1,2), is presented as quite literal, with two of its *four heads* (10, AV, RV) the well-known Tigris (*Hiddekel*, *cf.* Dn. 10:4) and *Euphrates* (14). Since these two are listed as if

---

[1] *Cf.* R. Gordis, 'The Knowledge of Good and Evil in the Old Testament and the Qumran Scrolls', in *JBL*, LXXVI, 1957, pp. 123–138.
[2] *Cf.* 2 Sa. 14:17 with 20 (Skinner, p. 95n.). So, *e.g.*, C. H. Gordon, *The World of the Old Testament* (Phoenix, 1960), p. 36.
[3] *Art. cit.*
[4] *Cf.*, *e.g.*, Skinner, p. 96; H. S. Stern, 'The Knowledge of Good and Evil' in *VT*, VIII, 1958, pp. 405–418.

reading from east to west, the unknown *Pishon* (11) and *Giho* (13) seem implied to lie still further east, which is consisten with the name *Cush* (13, RV, RSV), understood as the Kassite territory east of the Tigris, not the remote *Ethiopia* (AV) which is another Cush. *Havilah* (11; sandy land?) is linked with Cush in Genesis 10:7, and Cush with Babylon (10:8,10) which the Kassites invaded at one period.[1] The area, then, may be a relatively compact one, above the Persian Gulf into which the rivers Tigris and Euphrates, among others, make their way. This gulf, whose tidal flow sets up 'a natural irrigation and drainage' of the estuary region, according to P. Buringh,[2] fitting it for 'vegetation' and 'fruit trees' even in primitive times, could be the 'river' of verse 10 – for an ancient name for the Gulf was *nar marratum*, bitter river – and the 'four heads' would then be the four mouths from which the respective rivers are traced here, explorer fashion, upstream.[3]

12. *Bdellium*, a word not unlike the Hebrew (*bᵉdōlaḥ*), is a yellowish aromatic resin, which would seem ill-matched with *gold* and *onyx*. Since *bᵉdōlaḥ* was evidently white rather than yellow (Nu. 11:7; *cf.* Ex. 16:31) there is little but the sound of the word to suggest bdellium, and the old conjecture that it should be translated 'pearl'[4] has some plausibility, if nothing more. There is also uncertainty over *onyx*. The Hebrew is *šōham*, which reappears as the stone on which the names of the twelve tribes were to be engraved for the ephod (Ex. 28:9, *etc.*), and an object of some value (Jb. 28:16; Ezk. 28:13). There is reason to identify it with lapis lazuli, but not with certainty.[5]

17. The full implications of the warning, *thou shalt surely die* (AV, RV), will slowly unfold to the last pages of the New Testament. They are briefly discussed at 3:7; meanwhile it may be pointed out that these words do not necessarily imply that

[1] But Seba in Gn. 10:7 could point to South Arabia, where the (other?) Havilah of 10:29 is located.
[2] 'Living Conditions in the lower Mesopotamian Plain in Ancient Times': article in *Sumer*, XIII, 1957, pp. 31–46, referred to by E. A. Speiser, *The Rivers of Paradise: Festschrift J. Friedrich* (Heidelberg, 1959).
[3] Speiser, *loc. cit.*, pp. 477–482; *cf.* A. H. Sayce, *HDB*, I, pp. 643ff.; T. C. Mitchell, *NBD*, p. 333b.
[4] *Cf.* E. Hull, *HDB*, I, p. 259.
[5] Speiser, *loc. cit.*, pp. 480f.

man was not naturally mortal. God 'alone has immortality' (1 Tim. 6:16, RSV), and the presence of the tree of life in the garden indicates that if man is to share the boon it must be an added gift. As R. Martin-Achard has put it: 'Before the Fall, between Adam and death, which is part of his natural lot as an element in his human heritage, there stands the Living God; His presence is sufficient to ward death off . . .'.[1] The translation of Enoch, 'that he should not see death' (Heb. 11:5), perhaps illustrates what God had prepared for man.

18-25. The making of the woman. The New Testament draws much of its teaching on the sexes from this crowning paragraph of the chapter, which is the dynamic, or dramatic, counterpart of 1:27,28. The naming of the animals, a scene which portrays man as monarch of all he surveys, poignantly reveals him as a social being, made for fellowship, not power: he will not live until he loves, giving himself away (24) to another on his own level. So the woman is presented wholly as his partner and counterpart; nothing is yet said of her as childbearer. She is valued for herself alone.

In more detail, we may find the following emphases here. First, man is prior to woman (1 Cor. 11:8,9; 1 Tim. 2:13).[2] Secondly, the sexes are complementary: the true partnership is expounded by the terms that are used (*a helper fit for him*, 18,20, RSV; literally 'a help as opposite him', *i.e.*, 'corresponding to him'), by the fruitless search elsewhere, as man discerns the natures (expressing them in the *names*, 20) of other creatures, and by the fact that Eve is of the very stuff of Adam[3] and yet a

---

[1] *From Death to Life* (Oliver and Boyd, 1960), p. 19.

[2] This priority, like that of, *e.g.*, parents to children, is built into this world, not the next (Lk. 20:35f.). God's people, living in both time and eternity, are under His temporal order for their practice (Eph. 5:22f.; 1 Cor. 11:8f.; 1 Pet. 3:6,7) and His eternal one for their fundamental attitudes (Gal. 3:28).

[3] Attention has been drawn to the connection between a rib and the creation of a woman in the Sumerian story of Enki, for whose healing Nin-ti was made. The latter name can mean both 'lady of the rib' and 'lady who makes live'. See S. N. Kramer, *History begins at Sumer* (Thames and Hudson, 1958), pp. 194-196; D. J. Wiseman, *Illustrations from Biblical Archaeology* (Tyndale Press, 1958), p. 9. But apart from the two themes of rib and life-making (verbally linked in Sumerian but not Hebrew) the

wholly new being. Adam's joyful '*at last...*' (23, RSV) grows into the first poetic couplet in the Bible, and his work of naming is triumphantly concluded in a title that echoes his own. Thirdly, the union of the two in marriage is to be an exclusive (*a man leaves...*,[1] 24, RSV), permanent (*...and cleaves*), God-sealed bond (*one flesh: cf.* Mk. 10:8f.); for 'God himself, like a father of the bride, leads the woman to the man' (G. von Rad).[2] Fourthly, there is, in God's true pattern, perfect ease between them (25). But it is the fruit of perfect love, which has no alloy of greed, distrust or dishonour; it was understandably an immediate casualty of the Fall (see further on 3:7), and the chapter ends with a pointed reminder of our vanished concord.

3:1-24. Man's fall and expulsion

Certain details of this story have been discussed already in the comment at 2:9 on the trees and the knowledge of good and evil.

On its *historicity* two things should be said. First, the New Testament assumes it and argues from it, making the first Adam as literal as the last, whose genealogy is indeed traced back to him in Luke 3:23ff. According to Romans 5:18,19; 1 Corinthians 15:20,21, Adam was 'one man', and his sin 'one trespass', as factual as the cross and resurrection. But secondly, granted this historicity, it may still be an open question whether the account transcribes the facts or translates them: *i.e.*, whether it is a narrative comparable to such a passage as 2 Samuel 11 (which is the straight story of David's sin) or to 2 Samuel 12:1-6 (which presents the same event translated into quite other terms that interpret it).

The *doctrine* latent in the chapter, that 'sin came into the

---

stories have little in common. Enki was a god who had brought eight diseases on himself, and Nin-ti was one of eight goddesses created to heal the eight affected parts (in this case, his rib). If this originated in the Eden story it has travelled very far from it.

[1] Note the order: 'leaving' before 'cleaving'; marriage, nothing less, before intercourse. So this question, as well as divorce, was settled 'from the beginning' (Mk. 10:6ff.). See also on 34:7.

[2] *Genesis*, p. 82.

world through one man and death through sin' (Rom.
5:12, RSV), emerges in sharp focus only in the New Testament.
The Old Testament uses the story little, though it witnesses
to man's bondage; it has the materials of the doctrine but has
not formulated it. Jewry, on the other hand, knows and rejects
it. According to Isidore Epstein, 'Judaism denies the existence
of original sin. . . . True, the idea that the sin of Adam had
brought death on all mankind is not unknown in Jewish
teaching, but the reference is invariably to physical death, and
is not to be confused with the spiritual death from which in
Christian doctrine none can be saved except through faith
in the risen Saviour. Man can therefore achieve his own
redemption by penitence . . .'[1]

It took the work of the last Adam to bring home to us our
full downfall in the first Adam.

1-7. Temptation and disobedience. In verse 1, *the
serpent* is explicitly God's handiwork, subtle as he is (for the
predominant sense of *subtle* is 'shrewd', as in Pr. 12:23; 14:18,
etc.), and the chapter speaks not of evil invading, as though it
had its own existence, but of creatures rebelling. His malevo-
lent brilliance raises the question, which is not pursued,
whether he is the tool of a more formidable rebel; the inference becomes compelling in 15, where see comment. But
Eve must not be under duress: her temptation comes through
a subordinate (*cf.* Mt. 16:22,23, concerning Jesus and Peter),
which strengthens its appeal to pride but carries no compulsion.

The tempter begins with suggestion rather than argument.
The incredulous tone – 'So God has actually said . . .?' – is
both disturbing and flattering: it smuggles in the assumption
that God's word is subject to our judgment. The exaggeration,
Ye shall not eat of any tree (RV, RSV, rightly), is a further and
favourite device: dangled before Eve it will draw her into
debate on her opponent's terms.

2, 3. Eve is duly drawn, and by adding *neither shall ye touch it*

---

[1] *Judaism* (Pelican, 1959), p. 142. *Cf.* J. Klausner, *The Messianic Idea in
Israel* (Allen and Unwin, 1956), p. 530.

she over-corrects the error, magnifying God's strictness (she was to have many successors).

4. After the query, the flat contradiction: *Ye shall not surely die* (AV, RV). It is the serpent's word against God's, and the first doctrine to be denied is judgment. If modern denials of it are very differently motivated, they are equally at odds with revelation: Jesus fully reaffirmed the doctrine (*e.g.* Mt. 7:13–27).

5. The climax is a lie big enough to reinterpret life (this breadth is the power of a false system) and dynamic enough to redirect the flow of affection and ambition. To be *as God*,[1] and to achieve it by outwitting Him, is an intoxicating programme. God will henceforth be regarded, consciously or not, as rival and enemy. Against this human arrogance 'the obedience of the one' and His taking 'the form of a servant' show up in their true colours (Rom. 5:19; Phil. 2:7).

So the tempter pits his bare assertion against the word and works of God, presenting divine love as envy, service as servility, and a suicidal plunge as a leap into life, 'All these things will I give thee . . .'; the pattern repeats in Christ's temptations, and in ours.

On *knowing good and evil*, see on 2:9.

6. . . . *the woman saw* . . . – and visual evidence is potent: God allows the forbidden its full appeal. The pattern of sin runs right through the act, for Eve listened to a creature instead of the Creator, followed her impressions against her instructions, and made self-fulfilment her goal. This prospect of material, aesthetic and mental enrichment (6a) seemed to add up to life itself; the world still offers it (1 Jn. 2:16). But man's lifeline is spiritual, namely God's word and the response of faith (Dt. 8:3; Hab. 2:4); to break it is death.

She took . . . and ate: so simple the act, so hard its undoing. God will taste poverty and death before 'take and eat' become verbs of salvation.

. . . *and he ate*: led, as the woman had been, instead of leading; a curious way to achieve divinity. The man and the

---

[1] Or, *gods* (AV). The word *'elōhîm* can be used generically to include the angelic orders; see on 1:26.

woman have been sold a false idea of evil, as something beyond good; of wisdom, as sophistication; and now of greatness, as greed.

7. The opening of the verse, utterly unexpected after 2:17, forces the reader to re-examine the meaning of the death that was threatened there. Augustine comments: 'If . . . it be asked what death God threatened man with . . . , whether . . . bodily or spiritual or that second death, we answer: It was all . . . He comprehends therein, not only the first part of the first death, wheresoever the soul loses God, nor the latter only, wherein the soul leaves the body, . . . but also . . . the second which is the last of deaths, eternal, and following after all.'[1]

The serpent's promise of *eyes . . . opened* came true in its fashion (and *cf.* 22), but it was a grotesque anticlimax to the dream of enlightenment. Man saw the familiar world and spoilt it now in the seeing, projecting evil on to innocence (*cf.* Tit. 1:15) and reacting to good with shame and flight. His new consciousness of good and evil was both like and unlike the divine knowledge (3:22), differing from it and from innocence as a sick man's aching awareness of his body differs both from the insight of the physician and the unconcern of the man in health.

The *fig leaves* were pathetic enough, as human expedients tend to be, but the instinct was sound and God confirmed it (21), for sin's proper fruit is shame. The couple, now ill at ease together, experienced a foretaste of fallen human relations in general. There is no road back, as the nudists and those who make a cult of frankness, the spiritual nudists, suppose. God's way is forward, for when the body is redeemed (Rom. 8:23) and love is perfect we shall be not back in Eden but clothed with glory (2 Cor. 5:4).

8-13. Confrontation. In verse 8, it is the *sound* (RSV), not the *voice* (AV, RV) that they first hear. With the impulse to hide from the *presence* (literally 'face') of the Lord, compare ultimately Revelation 6:16, and in contrast, Revelation 22:4.

---

[1] *The City of God*, XIII. xii (Dent, Everyman edition, 1945: Vol. II, pp. 9f.).

9. God's first word to fallen man has all the marks of grace. It is a question, since to help him He must draw rather than drive him out of hiding. Only a voice penetrates his concealment. With this '*Where . . .?*', *cf.* the searching 'Why . . .?' to Saul, and 'What . . .?' to Legion. Cain was to hear all three (4:6,9,10).

10. Adam's answer conceals the cause behind the symptoms; but *afraid* (the first mention of fear) is significant: this shrinking from God remains part of our fallen condition.

12, 13. The second answer admits the truth, but angles it against the woman and ultimately God. Man is learning quickly, but his retreat into verbal hiding only puts a fresh obstacle in the way of mercy. God, by addressing man, woman and serpent in that order, has shown how He regards their degrees of responsibility.

14–19. Sentence. Prose here gives way to rhythmic speech, as in 2:23 and in oracles generally. Note, in all that follows, the undiminished sovereignty of God. Man's dominion (chapter 2) and man's sin (chapter 3) 'simply set sovereignty in a different context'[1]: they do not threaten it.

14. No question is put to the serpent: only his sentence. These words do not imply that hitherto serpents had not been reptiles (still less that the story is merely aetiological, *i.e.*, a 'Just So Story' on how the serpent lost its legs[2] – an interest belied by the tragic context), but that the crawling is henceforth symbolic (*cf.* Is. 65:25) – just as in 9:13 a new significance, not new existence, will be decreed for the rainbow.

15. There is good New Testament authority for seeing here the *protevangelium*, the first glimmer of the gospel. Remarkably, it makes its début as a sentence passed on the enemy (*cf.* Col. 2:15), not a direct promise to man, for redemption is about God's rule as much as about man's need (*cf.* Ezk. 36:22, 'not . . . for your sake . . .'). The prospect of struggle, suffering and human triumph is clear enough,[3] but only the New Testament

---

[1] J. A. Motyer, in a private communication.
[2] *Cf.*, *e.g.*, *IB*, p. 508, and most modern commentaries.
[3] In addition to the contrast between head and heel, the second 'bruise'

will unmask the figure of Satan behind the serpent (Rom. 16:20; Rev. 12:9; 20:2), and show how significant was the passing over of Adam for *the woman*[1] and *her seed* (*cf.* Mt. 1:23; Gal. 4:4; ?1 Tim. 2:15). The latter, like the seed of Abraham, is both collective (*cf.* Rom. 16:20) and, in the crucial struggle, individual (*cf.* Gal. 3:16),[2] since Jesus as the last Adam summed up mankind in Himself. RSV's personal pronoun *he*, allowed but not required by the Hebrew, has a pre-Christian precedent in the LXX here.[3]

16. Pain and bondage now appear on the horizon. Two kindred words are used in 16 for the repeated *sorrow* (AV, RV) or *pain* (RSV), the first of which exactly recurs in 17c for the 'toil' (RV, RSV) or 'sorrow' (AV) imposed on Adam. A possible rendering each time would be 'travail'.

RSV's *your pain in childbearing* catches the meaning of the Hebrew idiom which AV, RV render too literally.[4] The phrase *your desire shall be for your husband* (RSV), with the reciprocating *he shall rule over you*, portrays a marriage relation in which control has slipped from the fully personal realm to that of instinctive urges passive and active. 'To love and to cherish' becomes 'To desire and to dominate'. While even pagan marriage can rise far above this, the pull of sin is always towards it. An echo of the phrase, in 4:7b, conjures up still more vividly its suggestion of the jungle.

17. In mercy, the curse is on man's realm, not man himself; but nothing constructive is said to Adam, in whom all die. *Sorrow . . . sweat . . . and dust* answer the fantasy 'you will be like God', and lead to the cry 'all things are full of weariness' (Ec. 1:8, RSV).

---

should possibly be translated as merely 'snap at', a punning sense suggested by the proximity of 'heel' (*cf.* K-B, *s.v. šwp* II). Such verbal subtleties are a feature of some oracles of destiny: *cf.* 16:12; 27:28,39; 40:13,19.

[1] The expression itself would not suggest virgin birth until the event: *cf.* Lk. 7:28.

[2] 'Seed' refers to an individual also in Gn. 4:25; 1 Sa. 1:11 (Heb.).

[3] See R. A. Martin, *JBL*, LXXXIV, 1965, pp. 424ff.

[4] See E. A. Speiser's remarks on hendiadys, *Genesis*, p. LXX. A more precarious suggestion is that the second noun means sexual desire, on the basis of an Ugaritic root *h-r-r* (C. Rabin, *Scripta Hierosolymitana*, VIII (Magnes; O.U.P., 1961), p. 390).

18. *Thorns . . . and thistles* are eloquent signs of nature un-tamed and encroaching; in the Old Testament they mark the scenes of man's self-defeat and God's judgment, *e.g.* in the slug-gard's field (Pr. 24:31) and the ruined city (Is. 34:13). They need not be envisaged here as newly created, but as henceforth a perennial threat (as the unconquered Canaanites would be to Israel, Nu. 33:55); for man in his own disorder would never now 'subdue' the earth. The nature-miracles of Jesus give some idea of the control which man under God might have exercised (*cf.* Heb. 2:8,9).

20. The naming of Eve. After the sentence of death, this name, 'life', with its play on the word *living*, is very striking; its connection with Eve's role as *mother* further suggests that Adam heard the promise of 15 in faith.

21. The coats of skins. It is unduly subtle, and a dis-traction, to foresee the atonement here: God is meeting im-mediate rather than ultimate needs, for both are His concern. The coats of skins are forerunners of the many measures of welfare, both moral[1] and physical, which man's sin makes necessary. Social action, now delegated to human hands (Rom. 13:1–7; Jas. 2:16), could not have had an earlier or more exalted inauguration.

22–24. Paradise lost. On man's new knowledge, see the middle comment on 7. The expulsion is by decree; it could also be expressed as by logical necessity, since eternal life is fellow-ship with God (Jn. 17:3), which man has now repudiated. The point is re-emphasized in the phrase *the ground from which he was taken*, an echo of 19; it is that half of the truth about him (2:7) by which he has chosen to live; and he must end where he belongs. (*Cf.* Phil. 3:19–21.)

24. Every detail of this verse, with its *flame* and *sword* and the turning *every way*, actively excludes the sinner. His way back is more than hard, it is resisted: he cannot save himself. The *cherubim*,[2] God's multiform and awesome thronebearers

[1] See the final comment on 7.
[2] See, further, the article 'Cherubim' in *NBD*, p. 208.

in Ezekiel's visions (*cf.* Ezk. 1:5 with Ezk. 10:15), are seen elsewhere as symbolic guardians of the holy of holies, their forms embroidered on the veil that barred access to it, and modelled above the ark (Ex. 36:35; 37:7–9). At the death of Christ this veil was rent in two (Mt. 27:51) and the way to God thrown open (Heb. 10:19–22) in fact as well as symbol.

Additional Note on sin and suffering

Three kinds of disorder, covering the greater part of human suffering, make their germinal appearance in this chapter.

In *personal* relations there are the first signs of mutual estrangement (7) and the brutalizing of sexual love (16b). Here in embryo are the mistrusts and passions which will ravage society. In the *spiritual* realm man has become, in his self-contradiction, simultaneously in flight (and banishment) from God (8,24) and in battle with evil (15). On the *physical* plane, his life is to be a painful struggle to renew (16) and sustain (19) its basic processes, which are in some degree disturbed.

This multiple disarray is, from one aspect, his punishment, pronounced by God; from another, it is the plain outcome of his anarchy. Leaderless, the choir of creation can only grind on in discord. It seems, indeed, from Romans 8:19–23 and from what is known of the pre-human world, that there was a state of travail in nature from the first, which man was empowered to 'subdue' (1:28) (perhaps little by little as he spread abroad to 'fill the earth'), until he relapsed instead into disorder himself. Even now his power over nature (Ps. 8:6–8; Jas. 3:7) reflects this primal ability; the ordering influence of *the* Man, Christ Jesus, shows what was its full potential, one day to be realized everywhere and for ever (Rom. 8:19).

III. MAN UNDER SIN AND DEATH (4:1 – 6:8)

4:1-15. The murder of Abel

If, behind the serpent, the devil was discernible in chapter 3, the flesh and the world come into view in the present chapter (see further on 16–24). Sin is shown with its own growth-cycle as in James 1:15, and in 7b it is personified in almost Pauline fashion (*cf.* Rom. 7:8ff.). Many details emphasize the depth of Cain's crime, and therefore of the Fall: the context is worship, the victim a brother; and while Eve had been talked into her sin, Cain will not have even God talk him out of it; nor will he confess to it, nor yet accept his punishment.

1. The word *knew*, in this special sense, conveys very well the fully personal level of true sexual union, although it can lose this higher content altogether (*cf.* 19:5).

Cain has something of the sound of *qānâ*, 'to get'. Such comments on names are usually word-plays rather than etymologies, overlaying a standard name with a particular significance. So, *e.g.*, in 17:17,19 an existing name Isaac ('may [God] smile') was chosen to commemorate a certain human smile and the promise that provoked it.

The expression *with the help of* (RV, RSV) is literally just 'with'; and although this Hebrew word allows other interpretations, that of RV, RSV is simplest; *cf.* 1 Samuel 14:45 (another word for 'with').

Eve's cry of faith, here as in 25, lifts the situation out of the rut of the purely natural, to its true level (as faith always does: 1 Tim. 4:4,5), whether she is touching on the oracle of 3:15 or not.

2. The name *Abel* is identical in form with the Hebrew for vanity or a mere breath (*e.g.* Ec. 1:2, *etc.*); but the connection is probably fortuitous since nothing is made of it. The name may be cognate with the Sumerian *ibil(a)*, Akkadian *ab/plu*, 'son'.

Scholars have tended to read back the rivalries between two ways of life, pastoral and agricultural,[1] into this story. Such a theme is found in the Old Testament (*e.g.* Je. 35:6ff.), but here the contrast of cultures plays a quite subordinate role. God has room for both ways (*cf.* Dt. 8), and there are the makings of a rich pattern in these complementary skills and the attempted interweaving of work and worship. The pattern

---

[1] *Cf., e.g.*, the Sumerian contest-tale of Dumuzi and Enkimdu, shepherd-god and farmer-god: *ANET*, pp. 41f.

goes to pieces solely through the human material, and it is the exposure to God's truth that disrupts it, uncovering for the first time the deadly antipathy of carnal religion to spiritual.

3-5. The *offering* is a *minhâ*, which in human affairs was a gift of homage or allegiance and, as a ritual term, could describe either animal or more often cereal offerings (*e.g.* 1 Sa. 2:17; Lv. 2:1). It is precarious to claim that the absence of blood disqualified Cain's gift (*cf.* Dt. 26:1-11); all that is explicit here is that Abel offered the pick of his flock and that Cain's spirit was arrogant (5b; *cf.* Pr. 21:27). The New Testament draws out the further important implications that Cain's life, unlike Abel's, gave the lie to his offering (1 Jn. 3:12) and that Abel's faith was decisive for his acceptance (Heb. 11:4).

6. In the Lord's repeated '*Why . . .?*' and '*If . . .*', His appeal to reason and His concern for the sinner are as strongly marked as His concern for truth (5a) and justice (10).

7. In the Hebrew, *accepted* (7) is literally 'a lifting up' (*cf.* RVmg), an expression that can indicate a smiling as against a frowning (*fallen*, 6) face: *cf.* Numbers 6:26. The sense may be that the very look on Cain's face gives him away;[1] more probably it goes further, to promise God's restoration (*cf.* 40:13) on a change of heart. The picture of *sin . . . couching at the door* (RSV) is developed in the striking metaphor of taming a wild beast: so RSV, *its desire is for you* (Moffatt 'eager to be at you'), *but you must master it*. The phrase is adapted from 3:16b, on which it throws back a sombre light.[2]

8. RV correctly translates the Hebrew: *And Cain told Abel his brother* (*cf.* Ex. 19:25). If this is (as it seems to be) the true text, Cain shows a lifelike oscillation between accepting and defying God's remonstrance. LXX however has . . . *said to Abel . . . 'Let us go out to the field'* (RSV), making the murder doubly deliberate if these words are indeed an authentic part of the original text.

---

[1] *Cf.* Moffatt.

[2] A possible alternative is: 'a sin-offering is couching . . .' (*cf.* 22:13?), in which case the final phrase ('his desire . . .') would refer to Abel, and the whole verse be assuring Cain that neither God's displeasure nor Abel's ascendancy need be permanent. It would be, however, a very cryptic way of saying it.

9. *Where is . . . thy brother?* matches the 'Where art thou?' of 3:9, as God's perennially searching inquiry of man. The truculent reply, equally in character, betrays a hardening in comparison with the shuffling answers of 3:10ff.

10. We ourselves speak of wrongs that 'cry out' to be righted. The New Testament concurs with the Old in this, and develops the metaphor (*e.g.* Rev. 6:9,10; Lk. 18:7,8), which should still however be read as metaphor. In striking contrast, the blood of Jesus cries out for grace (Heb. 12:24).

11, 12. The impenitent Cain is addressed more sharply than Adam, for whom the curse was indirect, not 'cursed art *thou*'.

13, 14. Cain's protest[1] is echoed in the injured tones of Dives (Lk. 16:24,27,28; *cf.* Rev. 16:11), in contrast to the penitent thief's admission that 'we receive the due reward of our deeds'. The last phrase of 14, *whoever finds me . . .* (RSV), suggests an expanding population, present or future; it could also imply that every person encountered would be a near kinsman of Abel – consistently enough with the context. See, however, Introduction, Human Beginnings, pp. 26ff.

15. God's concern for the innocent (10) is matched only by His care for the sinner. Even the querulous prayer of Cain had contained a germ of entreaty; God's answering pledge, together with His *mark* or *sign* (the same word as in 9:13; 17:11) – not a stigma but a safe-conduct – is almost a covenant, making Him virtually Cain's *gō'ēl* or protector; *cf.* 2 Samuel 14:14b, AV, RV. It is the utmost that mercy can do for the unrepentant.

4:16–24. The family of Cain
The beginnings of civilized life show a characteristic potentiality for good and evil, with the arts that will bless mankind flanked by abuses (19,23,24) that will curse it. Culture, used or abused, offers no redemption; the one gleam of hope is in God's gift and man's belated response, recorded in the chapter's closing pair of verses.

[1] The Hebrew *could* be construed as LXX: 'my sin is too great for forgiveness': but the context gives no support to this.

16. It was in *the presence of the Lord* that the crisis had arisen (5); Cain's departure was both his sentence and his choice. On the one hand, he had feared banishment 'from thy face' (14) and the 'wandering' now expressed in the name *Nod* ('wandering'); on the other hand, he had disdained contrition and now set himself to make some success of his independence. The ensuing account gives a first taste of a self-sufficient society, which is the essence of what the New Testament calls 'the world'.

17. The opening phrase suggests that Cain was already married at this time, and 14,15 with 5:3 give the impression that the human family had begun to multiply, unless in 14 (see comment) Cain's fears were only for the future. See Introduction, Human Beginnings, pp. 29f.

The name *Enoch* (*ḥᵃnôḵ*) is akin to the verb 'to initiate':[1] there may be the thought of a new beginning in the naming of the first son and first city of Cain's independence. *City* is a term, in the Hebrew, that can be applied to any human settlement, small or great. The respective claims of the two Enochs to fame (*cf.* 5:22-24) make a not unfair comparison between the two branches of humanity, which are traced down to the families of warlike Lamech (4:24) and godly Noah (5:32).

18. Two of the names here, Enoch and Lamech, are used in both families (*cf.* 5:18,25); the resemblances between others are more apparent in English than Hebrew.

19-24. A biased account would have ascribed nothing good to Cain. The truth is more complex: God was to make much use of Cainite techniques for His people, from the semi-nomadic discipline itself (20; *cf.* Heb. 11:9) to the civilized arts and crafts (*e.g.* Ex. 35:35).[2] The phrase *he was the father*

[1] W. F. Albright, however, argues for the meaning 'follower' (*i.e.*, 'successor'), in *JBL*, LVIII, 1939, p. 96.

[2] In 22 the translation *forger* (RV, RSV) implies more than the Hebrew *lōṭēš*, 'hammerer' or 'sharpener'. Meteoric iron and surface deposits of copper were hammered and filed long before smelting and forging were heard of. Perishable as these metals are, some examples have survived from the third millennium BC (iron) and even the fifth or earlier (copper); *cf. JASA*, XVIII, 1966, pp. 31f. See also Introduction, Human Beginnings, p. 28.

of all such acknowledges the debt and prepares us to accept for ourselves a similar indebtedness to secular enterprise; for the Bible nowhere teaches that the godly should have all the gifts. At the same time we are saved from over-valuing these skills: the family of Lamech could handle its environment but not itself. The attempt to improve on God's marriage ordinance (19; *cf.* 2:24) set a disastrous precedent, on which the rest of Genesis is comment enough; and the immediate conversion of metal-working to weapon-making is equally ominous. Cain's family is a microcosm: its pattern of technical prowess and moral failure is that of humanity.

Lamech's taunt-song reveals the swift progress of sin. Where Cain had succumbed to it (7) Lamech exults in it; where Cain had sought protection (14,15) Lamech looks round for provocation: the savage disproportion of killing a mere lad (Hebrew *yeled*, 'child') for a mere wound is the whole point of his boast (*cf.* 24). On this note of bravado the family disappears from the story.[1] By contrast, Jesus may well have had this 'seventy-seven' saying in mind when He spoke of forgiveness 'unto seventy *times* seven'.

4:25, 26. Seth replaces Abel

Eve's faith, emphasizing God's will by the name *Seth* ('appointing'), is even clearer now than in verse 1. The mention of *another seed* (AV, RV) also seems to take up the promise of 3:15.

26. *Enosh* means 'man' (*cf.* Ps. 8:4a,5a), perhaps with a tinge of emphasis on his frailty.

The final note, *then began men . . .* , is of twofold interest, recording the first shoot of spiritual growth since Abel and the first disclosure of the name Yahweh (*the Lord*). In Genesis it is one of various divine names on people's lips,[2] but still a *mere* name, not yet revealing any of God's characteristics as other terms did (*e.g.* El 'Elyon, 'God most high'). In this sense God was not made 'known' by the name Yahweh until He gave

---

[1] See Additional Note on the Cainites, below.
[2] In the common critical analysis its use in Genesis is mostly, by definition, found in passages assigned to the Yahwist (J); yet even so, not exclusively. See Introduction, pp. 16ff.

content to it in the message at the burning bush (Ex. 3:13b,14; 6:3).[1]

Additional Note on the Cainites

A case has been made out for identifying the Cainites with the Kenites. The Hebrew terms are identical (*cf.* Nu. 24:21,22, RV, RSV), and the Arabic equivalent means 'smith'. There is evidence of the ancient existence of travelling groups such as the family described in Genesis 4: chiefly tent-dwellers, moving from place to place as craftsmen and musicians. A famous patriarchal-age tomb-painting at Beni Hasan shows such a group equipped with weapons, musical instruments and bellows. It is therefore commonly suggested that the facts of this chapter were drawn from tribal memories, together with a story to account for the beginnings of this roving existence, and were put to a new use by the compiler of Genesis.

The theory is of course incompatible with the Flood story, which shows a clean break with the early families named here, except through Noah. It has value, however, in calling attention to a known pattern of life embodying all the features of Genesis 4:16ff. The term *qayin*, 'smith', would be cause enough to give the Kenites their name, and it in turn could have originated from the name Cain, just as in modern times a pioneer (*e.g.* Watt, Ohm, Volt) may leave a permanent mark on the terminology of his craft. The Cain-Kenite succession was real enough, we may conclude, but it was occupational, not hereditary.

5:1-32. The family of Seth

This chapter serves at least three ends in the scheme of Genesis. First, it bears witness to man's value to God, by naming individuals and stages in this early human phase: each is known and remembered. Secondly, it shows how the line of Seth the 'appointed' (4:25) led on to Noah the deliverer. Thirdly, it both demonstrates the reign of death, by its in-

---

[1] *Cf.* J. A. Motyer, *The Revelation of the Divine Name.* See also Introduction, p. 33.

sistent refrain (5b,8b, *etc.*), and conspicuously breaks the rhythm to tell of Enoch, the standing pledge of death's defeat.

1. The opening, *This is the book . . .* , seems to indicate that the chapter was originally a self-contained unit ('book' means 'written account', of whatever length), and the impression is strengthened by its opening with a creation summary, and by the set pattern of its paragraphs.[1]

2. The words *and called their name Adam* (AV, RV), or *Man* (RSV), emphasize the fact that though the male, as head, bore the name of the race, it takes the two sexes together to express what God means by 'human' (*cf.* 1 Cor. 11:11).

3. On the *hundred and thirty years*, and other figures in this passage, see the Additional Note to the chapter. The contrast between *his own likeness* (RV, RSV) in this verse, and the likeness of God in verse 1, should not be pressed too far: see the discussion at 1:26.

It is striking that of Adam's sons only Seth is named here. No doubt the chapter first existed as a pedigree of this one family, but placed here in the context of the Cainites and their achievements its silence regarding them is pointed. In the history of salvation the family of Cain is an irrelevance.

9. On *Enosh* ('*enôš*), see 4:26 and note.

12. The name *Kenan* (*qênān*) is closely similar to Cain, as in AV's spelling, *Cainan* (not to be confused with Ham's son Canaan (*kᵉna'an*) in 10:6). It is not impossible that the name attached itself to this man as the introducer of Cainite skills to his fellow Sethites (*cf.* 4:20-22).

15. *Mahalalel* (*mahᵃlal-'ēl*) means 'praise of God'.

18. *Jared* (*yereḏ*) could mean 'descent', if of Hebrew origin;[2] it has no true resemblance to Irad ('*îrāḏ*) in 4:18.

21-24. This astonishing paragraph 'shines', as W. R. Bowie puts it, 'like a single brilliant star above the earthy record of this chapter'.[3] The simplicity of the repeated *walked with*

---

[1] On P. J. Wiseman's theory that verse 1a concludes rather than opens a section, see Introduction IIc, pp. 23f.

[2] Skinner calls attention to, *e.g.*, the Book of Enoch 6:6 which places the 'descent' of the fallen angels (see on Gn. 6:2) in Jared's days.

[3] *IB*, I, p. 530. A distorted memory of Enoch seems to be preserved in

God, suddenly breaking the formula that had begun to close round Enoch like the rest, portrays the intimacy that is the essence of Old Testament piety. This, rather than the harsh moralism popularly associated with the Old Testament, is Enoch's common ground with Noah (of whom alone this particular phrase recurs, 6:9), with Abraham the friend of God, Moses who spoke with Him 'face to face', and such men as Jacob, Job and Jeremiah who wrestled with Him.

The Hebrew allows, but hardly calls for, the view that Enoch's piety began with the birth of Methuselah: rather, *walked with God* is the counterpart of 'lived (on)' in 19,26, *etc.* This, to him, was life.

In the LXX, 'walked with' is paraphrased as 'pleased', and 'was not' becomes 'was not found'. It is the version used in Hebrews 11:5.

The phrase *God took him* left its mark on the Old Testament, it seems, in two places: Psalms 49:15 (MT 16); 73:24 (where 'receive' = 'take'), both of them remarkable affirmations. As Enochs and Elijahs are rare, this hope did not easily become general; but at least twice the gates of Sheol had not prevailed.

25. *Methuselah (mᵉṯûšelaḥ)* is of uncertain meaning; possibly 'man of the javelin'. No special attention is drawn to his length of life, which overtops Jared's by only seven years (20,27).

28, 29. We have no clue to the meaning of the name *Lamech (lemeḵ),* but both its bearers are remembered by their words, the Cainite one for his arrogance (4:23f.), the Sethite for his yearning. His oracle on the birth of his son is a word-play (see on 4:1), passing over the obvious etymology of the name *Noah* ('rest')[1] for the somewhat similar verb *naḥēm,* 'comfort'. The allusion to 3:17 may be a sign that he treasured the promise of 3:15. As often in Genesis, and on a still higher plane in Isaiah, a birth is the occasion for prophecy; no other subject has such hopes centred upon it. The Bible, in its

---

the seventh of the Sumerian antediluvians, a king intimate with the gods and versed in occult wisdom.

[1] But LXX has 'shall give us rest', reading the expected Hebrew verb.

orientation to the birth of a saviour in one capacity or another, is consistently personal in its expectation. Noah's mission, however, was to be more radical than anything Lamech envisaged, and this oracle was to be taken up in a new form at 6:6 (where see note).

Additional Note on the long-lived antediluvians

Two problems of interpretation lie on the surface of this chapter: in simple terms, the period as a whole looks too short, and the individual life-spans too long, to harmonize with other data. Common sense and present knowledge deserve a careful hearing on such a matter: they will sometimes point to the true intention of a passage, against a naïve or fanciful interpretation. But the passage itself, in its total context of Scripture, must have the last word.

a. The total period

Our present knowledge of civilization, *e.g.* at Jericho, goes back to at least 7000 BC, and of man himself very much further. When Ussher dated Adam at 4004 BC he assumed that the generations in this chapter were an unbroken chain: but the chapter neither adds its figures together nor gives the impression that the men it names overlapped each other's lives to any unusual extent (*e.g.* that Adam lived almost to the birth of Noah). If it has selected ten names (and in 11:10ff. another ten from Noah to Abraham) as separate landmarks rather than continuous links, it has genealogical custom both within and without the Bible to support it. Within Scripture, note the stylized scheme of three fourteens in Matthew 1 (involving the omission of three successive kings in Mt. 1:8). Outside it, anthropologists and others have drawn attention to similar genealogical methods in the Sudan, Arabia, and elsewhere.[1] On this understanding of the scheme, Seth, for example, produced at 105 either a forbear of Enosh or Enosh

[1] See W. F. Albright, *The Biblical Period from Abraham to Ezra* (Harper, 1963), p. 9.

himself[1] (*cf.* Mt. 1:8b, where Joram 'begat' his great-great-grandson); and so on. This leaves the total period undetermined.

b. The life-spans

Reinterpretations of the longevity of these men are less happy. At first sight the fact that a name can mean both an individual and his tribe (*cf.* chapter 10) could account for some of the great ages if the first figure in the record (3,6, *etc.*) were taken to denote a man's personal life-span, while the second figure (4,7, *etc.*) gave that of the family he founded;[2] but Enoch and Noah are fatal exceptions, for they are clearly portrayed as individuals to the end. The idea that units of time may have changed their meaning is equally unfruitful: apart from creating fresh difficulties in 12,15,21, it breaks down in the detailed chronology between 7:6 and 8:13.

As far as we can tell, then, the life-spans are intended literally. It may be worth pointing out that our familiar rate of growth is not the only conceivable one; also that various races have traditions of primitive longevity[3] which could stem from authentic memories. See also on 12:14. But further study of the conventions of ancient genealogy writing may throw new light on the intention of the chapter.

6:1–8. The approaching crisis

1–4. Sons of God and daughters of men. The point of this cryptic passage, whichever way we take it, is that a new stage has been reached in the progress of evil, with God's bounds overstepped in yet another realm.

2. *The sons of God* are identified by some interpreters as

---

[1] See article 'Chronology' in *Westminster Dictionary of the Bible* (Collins, 1944), p. 103, based on J. D. Davis, 'Antediluvian Patriarchs' in *ISBE*, I, pp. 139–143.

[2] So A. Winchell, *Pre-adamites*, pp. 449ff., cited by G. F. Wright, article 'Antediluvians', *ISBE*, I, p. 143.

[3] The Sumerian king-list names eight or ten antediluvians, reigning on an average some thirty thousand years apiece. Some grain of truth could lie behind these vast numbers, as truth evidently lies behind the actual names (*cf.* M. E. L. Mallowan in *Iraq*, XXVI, 1964, pp. 68f.).

the sons of Seth, over against those of Cain.[1] By others, including early Jewish writers,[2] they are taken to mean angels. If the second view defies the normalities of experience, the first defies those of language (and our task is to find the author's meaning); for while the Old Testament can declare God's people to be His sons,[3] the normal meaning of the actual term 'sons of God' is 'angels',[4] and nothing has prepared the reader to assume that 'men' now means Cainites only.[5] Possible New Testament support for 'angels' may be seen in 1 Peter 3:19,20;[6] also in 2 Peter 2:4–6, where the fallen angels, the Flood, and the doom of Sodom form a series that could be based on Genesis, and in Jude 6, where the angels' offence is that they 'left their proper habitation'. The craving of demons for a body, evident in the Gospels, offers at least some parallel to this hunger for sexual experience. But where Scripture is as reticent as here, both Peter and Jude warn us away. We have our proper place as well! More important than the detail of this episode is its indication that man is beyond self-help, whether the Seth-ites have betrayed their calling, or demonic powers have gained a stranglehold.

3. In this much debated verse, follow RSV: '*My spirit shall not abide in man for ever, for he is flesh, but . . .* '. The word *abide* (*yāḏôn*) is supported by the chief ancient versions, although its etymology is uncertain.[7] AV, RV's *strive* would seem to require the form *yāḏîn* or possibly *yāḏûn*.[8] Even the word *for* (*bᵉšaggam*, 'inasmuch as also') is not unchallenged (see RVmg), but the best MSS support it.

---

[1] *E.g.*, J. Murray, *Principles of Conduct* (Tyndale Press, 1957), pp. 243–249.

[2] See Enoch 6:2; also the Qumran Genesis Apocryphon, col. II.

[3] Dt. 14:1; Is. 1:2; Ho. 1:10 (MT 2:1).

[4] Jb. 1:6; 2:1; 38:7; Dn. 3:25.

[5] A third view, that of M. G. Kline in *WTJ*, XXIV, 1962, pp. 187–204, makes 'sons of God' a term for kings, and 2b a reference to royal polygamy. But it is hard to see why matters as familiar as kingship and polygamy should be expressed so indirectly. For another suggested link with kingship, *cf.* E. G. Kraeling in *JNES*, VI, 1947, pp. 193–208.

[6] *Cf.* A. M. Stibbs, *1 Peter* (Tyndale Press, 1959), pp. 142f.

[7] The vocalization indicates the root *d-n-n*, for which there is some evidence of a meaning 'remain': *cf.* Cassuto, I, pp. 295f.

[8] But Akkadian *danānu*, to become strong, reinforce, speak severely to, may point to a Hebrew *d – n – n* of similar meaning.

The *hundred and twenty years* could be the time of respite before the Flood (*cf.* 1 Pet. 3:20), or the shortened average life-span now to be expected. Either of these meanings would be consonant with what follows in Genesis.

It seems, then, that God is concerned at this point not with depravity, which verse 5 will introduce, but with presumption. This was the theme of 3:5 ('as gods') and of 3:22b ('and live for ever'); it recurs in 11:4 ('reach unto heaven'), and the present episode could well belong to the series as an attempt, this time on angelic initiative, to bring supernatural power, or even immortality, illicitly to earth. Hence the contrast between *spirit* and *flesh*, in God's comment. Man is still a mere mortal, sustained by God's animating spirit (as in Ps. 104:29,30) only at His good pleasure.

4. AV's famous phrase, *There were giants* . . . is derived from LXX, Vulg., but RV, RSV confess the obscurity of the key word by transliterating it *the Nephilim*. The expression *mighty men*, however, together with Numbers 13:33, tends to support the familiar translation. It is worth noting that the giants are not said to have sprung solely from this origin: if some arose in this way (*also after that*), others existed already (*in those days*).

5–8. Sin full-grown. In verse 5, the expression *the Lord saw* invites bitter comparison with the creation story, 1:31. In the two halves of the verse man's evil is presented extensively and intensively, the latter with devastating force in the words *every . . . only . . . continually*. 'A more emphatic statement of the wickedness of the human heart is hardly conceivable.'[1]

The term for *imagination* (*yēṣer*) is closer to action than the English suggests: it is derived from the potter's verb 'to form' (*cf.* 2:7), and implies design or purpose. Later Judaism made it a technical term for each of the twin impulses, towards good and evil, which it considers to coexist in man; but the New Testament is the true exponent of the passage, finding 'no good thing' in our fallen nature (Rom. 7:18).

6. This very human description conveys the poignancy of

[1] Th. C. Vriezen, *An Outline of Old Testament Theology* (Blackwell, 1960), p. 210.

the situation, leaving the word *repented* (*sorry*, RSV) to be safe-guarded on another occasion against the implication of caprice (1 Sa. 15:29,35). This is the Old Testament way of speaking, using the boldest terms, counterpoised elsewhere if need be, but not weakened. The word *grieved* is akin to the 'sorrow' ('pain', RSV) and 'toil' of 3:16,17: already God suffers on man's account. Further, U. Cassuto has pointed out[1] that the three verbs here, *repented . . . made . . . grieved*, reproduce the three Hebrew roots of 'comfort . . . work . . . toil' at 5:29, immeasurably widening the scope of Lamech's words. Man longs for temporal relief; God must have things *right*. 'The hopes that Lamech set on his son were realized in a manner far different from that which he had imagined.'[2]

7, 8. The simple brevity of 8 is extremely telling after the sweeping terms of 7. Together the two verses show God's characteristic way with evil: to meet it not with half-measures but with the simultaneous extremes of judgment and salvation. Grace (8) is still sheer bounty, whether its recipient is a Noah or (*cf.* 19:19) a Lot. The further fact that all life is bound together is made equally plain, with man's fellow creatures sharing his doom and, as the story develops, his deliverance – a theme taken further in Romans 8:19–21.

IV. THE WORLD UNDER JUDGMENT (6:9 – 8:14)

The phrase, *These are the generations*, opens a new section of the book (*cf.* 2:4; 5:1) for which the reader's appetite has been whetted by the sudden turn of the narrative in verse 8. Here is the transition from the old world to the new, in a pattern which the New Testament finds significant for all time, both 'now' (1 Pet. 3:20,21) and in the end (Lk. 17:26ff.; 2 Pet. 3:6,7). Sin, now at full spread, must bring forth death, and the first full-scale exercise of judgment demonstrates that with God the truth of a situation prevails, regardless of majorities and minorities. If as 'few' as eight souls are saved (1 Pet. 3:20), seven of these owe it to a single one (Heb. 11:7), and this minority inherits the new earth.

[1] *Genesis*, I, p. 303. [2] *Ibid.*

6:9–12. One man in step with God

9. In a corrupt world *Noah* emerges not merely as the best of a bad generation, but as a remarkably complete man of God. Of the two adjectives, *righteous* (RV, RSV) is primarily manward, *perfect* (AV, RV; *i.e.*, whole-hearted)[1] is Godward. The phrase *in his generations* is not related to his pedigree (it is a different word from that of the opening clause): it could be rendered '(alone) among his contemporaries', and possibly belongs, in spite of the punctuation, to the words that follow.

The final clause is matched only by the praise of Enoch (5:24), which it echoes with an added emphasis: 'It was with God that Noah walked.'

10–12. Much of what is said here has arisen in the genealogy and closing record of the old world; its repetition adds to its solemnity. But the words *corrupt(ed)* and *violence* give new insight into the prevailing anarchy (and into the ugly side of the might and fame noted in verse 4). The Hebrew for *corrupt(ed)* (or 'destroyed') also makes it plain that what God decided to 'destroy' (13) had been virtually self-destroyed already.

6:13–22. The ark commissioned

Noah's close walk with God makes it fitting that he is taken into his Master's confidence, as Abraham was to be concerning Sodom (18:17). This relationship, and the reasoned verdict, are in strong contrast to the atmosphere of rivalries and caprice which pervades the Babylonian flood stories.

The earth's share in the destruction (13c) was to be only in measure: 2 Peter 3:5–13 points out how different will be the final annihilation. In fact the whole act of judgment was partial: the survivors passed through a mere token of judgment, only to carry into the new world the sin of the old, as if to demonstrate that nothing less than complete death and rebirth will meet our situation.

14. The *ark*'s general features and name – for it is called a 'chest', not a ship – emphasize its sole purpose, to provide

---

[1] Used of one's attitude, *tāmîm* (whole) has this sense; used strictly, as a sacrificial term, it means 'without blemish' (*e.g.* Ex. 12:5).

shelter and orderly existence for a variety of creatures. Hence the three decks of 16, and, in the received text, the rooms or cabins, here rather charmingly called 'nests'. But perhaps *qinnîm*, 'nests', should be revocalized as *qānîm*:[1] '*of reeds* shalt thou make the ark', which is an easier Hebrew sentence. Some advocates of this reading think it a merely verbal relic of the Gilgamesh epic, in which a reed shrine is prominent; it is more meaningful to view the reeds as functional, both caulking the vessel and binding its wooden frame together, as is done with the papyrus boats of the Nile and Euphrates to this day. This material would be abundant, and easy to handle.[2] Incidentally, the only other ark (*tēḇâ*) in Scripture, that of Exodus 2, was made of rushes and pitch.

Nothing certain is known about *gopher wood*, a name found only here: LXX's 'square timber' is a guess; a more plausible conjecture is 'cypress' (Moffatt, von Rad, *etc.*). Both the verb and noun for pitch (*k-p-r*) are, it seems, closely related to the Hebrew for atone(ment). This may be more than a happy verbal coincidence (well suited to a story of judgment and salvation), for both words probably rest on a common basic meaning, 'to cover'.[3]

15. The size is vast (a cubit is about eighteen inches) but the shape is simple, and buildings of such a size were not unknown in antiquity. Also it would need no launching. As to its proportions, Augustine, allegorizing it, pointed out that they were those of a man;[4] he would have been nearer the mark to designate them those of a coffin. A similar root in Egyptian means chest or coffin, and the only other *tēḇâ* in the Old Testament was that in which the infant Moses, committed to death, voyaged into life.

16. *A roof* (RSV), or a *window* (AV) or *light* (RV) (it is a rare word), was to top the structure; the meaning of *finish it to a cubit above* (RSV) is obscure, but it may mean that an opening

---

[1] *Cf.* E. Ullendorff in *VT*, IV, 1954, pp. 95f.

[2] See T. C. Mitchell, 'Archaeology and Genesis I–XI' in *Faith and Thought*, XCI, No. 1, 1959, pp. 43f.

[3] 'To atone', however, may come from an Akkadian word, 'to wipe away'; if so, the two roots *k-p-r* are presumably unrelated.

[4] *The City of God*, XV. xxvi.

of this depth was to be left near the roof, as in some buildings of the Ancient Near East, perhaps running right round the vessel.

The door is of obvious importance, literally and in symbol (*cf.* 7:16): our Lord made much of the figure in the metaphor of the sheepfold (Jn. 10:1–9). The three *decks* (RSV) have tempted the allegorists; but they are expressive enough in their own right of God's care for what is orderly and differentiated.

17. There is strong emphasis, missed in RSV, on the opening pronoun: the whole design of judgment and covenant is the Lord's. Psalm 29:10 reiterates His sovereignty over the flood,[1] and uses for *flood* the word *mabbûl* which is otherwise confined to these chapters. It may be a term picturing the 'waters . . . above the firmament' as a kind of heavenly ocean.[2] This way of speaking is in any case used at 7:11, where it powerfully emphasizes the gravity of the judgment as a cosmic event and, in token, a reversal of the creation process of 1:7.[3]

18. This first mention of *covenant* in the Bible has salvation for its starting-point (like the Mosaic covenant, Ex. 19:4,5, and the new covenant, Mt. 26:28), but assures Noah of much more than his escape with his life. He goes into the ark not as a mere survivor but as the bearer of God's promise for the new age. The content of the covenant will be unfolded in chapter 9, and will embrace the whole company; but meanwhile it is directed to the one man through whom the many will be spared. God's will to save the family with its head (*cf.* 1 Cor. 7:14) is evident here, yet it waits on response: the same saving will is seen rejected in 19:12–14.

19, 20. A pair of each kind was the norm; the further detail, that sacrificial animals went in by sevens (7:2), of which a pair was for preserving the species (7:8,9), is not yet allowed to intrude. The concern is with the rule, not the exception.[4]

---

[1] A. Weiser translates Ps. 29:10: 'As the Lord sat enthroned over the flood, thus the Lord sits enthroned as king for ever' (*The Psalms* (S.C.M. Press, 1962), *in loc.*).

[2] W. F. Albright argues for this meaning in *JBL*, LVIII, 1939, p. 98.

[3] *Cf.* von Rad, p. 124.

[4] It is gratuitous to treat this exception (7:2) as a contradiction, as is

22. Noah's entire obedience expressed entirety of faith; it is this that Hebrews 11:7 finds significant. It is also significant that God gave so crucial a task not to an angel but to a man, and one man at that; it agrees with His greater deliverance 'through the obedience of the one' (Rom. 5:19, RV). The initiative throughout is God's: hence the reiterated *God commanded* (*cf.* 7:5,9,16), and the eventual 'God remembered' (8:1).

7:1-5. The order to embark

The effect of amplifying the instructions of 6:18f., only to retell them a third time on their fulfilment (8,9), is to emphasize God's careful provision and the steady approach of the crisis. The reiterations are deliberate and highly effective.

1. The apparent note of welcome in God's *'Come'* (AV, RV) should not be pressed: the word is as neutral as 'enter' (*cf.* RSV), as in 7. More significant is the phrase *thou and all thy house*, with the explanation, *for thee* (not 'for them') *have I seen righteous*: *cf.* on 6:18.

4. There is urgency, yet no haste, in the *seven days*; time for the whole task, but none for postponements. In visions of the end (*e.g.* Dn. 9:27) the symbol of a final seven days or years, and of its shortening, may be intended to call to mind this first closing of a day of grace.

5. See on 6:22.

7:6-24. The awaited flood

9. *Two and two*: see on 6:19,20.

11. The precise date, with its lack of obvious symbolism, has the mark of a plain fact well remembered; and this is borne out by the further careful notes of time in the story, which are characteristic of the Bible's texture, knitting together the local and the cosmic; *cf.* the precise dating of the gospel era in Luke 3:1,2. We can infer from the statement

---

sometimes done. The provision of extra animals for sacrifice cannot be made to conflict with the requirement of a pair for breeding. See Additional Note on the Flood, section *c*, pp. 97f.

about *the great deep* and *the windows of heaven* a vast upheaval of the sea-bed, and torrential rain; but the expressions are deliberately evocative of chapter 1: the waters above and below the firmament are, in token, merged again, as if to reverse the very work of creation and bring back the feature-less waste of waters.

12. On the *forty days* . . . , see the Additional Note on the Flood, section *c*, pp. 98f.

13. In spite of the early example of Lamech (4:19) and the general moral decline, Noah and his sons were mono-gamous: the family numbered eight in all (1 Pet. 3:20). Among the godly the first mention of polygamy is in the story of Abraham.

16. *And the Lord shut him in*: the expression beautifully shows God's fatherly touch, at the very brink of judgment. The same care that saw this matter through carries our salvation to its conclusion.

19-24. In themselves, these verses are not decisive for or against a localized flood (see Additional Note on the Flood, section *a*, pp. 93ff.): even *the whole heaven* (19) is likely, on the analogy of these chapters, to be the language of appearance (Paul uses similar speech hyperbolically in Col. 1:23). The concern of the story is to record the judgment which man brought on his whole world, not to dilate on geography. The very fact that a single word in Hebrew normally serves for either 'country' or 'earth' reflects a practical rather than theoretical interest.

20. *Fifteen cubits deep* refers to the clearance above the mountains, not the total depth. Possibly, as many have suggested, the measurement was learnt from the draught of the laden ark (*i.e.*, half its height of thirty cubits), which had cleared all obstacles. It should perhaps be added that some of the writers who consider the Flood to have been global conjecture that in the pre-diluvian world the main mountain ranges had not yet been thrust up (see, *e.g.*, Whitcomb and Morris, *The Genesis Flood*, pp. 267ff.).

22. On the meaning of *breath*, see footnote to 2:7.

8:1–14. The flood abates

1. When the Old Testament says that *God remembered*, it combines the ideas of faithful love (*cf.* Je. 2:2; 31:20) and timely intervention: 'God's remembering always implies his movement towards the object of his memory.'[1] *Cf.* 19:29; Exodus 2:24; Luke 1:54,55.

4. Mount Ararat itself is 17,000 feet high; but the account says no more than *upon the mountains* (or hills) *of Ararat, i.e.,* somewhere in the country of that name. This is thought to be Urartu, a mountainous land north of Mesopotamia, near Lake Van.

6. This word for *window* is not the rare term of av's 6:16; its meaning is not in doubt.

7–12. The *raven* and the *dove* almost ask to be treated as a parable; indeed the Holy Spirit, by taking the form of a dove, probably pointed to this episode with its suggestion of that which is sensitive and discriminating, the harbinger of the new creation (this, rather than peace, is the promise of the *freshly plucked olive leaf*, 11, rsv) and the guide of those who await it. The raven, in contrast, content with its carrion, was no harbinger of anything: its failure to return was as uninformative as would have been the report of a Demas (2 Tim. 4:10) on the state of society.

The little sequence, as von Rad points out,[2] 'subtly lets us witness the waiting and hoping of those enclosed in the ark'. Noah's resourcefulness comes to light, and above all, in 13,14, his self-discipline as he patiently awaits God's time and word.

V. RENEWAL AND REPEOPLING (8:15 – 10:32)

8:15–19. The new commission

It is still Noah with whom God deals. The whole scheme of salvation has centred on him; his sons are beneficiaries, but not partners until chapter 9. As almost a second Adam (9:1) he steps into a virgin world washed clean by judgment, and the spectacular deliverance in the ark is seen as a mere

[1] B. S. Childs, *Memory and Tradition in Israel* (S.C.M. Studies in Biblical Theology, No. 37, 1962), p. 34.

[2] *Genesis*, p. 117.

preliminary to salvation proper, which is a new creation. The New Testament sees the Flood and the rite of baptism as twin expressions of this reality (1 Pet. 3:18–22): that is, of the provision of a way through death into life.

8:20–22. The accepted sacrifice

20. Malachi 4:2 conjures up the sheer physical joy of release after confinement, but Noah's first thought is Godward. Homage, dedication and atonement are all expressed in the *burnt offerings*: the new earth is to be God's, if He will have it.

21. It is especially bold to speak of the *sweet savour* (AV, RV), since the Babylonian version crudely made the hunger of the gods, ravenous without man's gifts, a reason for their ending the flood. But the Old Testament, with no fear of giving such an impression (*cf.* Ps. 50:8–15), can use this vivid language which the New is glad to take up (Eph. 5:2).

Grammatically, the clause *for the imagination . . .* could be either an expansion of *for man's sake* or else the reason for saying 'never again'. Theologically it must be the former: the Lord's resolve not to renew the judgment is based on the accepted sacrifice (*cf.* 1 Sa. 26:19; Col. 1:20), not on man's incorrigibility, which had been the very ground of the judgment (6:5–7) and still called for its renewal; it never counts in the sinner's favour. If God seems too lightly propitiated, this arises partly from the simplicity of the style, partly from the inherent limitation of all Old Testament sacrifices, 'which can never take away sins'. The real propitiation, in the mind of God, was the sacrifice of Jesus (Rom. 3:25,26).

22. The assurance goes far beyond 21. It does not abolish disasters, but it does localize them, so that the human family may overcome them by forethought such as Joseph's and by compassion such as Paul's (2 Cor. 8:14).

Additional Note on the Flood

a. The extent and approximate date of the Flood

If we possessed no physical clues to the early history of the earth and the primitive distribution of mankind, it would have to be left an open question whether such expressions in the Flood story as 'the earth', 'all the high mountains under the whole heaven', and 'all flesh', in Genesis 7:19,21, were to be understood in their modern or their ancient sense.[1] As it is, the various geological data that have been thought to favour a strictly universal flood have been successively found wanting, in the opinion of most experts, and little reasonable doubt remains (although some would dispute this)[2] that the events of Genesis 6–8 must have taken place within a limited though indeed a vast area, covering not the entire globe but the scene of the human story of the previous chapters. Some opinions would confine this to Mesopotamia, others envisage a still larger tract;[3] there is certainly room for further investigation.[4]

But it also appears, from the distribution and generally accepted dating of human remains, that certain branches of mankind had been settled in countries far beyond the specific Old Testament horizon since the palaeolithic age,[5] and unless this world population was drawn back into the vicinity of Mesopotamia before the Flood, or unless the palaeontological data need drastic reinterpretation,[6] it seems to follow that the destruction of life was, like the inundation of the earth, complete in the relative and not the absolute sense. By 'relative' we mean related to the area of direct Old Testament interest. To quote Bernard Ramm: 'The record neither affirms nor denies that man existed beyond the Mesopotamian valley. Noah was certainly not a preacher of righteousness to the peoples of Africa, of India, of China or of America – places

---

[1] As examples of the latter, *cf.* 'all the face of the earth . . . all countries . . . all the earth', in 41:56,57, and Paul's words in Col. 1: 23: 'the gospel . . . has been preached to every creature under heaven.' *Cf.* also Acts 2:5 ('every nation under heaven') in relation to the list in Acts 2:9–11.

[2] *E.g.* J. C. Whitcomb and H. M. Morris, *The Genesis Flood* (Presbyterian and Reformed Publishing Company, 1961).

[3] *Cf.* R. Jamieson, quoted in B. Ramm, *The Christian View of Science and Scripture*, p. 162. The whole section, pp. 156–169, is a most valuable survey. See also T. C. Mitchell, in *NBD*, *s.v.* 'Flood'.

[4] *Cf.* R. L. Raikes in *Iraq*, XXVIII, 1966, pp. 62f.

[5] See Introduction, Human Beginnings, pp. 26ff.

[6] One such reinterpretation is offered in Whitcomb and Morris, *op. cit.*

where there is evidence for the existence of man many thousands of years before the flood. . . . The emphasis in Genesis is upon that group of cultures from which Abraham eventually came.'[1] If this is so, the language of this story is in fact the everyday language normally used in Scripture, describing matters from the narrator's own vantage-point and within the customary frame of reference of his readers. See also the commentary on 7:19–24.

Whether this is the right assessment of the evidence or not, we should be careful to read the account whole-heartedly in its own terms, which depict a *total* judgment on the ungodly world already set before us in Genesis – not an event of debatable dimensions in a world we may try to reconstruct. The whole living scene is blotted out, and the New Testament makes us learn from it the greater judgment that awaits not only our entire globe but the universe itself (2 Pet. 3:5–7).

For the approximate date of the Flood the chief biblical clue, apart from the genealogies of Genesis 5 and 11 (which are open to more than one interpretation; *cf.* the Additional Note to chapter 5), is the statement that the nations of chapter 10 sprang from the sons of Noah. This seems to imply a very early date indeed, some millennia before the Babylonian floods of around 3000 BC which left their physical traces at different times at Ur, Shuruppak, Kish and elsewhere.[2] But it would be guess-work to be more specific than this.

b. Flood stories outside the Bible

Stories of great flooding are found in most parts of the world, from Europe to the South Seas, and from the Americas to the Far East. Only in Africa are they noticeably rare.

Scattered details in them may bring Noah's flood to mind, in varying degrees. A deluge may be sent in divine anger, and one man be warned of it. In the Greek story, Deucalion's vessel, like Noah's, was a chest (but not of the same vast

[1] *Op. cit.*, p. 163.
[2] See, *e.g.*, the tables in A. Parrot, *The Flood and Noah's Ark* (S.C.M. Press, 1955), p. 52, and in M. E. L. Mallowan, 'Noah's Flood Reconsidered', *Iraq*, XXVI, 1964, facing p. 82. See, again, T. C. Mitchell in *NBD*, *s.v.* 'Flood'.

size) which eventually grounded on a mountain. Some North American Indian tales speak of pairs of animals taken on board a raft, and of birds sent out as means of reconnaissance. It is reasonable to think that some memories of Noah's flood were carried into distant parts by the expanding circle of his descendants; yet it must be remembered that floods are not the rarest of disasters, and survivors' experiences will have much in common. The specific similarities between the Genesis story and most others are utterly outweighed by the differences, and it is only the Babylonian legend that shows any close resemblances to the story of Noah.

There are several versions of this Babylonian tradition,[1] in which the hero is variously described as Ziusudra, Utnapishtim and Atrahasis (names on the themes of life and wisdom; Noah's name is derived from the root 'rest'). The flood is decreed by the council of gods; it is a last resort, according to the Atrahasis version, to silence the rowdiness of man, so that heaven may get a little sleep. However, one dissentient god warns the hero, who is a worshipper of his, to build himself a ship; but he is to keep its purpose secret, putting off enquirers with some reassuring story.

The Babylonian ship is a seven-decked cube, 120 cubits each way, and is proofed with pitch, stocked with money and provisions, and boarded by the hero's family together with animals and craftsmen. Then the storm breaks, with such violence that the gods themselves are terrified at what they have done. After seven days the hero opens a window, eventually to see land in the distance. The ship comes to rest on mount Niṣir, and after seven more days three birds are released in succession. The first two, a dove and a swallow, have to return; but the third, a raven, finding the waters abated, returns no more. Then the hero disembarks and makes sacrifice to the gods, who are famished by now for lack of offerings. So 'the gods smelled the sweet savour; the gods gathered like flies over the sacrificer'. Heaven has learnt its lesson, and the chief instigator of the plot is rebuked. To make amends, he confers deity on the flood-hero.

[1] See the first footnote to the Introduction, p. 13.

By common consent this version of events is altogether put to shame by Genesis. Even the incidentals, the dice-shaped ark and the sequence of the birds, suffer in the comparison, while the theology flounders from one ineptitude to the next. But opinions differ over the literary relation of the one story to the other. In the majority view, some version of the Babylonian stories, which were certainly copied and recopied for centuries before Moses, must be the raw material of which Genesis is the finished product.[1] The setting seems Babylonian, and even the word for 'pitch' in 6:14, found only here, is the Hebrew equivalent of the Babylonian term in the Gilgamesh epic.

But another view is that the two have ultimately a common origin, which Genesis reflects faithfully and Babylon corruptly. The fact that Genesis tells a simpler, more coherent story favours this, if we accept that a real event lies behind these traditions. The arguments brought against this view are very indecisive: the Mesopotamian setting is what the Bible itself affirms for this period (*cf.* 11:2,28), and the word for 'pitch' (*kōper, cf.* Babylonian *kupru*) is one of three Hebrew synonyms, of which the other two occur only three times each in the Old Testament – a statistical foundation far too meagre to build on.[2] It remains fully self-consistent to hold that a family tenacious enough of its traditions to preserve its genealogy from Shem to Moses could have handed down its own account of so memorable an event.

c. Documentary analysis of the Flood story

Genesis 6–8 is one of the showpieces of literary criticism, a textbook-example of the art of detecting and unravelling a composite narrative. Two traditions, Yahwistic (J) and Priestly (P), are claimed to be found here, and are considered to be so discrepant as to need separate treatment in most

[1] This view would make Genesis, whatever its other merits, an even less reliable witness to the original events than the Babylonian accounts.
[2] *Cf.* A. Heidel, *The Gilgamesh Epic and Old Testament Parallels*[2] (University of Chicago Press, 1949), pp. 265ff. The whole section, pp. 260–269, discusses the question of dependence.

modern commentaries. The following points are usually made.

First, in the ark J has sevens of clean animals and birds, as well as pairs of unclean; P makes no distinction. Secondly, J ascribes the flood to heavy rain, but P to waters from the great deep and the windows of heaven; thirdly, J's flood lasts forty days plus the three weeks in which the birds are sent out, while P's lasts a year and ten days. Fourthly, repetitions and tricks of style continually betray the presence of the two sources.

To each of these suggestions some reply is possible.

1. The question of sevens and pairs of animals could be at bottom a simple matter of style, a choice between a graceful and a tedious account; for a narrative which is always adding qualifying clauses soon becomes unbearable. The memorable 'two and two' is the guiding instruction to Noah about his livestock; once this has been settled in 6:19,20, and the exception made for clean animals in 7:2,3, it would kill the story to parade the exceptions at verses 9 and 15. (Incidentally the 'two and two' of 7:9 is an embarrassment to the analysis; see 4 below.) Silence therefore proves nothing except the author's literary common sense.

2. Three expressions for the multiple onslaught of the Deluge are hardly excessive. Without a prior assumption of double documents there is no case to answer here. But see further on the question of vocabulary and duplications, under 4.

3. The rival time-tables are manufactured by lifting two periods of forty days from the total (7:12; 8:6), reducing them to one period, adding three weeks (8:6–12) and setting this total of sixty-one days (which we might call the Shorter Cataclysm) against the year and ten days of the whole account, ascribing them to J and P respectively.[1] Yet the chronology as it stands contains only one difficulty, the relation of the forty days of 7:12,17 to the 150 days of 7:24. This is by no means insoluble. Heidel may be right in submitting that the

---

[1] The 'forty days' of 7:17 (P) are an embarrassment to the analysis, and are ascribed to a redactor. On this expedient *cf*. 4. below.

ADDITIONAL NOTE: THE FLOOD

first forty days were followed by a moderation of (particularly) the waters from above, but not a complete cessation until the 150th day.[1] But it seems more likely, as U. Cassuto[2] and E. Nielsen[3] suggest (apparently independently), that, in true Semitic style, chapter 7 rounds off its account of the first phase, namely the forty days and their continuing effects, by summing its duration (150 days); then chapter 8 describes the second phase, that of deliverance, starting from its logical beginning in the stopping of the forty days' downpour (8:2), but noting the intermediate period that elapsed before the grounding of the ark (8:3). (On this narrative method, over-lapping the end of a previous paragraph, see footnote to 12:1-9.)

The following table shows the self-consistency of the account. From 8:3,4 it appears that the months are reckoned as of thirty days each; and in 8:10 the expression 'other seven days' probably implies a week's interval between 8:7 and 8.

References in Genesis	Events	Dates (in terms of Noah's life)
7:11	The flood begins	17.ii.600
7:12 (cf. 17)	Cataclysm till the fortieth day	26.iii.600
7:24 (cf. 8:3)	Inundation till the 150th day	16.vii.600
8:4	The ark aground	17.vii.600
8:5	The hill-tops visible	1.x.600
8:6,7	The raven sent	10.xi.600
8:8	The dove sent	17.xi.600
8:10,11	The dove and the leaf	24.xi.600
8:12	The dove departs	1.xii.600
8:13	The ground appears dry	1.i.601
8:14ff.	The disembarking	27.ii.601

It is not too much to say, with Heidel, 'There is here no discrepancy whatever.'[4]

4. The argument from typical J and P expressions, and from

[1] *Op. cit.*, p. 246.
[2] *Genesis*, II, pp. 99f.
[3] *Oral Tradition*, p. 99.
[4] *Op. cit.*, p. 247.

repetitions, is weakened by many anomalies. To take 7:7-9 as a specific example, the first phrase is the elaborate 'Noah and his sons and his wife and his sons' wives', which is characteristically P (*cf.* 6:18), over against J's simple 'you and all your household' (7:1). But all are agreed that it should be a J verse. Perhaps the original has been altered, or the words are 'a pure insertion' (Skinner)? In the next two verses, however, J's clean and unclean beasts (a distinction which P will not admit before Sinai) are accompanied by a string of P terms, including 'two and two', 'male and female' (as against J's (literally) 'a man and his wife'), and 'Elohim'. With so little left to J one might wonder why he is allotted the passage at all. The reason is simply that it duplicates 13-16, which belong to P;[1] and duplications are *ex hypothesi* inadmissible in a single source, for they are one of the criteria by which one recognizes a narrative as composite. The analyst is caught between his upper and nether millstones of vocabulary and duplication. His only escape is to postulate the wholesale interference of a redactor writing in the style of P; yet this is to abandon the seen for the unseen. Nielsen remarks on this kind of dilemma, that the documentary hypothesis 'is only tenable when it occasionally comes into conflict with its own presuppositions'. He adds, with justifiable irony, 'It is reassuring and sometimes necessary to have a Redactor up one's sleeve.'[2]

To turn from these elaborate exercises to the narrative itself is, we may suggest, to move from the realm of the ingeniously improbable into the fresh air of simplicity and truth.

9:1-7. The new decrees

Although there are echoes here of the charge to Adam (1,7), sin has darkened the scene. The image of God remains (6) and man is still heaven's viceroy, but his régime will be largely one of fear (2), his fellow-creatures are now his food (3), and violence will be abroad in the earth (5,6).

[1] *Cf., e.g.,* Skinner, p. 154n.
[2] *Oral Tradition,* pp. 97f.

3, 4. The permission to eat flesh may or may not have been an innovation: possibly it was implicit before (see on 1:29,30), and only now explicit, but perhaps it is more natural to infer with RSV that for man this was newly conceded. What is certainly a fresh development is the law on *blood*, which is theologically far-reaching. It at once limited man's rights over God's creatures, since their *life* (4) was His. The Mosaic law reaffirmed this repeatedly (*e.g.* Lv. 3:17; Dt. 12:15,16). It also prepared men to appreciate the use of blood in sacrifice. Belonging to God, it could be seen as His atoning gift to sinners, not theirs to Him (Lv. 17:11).

5, 6. The theme of the sanctity of blood is now taken further and made memorable by the rhythmic form of 6, preserved in AV, RV: *Whoso sheddeth man's blood* . . . . Something more than retribution is in mind here. The execution of a man-killing animal is not to be explained in such terms, although that of the murderer could be. The clue is in verse 6b: the purpose is didactic, as was that of verse 4. If all life is God's, human life is supremely so. Both these lessons remain in force, although (as I have argued elsewhere)[1] the means of teaching them may change: one cannot simply transfer verse 6 to the statute book unless one is prepared to include verses 4 and 5a with it. Capital punishment has to be defended on wider grounds.

9:8-17. The universal covenant

This first explicit covenant (if we take 6:18 to refer to this) is remarkable for its breadth (embracing 'every living creature'), its permanence ('perpetual', 'everlasting', *etc.*) and its generosity – for it was as unconditional as it was undeserved. For good measure, its sign and seal, a feature of all covenants, was such as to emphasize God's sole initiative, far out of man's reach.

Any idea that a covenant is basically a bargain is forestalled by such an opening to the series. At the same time, the absence of any obligations laid on the recipients[2] makes this

---

[1] *The Death Penalty* (C.P.A.S. Falcon Booklets, 1963), pp. 13f.
[2] There are obligations in verses 4–6, but they are not attached explicitly to the covenant.

an extreme example and, as J. Murray has pointed out, one which could produce no close bond of fellowship, since 'where there is religious relationship there is mutuality'.[1] There is no mutuality here.

8. God speaks in this chapter to the whole family together, no longer indirectly through Noah. They are joint-heirs with him of the new age, and all creation benefits with them.

12, 13. The *sign* (RSV; *cf.* on 3:14) was well suited to fulfil the prime function of all covenant-signs, which is reassurance. Like the later sign of circumcision, it was the seal (Rom. 4:11) of an accomplished fact; unlike it, this could not for a moment be thought to procure it.

It has been attractively suggested that the *bow* would now picture to men God's battle-bow laid aside.[2] Certainly a single word is used for both, and lightnings are His arrows in the poetry of Psalm 18:14 (*cf.* Ps. 7:12; Hab. 3:9); yet one might have expected this thought to have been more explicit. The obvious glory of the rainbow, however, against the gloom of the cloud, seems enough to make it a token of grace, even without the reflection that it arises from the conjunction of sun and storm, as of mercy and judgment.

The rainbow was seen as an element in God's glory by Ezekiel (1:28) and John (Rev. 4:3; *cf.* 10:1), perhaps as a reminder of this first pledge of grace.

14, 15. The promise is not that a rainbow will be seen in every cloud (AV, RV), but that when it is seen (*cf.* RSV), God will remember His covenant. *Remember* is used in its common meaning, rather than that noted at 8:1; the whole tone of the paragraph is accommodated to our need of simple reassurance.

9:18–29. The destinies of Shem, Ham and Japheth

The statement of verse 19 introduces the comprehensiveness of chapter 10, while 20–27 prepare for the selectiveness of the rest of the Old Testament, from 11:10 on. The Bible preserves its emphasis both on the unity of mankind, as the prophets' oracles on the heathen show, and on the specializations within

---

[1] *The Covenant of Grace* (Tyndale Press, 1954), p. 17.
[2] von Rad, p. 130.

that unity. But racial roles are superseded in the New Testament, where 'there cannot be Greek and Jew, . . . barbarian, Scythian, slave, free man, but Christ is all, and in all' (Col. 3:11, RSV). Any attempt to grade the branches of mankind by an appeal to 25–27 is therefore a re-erecting of what God has demolished, not unlike the rebuilding for which Paul rebuked Peter in Galatians 2:18. See also on 25.

Noah's drunkenness is recounted without moral comment on his part in the scandal: the word *began* (20) could imply that only inexperience was to blame; we cannot be certain.[1]

The loss of decency and honour which marks this first biblical story of strong drink is severer still in the second, the degradation of Lot (19:30ff.). It is not its only aspect (*cf.* Dt. 14:26; Ps. 104:15; Pr. 31:6,7), but Proverbs 31:4,5 is comment enough on the last passage, with the formidable support of Proverbs 23:29–35. The law was to make provision for vows forswearing its use, as a witness to primitive simplicity (Nu. 6:1ff.), but such vows were a special vocation (see also Je. 35; Lk. 7:33f.). Here however the drunkenness is incidental: the point of the story is the marring of Ham's inheritance through his flagrantly unfilial act. It is the obverse of the fifth commandment, which makes the national destiny pivot on the same point – for that commandment is not a sociological prescription (except incidentally), but a call to uphold God's delegated authority and so retain His blessing.

24. *Youngest* (RV, RSV) is the natural sense of the Hebrew, and seems further supported by 10:21. AV's *younger* is barely possible. The close contact of the Shem and Ham peoples and the remoteness of Japheth throughout the Old Testament period may have led to the familiar grouping of verse 18, *etc.*

25. That the curse fell on Canaan, youngest son of the

---

[1] RSV's translation, *Noah was the first tiller of the soil. He planted a vineyard* . . . , is quite unwarranted. The Hebrew allows at most 'Noah, the tiller . . . , was the first to plant a vineyard.' Even this is a moderately rare use of the construction, which reads literally 'Noah, (the) man of the soil, began and planted. . .' The only other occurrence of 'began and' is in Ezra 3:8, while out of forty occurrences of the similar 'began to', only four (*viz.* Gn. 10:8; Jdg. 10:18; 1 Sa. 14:35; and perhaps 1 Sa. 22:15) can be rendered 'was the first (to) . . .' This can be appreciated by examining, *e.g.*, Gn. 6:1; 41:54; Nu. 25:1; *etc.*

offender (10:6), who was himself a youngest son, emphasizes its reference to Ham's succession rather than his person. For his breach of the family, his own family would falter. Since it confines the curse to this one branch within the Hamites, those who reckon the Hamitic peoples in general to be doomed to inferiority have therefore misread the Old Testament as well as the New. It is likely, too, that the subjugation of the Canaanites to Israel fulfilled the oracle sufficiently (*cf.* Jos. 9:23; I Ki. 9:21).

26. Of the three oracles, only that on Shem uses God's personal name Yahweh (*the Lord*); the significance of the fact begins to emerge at 12:1, and will dominate the Old Testament (*cf.* Dt. 4:35). Since Shem means 'Name', there may well be a play on words here; *cf.* on 27. The traditional text, *Blessed be the Lord, the God of Shem* (RV, *cf.* AV), suggests that Shem is himself already in covenant with Yahweh and that his blessing is wholly found in his Lord. RSV (*Blessed by the Lord my God be Shem*) could be right in revocalizing the same consonants to make Shem the direct recipient of the blessing; but this simpler, less pregnant construction is unsupported by the ancient versions.

27. The word *enlarge* (make space for) is the parent verb of the name Japheth (*cf.* comment on Shem, 26); the oracle evidently confirms the prayer made at his birth. The fulfilment of the words *let him dwell in* (or among) *the tents of Shem* (RV, RSV) is sought almost in vain in the Old Testament,[1] but leaps to the eye in the New Testament in the ingathering of the Gentiles (Eph. 3:6), predominantly from the west. The fact that this reading of the oracle makes it a prediction of great events, instead of a pious retrojection of twelfth-century politics, will disturb only the resolutely sceptical.

10:1–32. The family of nations
Not every nation known to the Old Testament is enrolled here,[2] but enough are present to make the point that mankind

---

[1] von Rad, p. 134, suggests the Philistines, as coming from Crete; but 10:14 classes them as Hamitic.
[2] *Cf., e.g.,* Dt. 2:10–12.

is one, for all its diversity, under the one Creator. Possibly the seventy names (LXX 72) influenced our Lord's choice of this apparently symbolic number of emissaries in Luke 10:1. Delitzsch comments that 'the idea of the people of God implies that they have to regard all nations as future partakers with them of the same salvation,[1] and to embrace them with an interest of hopeful love unheard of elsewhere in the ancient world'.

Most of the names appear to be those of individuals, although they meet us later in the Old Testament as peoples, just as do the personal names Israel, Edom, Moab, *etc.* The natural sense of the chapter seems to make these the founders of their respective groups; but the interest lies in the group so founded and its relation to other peoples. This is borne out by the sprinkling of plural (*e.g.* Kittim, Dodanim, 4; *cf.* 13,14), dual (Mizraim, 6) and adjectival (16–18) forms, which also show that the compiler of the list did not automatically ascribe ancestors to the groups he recorded. It is also worth noting that most of the city names in the list are clearly cities and not men (they are part of a 'kingdom', 10, or are 'built', 11); it is not hard to suppose that the exceptions, such as Asshur (11, see note) and Sidon (15), were founders who gave their names to their cities, as *e.g.* Alexander did to Alexandria.

Of the three families of humanity, Japheth (2–5) and Ham (6–20) are dealt with first, to leave a clear field to the history of Shem in the remainder of the book. This is the procedure in Genesis with secondary themes: it will be applied in 11:10ff. to Shem itself, disposing of the non-Abrahamic branches before concentrating on the patriarchal line.

2–5. Japheth. The peoples of this paragraph range from as far west as the Aegean to the vicinity of the Caspian Sea, stretching in a wide sweep north of the Fertile Crescent; but they are classified (as are the Hamites and Shemites, 20,31) not purely geographically (*their lands*, 5) but also by varied

[1] *Cf.* Gn. 12:3.

criteria of language,[1] race[2] and nation, which take into account the shifting and mingling to which human groups are subject.

Gomer (*cf.* Ezk. 38:6) is generally identified with the Cimmerians ('a name', adds E. A. Speiser,[3] 'still in use apparently for the Welsh (*Cymry*)'); *Magog, Tubal* and *Meschech* come 'from the uttermost parts of the north' in Ezekiel 38:2,6; 39:1,2; *Madai* are evidently the Medes, who are found west of the Caspian Sea in the ninth century BC; *Javan* the Ionians, a branch of the Greeks, for whom this is the standard name in the Old Testament (*e.g.* Dn. 8:21), its equivalent also occurring in the Ugaritic texts of the fourteenth century BC. *Tiras* may be the Etruscans.[4]

3, 4. *The sons of Gomer* (3) and of *Javan* (4) could be peoples either descended from or subordinate to these two: in 3 the firmest identification is of *Ashkenaz* with the Scythians, and in 4 of *Kittim* with the inhabitants of Cyprus and its neighbouring coasts, and *Rodanim* (rather than *Dodanim*: see 1 Ch. 1:7) with those of Rhodes.

5. The *isles* (AV, RV) or coastlands (*cf.* RSV) are a term, especially in Isaiah 40 onwards, for the distant parts of the earth, and particularly the west. If the word is taken in this more restricted sense, 5 will refer chiefly to 4; but this seems unlikely in view of 20,31.

6-20. Ham. Geographically, these are chiefly the nations from Canaan southwards; but they are not simply the African races, as 8-12 are enough to show. The scheme of the paragraph is to name four primary peoples in 6, and to trace the offshoots of three of them in (a) 7-12 (Cush), (b) 13,14 (Mizraim) and (c) 15-19 (Canaan).

(*a*) *The sons of Cush* (7-12). Two peoples seem to have borne this name: the Ethiopians, at one extreme, and the Kassites,

---

[1] The Japheth languages appear to have been mostly Indo-Aryan.
[2] But D. J. Wiseman, 'Genesis 10: Some Archaeological Considerations' (*JTVI*, LXXXVII, 1955), pp. 16f., points out that *mišpāḥôt*, families, may sometimes have a political rather than a genetic meaning.
[3] *Genesis, in loc.*
[4] E. Dhorme, *ap.* Wiseman, *art. cit.*, p. 18.

east of Assyria, at the other. This passage suggests that they are linked. Verse 7 shows most of this stock bordering the Red Sea: west of it the *Cush* that is Ethiopia, and on its eastern shores *Seba* (probably identical or closely linked with Sheba), *Havilah* (*cf.* 1 Sa. 15:7)[1] and *Dedan* (Is. 21:13), all in Arabia, reading from south to north. Verses 8–12, on the other hand, show another descendant of Cush striking out independently, to found a kingdom on the far side of the Fertile Crescent. Nimrod may have led a migration of Cushites, to dominate and leave their name on the Kassites (Cushites), much as the Philistine invaders were eventually to do to Palestine. D. J. Wiseman points out that the earliest known inhabitants of both Egypt (Mizraim, 6) and Canaan (6) were non-Semites who show affinities with the Sumerians of early Babylon, themselves non-Semitic.

Nimrod[2] looks out of antiquity as the first of 'the great men that are in the earth', remembered for two things the world admires, personal prowess and political power. The Bible does not underrate them: there is warmth in the reiterated *before the Lord* (9), marking God's estimate of his skill – it is more than a mere formula. At the same time there is tragic irony (that is, irony not yet apparent in the story) in the note of his further exploits: *The beginning of his kingdom was Babel. . . .* The next chapter, and the further progress of Babel (Babylon) to the catastrophe of Revelation 18, add their comment to the tale of earthly success.

10. *The beginning* should probably be translated 'the chief part';[3] the first three cities are well known in antiquity; *Calneh* (AV, RV) however may be a name for Nippur, or, revocalized, may mean *all of them* (RSV).

11. RV, RSV may be right in making Nimrod still the subject, and *Assyria* (*Asshur*, AV) his destination; the fact that the modern name for *Calah*[4] is Nimrud lends some slight support to it.

12. *The great city* may be a term for the three cities taken

---

[1] The Havilah of Gn. 2:11 appears to be quite distinct.
[2] For a discussion of his identity, see *NBD*, *s.v.* 'Nimrod'.
[3] *Cf.*, *e.g.*, Speiser, who refers to Je. 49:35.
[4] See article 'Calah' in *NBD*.

together, as its recurrence in Jonah 1:2; 3:2; 4:11, with the mention of its large area, may indicate.[1]

(*b*) *Egypt and its offshoots* (13,14). *Mizraim* (Egypt) is a dual (originally for Upper and Lower Egypt?), and the rest are plurals (see the opening remarks on the chapter). The name *Pathrusim* indicates dwellers in southern (Upper) Egypt. It is surprising to find the *Philistines* and *Caphtorim* (Cretans) linked with Egypt: this either points to a time before they settled in Crete (from which they invaded Palestine (Am. 9:7) after an attempt on Egypt), or else is an expression of their geographica and political subordination to Egypt when they occupied the south-west coastal strip of Palestine.

(*c*) *Canaan* (15–19). Our knowledge of the early Canaanites indicates that they were non-Semitic, as this paragraph shows. In accordance with the curse on Canaan in 9:25f., and because of their wickedness (15:16; Dt. 20:17f.), most of these peoples were to be dispossessed by Israel, and sooner still, the cities of 19b divinely destroyed.

21-31. Shem. The ground has been cleared for the family of peoples which will be the Old Testament's main concern, and of these *Eber* ('*ēḇer*, the apparent root of the name Hebrew; see on 24) is singled out at once (21). To this end the list quickly narrows to the line of Arpachshad (22,24) and so to Eber (24); but the more significant branch of this family (that of Peleg) is kept in reserve for the fuller treatment of 11:10ff., while that of *Joktan* (26ff., father of many of the Arab races) is first disposed of, according to the standard practice of the book (see the opening comment on the chapter).

22. *Elam* presents a difficulty, being apparently non-Semitic; and *Asshur* and *Lud* have already appeared in the Hamitic list (11, Assyria; 13, Ludim). D. J. Wiseman suggests 'that Semites early penetrated Elam even though they were later not . . . dominant, whereas in "Hamitic" Assyria . . . they later inherited the Sumerian culture'.[2]

Arpachshad (RV, RSV), a non-Semitic name, may perhaps have

[1] D. W. B. Robinson, *NBC*[1], p. 718.
[2] *Art. cit.*, p. 23.

a similar history; it is even possible that it conceals the name of Babylon.[1]

24. *Eber*, the apparent source of the word Hebrew (*'ibrî*), seems to be named from the verb *'ābar*, 'to pass over or through'; and in the Ancient Near East a somewhat similar name *habiru* designated a class with no secure place in society. Whether the term was originally ethnic and became social, and whether 'Hebrew' and *'habiru'* are related, are still debatable points.[2] What is clear is that 'Abram the Hebrew' (14:13) shared descent with other Semitic peoples from Eber.

25. *Peleg* is a name akin to *divided*: whether this refers to territorial divisions (*cf.* 11:8f.?) or to irrigation canals (Heb. *peleḡ*) is a matter for conjecture.

28, 29. *Sheba* (if it is the same as Seba) and *Havilah* have already appeared in the Hamitic list (7); this shows that these territories changed hands, or that the peoples were of mixed stock. A different Havilah (the name is descriptive, meaning perhaps 'sandy') is mentioned in 2:11.

VI. END AND BEGINNING: BABEL AND CANAAN
(11:1–32)

11:1–9. Babel
The primeval history reaches its fruitless climax as man, conscious of new abilities, prepares to glorify and fortify himself by collective effort. The elements of the story are timelessly characteristic of the spirit of the world. The project is typically grandiose; men describe it excitedly to one another as if it were the ultimate achievement – very much as modern man glories in his space projects. At the same time they betray their insecurity as they crowd together to preserve their identity and control their fortunes (4b).

[1] *Ibid.*

[2] *Cf., e.g.*, D. J. Wiseman, *The Word of God for Abraham and To-day* (Westminster Chapel Bookroom, 1959), pp. 11f. W. F. Albright, characteristically independent, proposes a derivation yielding 'donkey driver', in *The Biblical Period from Abraham to Ezra*, p. 5. For fuller discussions see J. Bottéro, *Le Problème des Habiru* (Paris, 1954); M. P. Gray in *HUCA*, XXIX, 1958, pp. 135–202; M. G. Kline in *WTJ*, XIX, 1956–7, pp. 1–24, 170–184; XX, 1957, pp. 46–70.

The narrative captures the simultaneous absurdity and gravity of it. Even the materials are makeshift, as verse 3 remarks, yet the builders are weaker still. There is irony in God's echo of their bustling 'Go to . . . Go to . . .' with His own 'Go to, let us go down . . .'; and the end is anticlimax: 'they left off . . .' The half-built city is all too apt a monument to this aspect of man.

Yet it is taken seriously too. To modern ears 6b is wholly apposite: 'this is only the beginning . . .; nothing that they propose . . . will now be impossible for them' (RSV). The note of foreboding marks a Creator's and Father's concern, not a rival's: it is like our Lord's saying, 'If they do these things in the green tree . . .' (Lk. 23:31). It makes it clear that unity and peace are not ultimate goods: better division than collective apostasy (*cf.* Lk. 12:51).

The end reveals the decisive hand of God in human affairs. Mutual incomprehension has admittedly its natural causes, such as the very attitudes of pride and fear expressed in verse 4 (which could be the motto of modern nationalism); but ultimately it is God's fit discipline of an unruly race.

Pentecost opened a new chapter of the story, in the articulating of one gospel in many tongues. The final reversal is promised in Zephaniah 3:9: 'Yea, at that time I will change the speech of the peoples to a pure speech, that all of them may call on the name of the Lord and serve him with one accord' (RSV).

1. *One speech* (AV, RV; literally 'one [set of] words') is preferable to RSV's *few words*, though either is possible (see Heb. of Ezk. 37:17; Gn. 27:44 respectively). The episode was either soon after the Flood (*cf.* 10:5, *etc.*) or else it was limited to a particular people, if *earth* here should be translated 'land'. (The impression that this is a group of settlers afraid of attack (2,4b) lends some support to the latter.)

9. *Babel* (Babylon) called itself Bab-ili, 'gate of God' (which may have been a flattering reinterpretation of its original meaning);[1] but by a play of words Scripture superimposes the truer label *bālal* ('he confused'). In the Bible this

[1] See I. J. Gelb, in *JIAS*, I, 1965, pp. 1–4.

city increasingly came to symbolize the godless society, with its pretensions (Gn. 11), persecutions (Dn. 3), pleasures, sins and superstitions (Is. 47:8–13), its riches and eventual doom (Rev. 17, 18). One of its glories was its huge *ziggurat*, a temple-crowned artificial mountain whose name, Etemenanki, suggested the linking of heaven and earth. But it was her sins that 'reached . . . unto heaven' (Rev. 18:5). In Revelation she is contrasted with the holy city which comes 'down out of heaven', whose open gates unite the nations (Rev. 21:10,24–27).

11:10–26. Towards the chosen people

The chosen line now leads out of the old world into that of the patriarchs. Of the names in 10:22ff. only the ancestors of Eber reappear; thereafter it is Peleg, not Joktan as in 10:25ff., who is the growing-point. Ten generations are shown, perhaps to match the ten named from Adam to Noah; but the growth of nations in chapter 10, apart from any other considerations, makes it clear that great intervals lie between them.[1]

The life-span is steadily contracting[2] from the antediluvian level towards the 175 years of Abraham and the 110 of Joseph. More significantly, in view of the promised birth of Isaac, the age of parenthood has dropped to a point not far above its present level.

11:27–32. Towards the promised land

Joshua 24:2 shows that Terah and his forbears 'served other gods'; his own name and those of Laban, Sarah and Milcah point towards the moon-god as perhaps the most prominent of these. Certainly Ur and Haran were centres of moon worship, which may suggest why the migration halted where it did (31). Terah's motive in leaving Ur may have been no more than prudence (the Elamites destroyed the city *c.* 1950 BC);[3] but Abram had already heard the call of God (Acts 7:2–4).

A comparison of 31b with 12:5b shows that Terah, lacking

[1] See Additional Note to chapter 5, pp. 82f.
[2] See comment on 6:3, and Additional Note to chapter 5.
[3] Albright, *FSAC²*, 1957, p. 236.

the vision, lost the will to persist; in Hebrews 11:9,10 the lesson is drawn that only faith will stay the course. So the chapter brings the primeval history to a doubly appropriate close, with man's self-effort issuing in confusion at Babel and in compromise here. On his own, man will get no further than this.

32. Terah's age at death presents a difficulty, since it makes his eldest son 135 years old (26), whereas Abram was only 75 (12:4, with Acts 7:4). One solution is to suppose Abram to have been the youngest son, born sixty years after the eldest but placed first in the list in 11:26,27 because of his prominence (like Ephraim before Manasseh). Another is to follow the Samaritan text, which gives Terah's age as 145 at death. This seems preferable, if only because Abram would scarcely have made the exclamation of 17:17 had his own father begotten him at 130.

B. The Chosen Family (chapters 12–50)

The great theme of these chapters will be the promised seed or posterity, and, to a lesser extent, the promised land, to which the little group clings tenaciously and in the final chapter looks back in the certainty of return.

The promise of a son dominates chapters 12 to 20 by its tantalizing delay, while Abram alternately jeopardizes it by failures of nerve and hope (chapters 12, 16, 20) and holds to it by faith (chapters 15, 17, 18).

After Isaac's birth in chapter 21 the interest centres on the slender line of succession to the promise; finally the story moves towards the phase beyond the patriarchs, as God leads the family to Egypt and reveals the beginnings of the tribal destinies. By the end of the book Israel's place among the nations who will remain her neighbours throughout the Old Testament, and her unique calling and prospect, have been clearly established, and the stage set for the great events of the Exodus.

I. ABRAM UNDER CALL AND PROMISE
(chapters 12–20)

12:1–9. Abram follows the call

The history of redemption, like that of creation, begins with God speaking: this, in a nutshell, differentiates Abram's story from his father's. The call to forsake all and follow finds its nearest parallels in the Gospels (which are in some ways nearer the patriarchal pattern than was the Law – *cf.* Gal. 3), and Abram's early history is partly that of his gradual disentanglement from *country*, *kindred* and *father's house*, a process not completed until the end of chapter 13.

The call had first been heard in Ur (Acts 7:2–4),[1] and some

---

[1] Hence AV's pluperfect here ('had said'). Normally this Hebrew construction simply means 'said' – which may point to a renewed call. But it can be 'amplifying the preceding narrative regarded as a *whole*, and not meant merely to be the continuation, chronologically, of its concluding stage' (S. R. Driver, *Hebrew Tenses*[3] (Oxford, 1892), p. 82). *Cf.* the pluperfect sense of, *e.g.*, Is. 37:5; Zc. 7:2.

interpreters censure Abram for not breaking at once with his father and nephew. But the account does not brand him a lingerer like Lot (19:16), and it is reasonable to think that he was biding God's time until the family ties could be honourably loosened. To wait on without surrendering the vision can be an exacting task (it is asked of many an intending minister or missionary). In due course the instructions were fulfilled, and the occasion was celebrated by a renewal of the promise (13:14ff.).

1–3. Abram's part is expressed in a single though searching command, while the heaped up *I will*'s reveal how much greater is the Lord's part. At the same time their futurity emphasizes the bare faith that was required: Abram must exchange the known for the unknown (Heb. 11:8), and find his reward in what he could not live to see (*a great nation*), in what was intangible (*thy name*) and in what he would impart (*blessing*). Grammatically, the last clause of verse 3 (*cf.* 18:18; 28:14) could be taken as either passive (AV, RV, RSVmg, *be blessed*) or reflexive (RSV, *bless themselves*; *i.e.*, 'may I/you be blessed like Abram . . .'); but the New Testament, following LXX, understands it as passive (Acts 3:25; Gal. 3:8); indeed LXX does so also at 22:18 and 26:4 where the verb is in a form which is nearly always[1] reflexive.

Blessing for the world was a vision fitfully seen at first (it disappears between the patriarchs and the kings, apart from a reminder of Israel's priestly role in Ex. 19:5,6). Later it reappeared in the psalms and prophets, and perhaps even at its faintest it always imparted some sense of mission to Israel; yet it never became a programme of concerted action until the ascension.

4, 5. On Abram's age, see on 11:32; on the relation between Terah's and Abram's migrations, see on the closing paragraph of chapter 11, and the opening of chapter 12.

6, 7. *Shechem* (AV *Sichem*), in the pass between mounts Ebal and Gerizim, at the crossroads of central Palestine, was marked out as a place of decision. Here the Israelites would be assembled to choose between blessing and cursing (Dt. 11:29,

---

[1] But see Hebrew of Pr. 31:30; Ec. 8:10 (G-K,54g).

30), here Joshua would give his last charge (Jos. 24), and here the kingdom of Solomon would one day break in two (1 Ki. 12) – an event leaving its trace in the Samaritan community still surviving at this spot (modern Nablus). The *oak* (not *the plain*, AV) *of Moreh* ('Teacher') may have gained its name from soothsaying (*cf.* Jdg. 9:37), and the term *the place* may indicate the presence of a Canaanite shrine, as the final sentence hints. If so, it was a foretaste of things to come that at this stronghold of other gods the Lord revealed His presence, allocated the land to His servant and received formal homage.

8. On the phrase *called upon the name of the Lord*, see comment at 4:26. Abram's action planted the flag, so to speak, at the heart of the promised land, and declared that Yahweh's writ runs everywhere. He renewed the homage as he journeyed (8; *cf.* 13:4,18), and there is force in the contrast between *pitched* and *builded* (8), the one for himself, the other for God. The only structures he left behind him were altars: no relics of his own wealth.

The name Ai (always carrying the article in Hebrew) means 'the ruin'. It seems likely that this (like Beth-el, *cf.* 28:19) is its acquired name (Jos. 8:28), its original Canaanite one being no longer preserved.[1]

9. *The South* (AV, RV) is *the Negeb* (RSV), the now dry area south-west of the Dead Sea, described by Nelson Glueck as 'a key part of the immensely strategic strip of land . . . binding Asia and Africa together'.[2] Ample evidence that the Negeb was well peopled in the age of Abraham has been brought to light by Glueck, who comments on the archaeological confirmation of 'the general validity of the historical memories of the Age of Abraham surviving in chapters 12, 13 and 14 of the Book of Genesis'.[3]

12:10-20. Abram in Egypt

It is unrealistic to regard Egypt as necessarily forbidden

---

[1] *Cf.* E. F. Campbell, *BA*, XXVIII, 1965, p. 27.
[2] *BA*, XXII, 1959, p. 84.
[3] *Art. cit.*, p. 88. See also *BA*, XVIII, 1955, pp. 2–9.

territory to God's people at this stage,[1] for it was soon to be expressly allotted them as a refuge, and their presence there would not invalidate their claim to Canaan. Abram had to feel his way forward (8,9) without a special revelation at every step, guided like us largely by circumstances (*cf.* Ru. 1:1; Mt. 12:14,15). In a famine it might well seem a providence that Egypt was near by, watered by the flooding of the Nile.

Yet all the indications are that Abram did not stop to enquire, but went on his own initiative, taking everything into account but God. His craven and tortuous calculations are doubly revealing, both of the natural character of this spiritual giant (*cf.* Jas. 5:17a) and of the sudden transition that can be made from the plane of faith to that of fear. Entangled in his deception, he found himself unable to refuse his questionable earnings (16), if indeed he wished to, and unable to answer Pharaoh's stinging rebuke. Yet if this experience lay behind his fine reply to the king of Sodom in 14:22f. there was something salvaged from it.

The prime importance of the story, however, is its bearing on the promise of land and people. This is the true theme of these chapters, with Abram's vision under constant challenge. Here, at the first touch of hunger, fear and riches, the vision was lost and the whole enterprise hazarded: it would need plagues to restore Sarai to her destiny (17), and deportation (20) to get Abram back to Canaan.

13. *Thou art my sister* was technically true (20:12), and E. A. Speiser has drawn attention[2] to the esteem in which the Hurrians (influential at Haran) held the wife-sister relationship: a husband would even legally adopt his wife as sister to increase his authority and the status of the marriage. But using one half of the truth to conceal the other was so clearly a lie that on this occasion Abram attempted no defence.

14. The problem of Sarai's great beauty is chiefly that of its apparent tension with the rest of the story: at this point

---

[1] Even the topographical words 'down' (10) and 'up' (13:1) are treated as moral terms by some expositors! Their ingenuity might be taxed by, *e.g.*, 19:30; 1 Ki. 22:20, *etc.*
[2] *Genesis*, pp. 91ff.

she seems an inordinately young sixty-five,[1] whereas at Isaac's birth she is undoubtedly old at ninety. To make matters more difficult, history repeats itself in chapter 20, apparently just before the birth of Isaac.

The key to the whole problem lies with the patriarchal life-span, which was still approximately double our own (this seems to have been a special providence (*cf.* Dt. 34:7): there is no indication that it was general). Abraham died at 175 and Sarah at 127; Jacob was to think 130 years 'few and evil'. Their continued vigour shows that this was no mere postponement of death but a spreading-out of the whole life process: *e.g.* Abraham at, say, 110 in chapter 22 has the vitality of a man of, at most, seventy. Sarai's sixties would therefore presumably correspond with our thirties or forties, and her ninety years at Isaac's birth with perhaps our late fifties. At the latter age she was past childbearing, yet not past all thought of matrimony, and it is significant that in chapter 20, unlike chapter 12, there is no mention of her beauty. To Abimelech she was marriageable for her wealth and for the alliance that would be cemented with her 'brother', as Abimelech's further approach to Abraham for a covenant, when this move had failed, suggests in 21:22ff.

13:1-18. The parting from Lot

The lifelong test of Abram's obedience to the vision takes a new turn in this chapter in the temptation to self-assertion against Lot, and in the lure of the cities of the plain. With the promised land failing him again (6), this time with what must have seemed a permanent inadequacy, the common-sense course was to abandon it for something more fertile. The fact that Abram rose to the occasion in faith is traceable to verses 1-4, which present his journey to Beth-el as a pilgrimage (note the phrases that go beyond mere geography in verses 3, 4, and the climax in 4b): a renewal of his lapsed obedience, not an

---

[1] *I.e.*, ten years younger than Abram (17:17); *cf.* 12:4. It may have been more than ten years: either her age at 17:17 or Isaac's at 25:20 is a round number.

attempt to recapture the luxury of a vision – he was not making for Shechem (*cf.* 12:6,7).

The test arose (as in 12:10; *cf.* Mk. 1:12) after the renewal. Abram's handling of it is a model of insight, good sense and generosity: his reminder, *we are brethren*, singled out the aspect that mattered in face of an alien world (*cf.* 7b), and his proposal, being selfless as well as practical, resolved the immediate tension without creating any future ones. This wisdom sprang from his faith. By faith he had already renounced everything; he could afford to refresh the choice: and by faith he had opted for the unseen; he had no need to judge, as Lot did, 'by the sight of his eyes'.

The sequel for both men is instructive. Lot, choosing the things that are seen, found them corrupt (13) and insecure; choosing selfishly, he was to grow ever more isolated and unloved. Abram, on the other hand, found liberation. With the call of 12:1 at last fulfilled, the promise of 'land' and 'seed' was now amplified (14), reiterated (note the threefold 'thy seed' in 15,16) and made, in token, tangible (17). Both sight and action followed believing: his blind choice (9) was rewarded by God's 'Lift up now thine eyes' (14); and what the eyes took in as panorama his steps were to explore in detail (17). We may perhaps compare the sequence of verses 14 and 17 with that of Ephesians 3:18 and 4:1.

18. *The oaks of Mamre* (*cf.* on 12:6), some twenty miles south of Bethlehem, became the chief centre of Abram's movements, near which he would purchase his only property, the burial cave of Machpelah. Meanwhile, *tent* and *altar* epitomized his way of life.

14:1–24. The battle of the kings, and the meeting with Melchizedek

For the first time, the biblical events are expressly co-ordinated with external history. But the centre of gravity remains the same, and Abram is seen 'in' the world but not 'of' it; ready to fight in a proper cause as a good kinsman (verse 14) and good ally (13c,24b), but watchful of his calling (20b–24). It is an instructive sequel to chapter 13, with Lot's prize so quickly lost, but Abram's small resources so effective and his moral stature still further enhanced.

The chapter has its own character and the stamp of great antiquity,[1] some of its words and topographical details 'carrying us directly back into the Middle Bronze Age',[2] *i.e.*, the early second millennium BC. E. A. Speiser[3] gives grounds for thinking it an extract or adaptation of a foreign document; if so, it is an independent witness to Abram's historicity.

1–12. The defeat of Sodom and capture of Lot. The course of events follows the pattern, often to be repeated in the Old Testament, of a group of petty states defying their overlord and incurring a swift punishment.

1. The names ring true to their various countries, but attempts to identify them more closely have so far broken down. *Amraphel*, a Semitic name, is not a clear verbal equivalent of Hammurabi, as was once thought. The name *Arioch* is Hurrian, *Chedorlaomer* follows the pattern of Elamite names, and *Tidal* is fairly certainly Tudhalia, a name borne by several Hittite kings; but four contemporaries bearing these names have yet to be traced.

2. Of the five rebel cities, only the last would escape the disaster of chapter 19. The first two royal names are, suitably enough (perhaps by a twist),[4] compounds of 'evil' and 'wicked'.

3. In preserving the name and the character (10a) of a valley since submerged (it would seem)[5] under the Dead Sea, the record gives fascinating evidence of its antiquity.

---

[1] An earlier generation of critics regarded it as a late document, an opinion now rarely held in the light of growing archaeological knowledge.

[2] W. F. Albright, *The Archaeology of Palestine* (Pelican, 1949), p. 236.

[3] *Genesis*, p. 108.

[4] *Cf.* the common changing of *-baal* into *-bosheth* ('shame') in names; *e.g.* 2 Sa. 2:8; 1 Ch. 8:33.

[5] This falls short of proof. In Old Testament times probably only the low-lying battlefield was as yet submerged, for there are signs that the shallow south extension of the Dead Sea (the most likely location) has developed mostly since Roman times. See, briefly, *NBD*, pp. 1003, 1184; more fully, J. P. Harland, *BA*, V, 1942, pp. 17–32; VI, 1943, pp. 41–54; *IBD*, IV, pp. 395–397. Against this identification see J. Simons, *The Geographical and Topographical Texts of the Old Testament* (E. J. Brill, 1959), pp. 222–229.

5-7. The detailed digression to tell of action against these border tribes (*cf.* Dt. 2:10-12,20) strongly suggests that we are reading an extract from the victors' record of the campaign, which had other matters to settle besides those of Sodom.

10. On the description of the valley, see on verse 3. Speiser captures the force of the Hebrew: 'Now the Valley of Siddim was one bitumen pit after another.' The Dead Sea region is rich in minerals, and the sea was known in Roman times as *Asphaltites*, from the lumps of bitumen often found floating on its surface, especially in the southern area. These can be quite massive objects.

13-16. Abram's rescue of Lot. In verse 13, the designation *Abram the Hebrew*, as if introducing him to the reader, is another of the signs that the chapter was an independent document. On the term *Hebrew*, see on 10:24.

Mamre, Eshcol and *Aner* are disclosed only in this chapter as personal or, more probably, clan-names. They were in 'covenant'[1] (AV, RV *confederate*, RSV *allies*) with Abram, sworn, that is, to mutual loyalty. Verse 24 shows that they honoured their pledge.

14. The word for *his trained men* (*ḥᵃnîkāw*), found nowhere else in the Bible, has come to light in the Egyptian execration texts of this period, denoting a Palestinian chieftain's retainers, exactly as here.[2] On *Dan*, see Introduction, p. 16.

15, 16. Abram's success with so small a company is viewed sceptically by, *e.g.*, von Rad, who seems to overlook not only Abram's allies (13) but the surprise and confusion which would reinforce, at the purely natural level, a well-planned (*divided*) night-attack, possibly against only an escort-group lagging behind (*cf.* 16) the main force. And were Abram's unseen resources inferior to Gideon's?

17-24. Abram, Melchizedek and the king of Sodom. For Abram the harder battle begins, for there is a profound contrast between the two kings who come to meet him.

[1] For other human covenants, *cf.* 21:22ff.; 26:23ff.; 31:43ff.
[2] *Cf.* W. F. Albright, *op. cit.*, p. 36.

Melchizedek, king and priest, his name and title expressive of the realm of right and good (see Heb. 7:2), offers him, in token, a simple sufficiency from God, pronounces an unspecified blessing (dwelling on the Giver, not the gift), and accepts costly tribute. All this is meaningful only to faith. The king of Sodom, on the other hand, makes a handsome and businesslike offer; its sole disadvantage is perceptible, again, only to faith. To these rival benefactors Abram signifies his Yes and his No, refusing to compromise his call.

Such a climax shows what was truly at stake in this chapter of international events. The struggle of kings, the far-ranging armies and the spoil of a city are the small-change of the story; the crux is the faith or failure of one man.

At this distance we can see that this is no artificial judgment. More hinged on this than on the most resounding victory or the fate of any kingdom.

17. The *defeat* (RSV) is more accurate than the *slaughter* (AV, RV): it is lit. 'the smiting'. The valley of Shaveh (*cf.* 2 Sa. 18:18), apparently quite near Jerusalem, was the scene of the meeting now to be described, not of the battle.

18, 19. *Salem* is Jerusalem;[1] on its name, 'peace', and that of Melchizedek,[2] 'king of righteousness', see Hebrews 7:2. The union of *king* and *priest* at Jerusalem was to move David (the first Israelite to sit on Melchizedek's throne) to sing of a greater Melchizedek to come (Ps. 110:4).

God Most High (*'ēl 'elyôn*), whatever the title meant to Melchizedek's predecessors and successors,[3] meant to him the true God, self-revealed in measure, as his next words show. In any case Abram's tithe (*cf.* Heb. 7:4-10) and his conjunction of the name Yahweh (*the Lord*, 22) with Melchizedek's

---

[1] Albright's emendation (*BASOR*, CLXIII, 1961, p. 52) of *šālēm* to *šelōmōh* ('a king *allied to him*') is uncalled for, since Salem is a known abbreviation for Jerusalem (Ps. 76:2).

[2] The similar name of a successor, Adoni-zedek (Jos. 10:1), suggests that the kings of Jerusalem officially worshipped Zedek, a god known elsewhere in Palestine. The royal names presumably meant in the first place 'Zedek is my king, my lord', *etc.*: but in Melchizedek's case the alternative sense, 'King of righteousness', became the appropriate one.

[3] Phoenicians and Canaanites used this term for their supreme God.

term, *God Most High*, settle the question. The latter title is used frequently in the Psalms.

Possessor (or *maker*, RSV) is from the verb of 4:1 ('I have gotten') and if 'get' is the basic sense, it varies with the manner of getting, to mean, *e.g.*, 'bear' (4:1), 'buy', 'learn', and here, 'make'.[1]

15:1-21. The faith of Abram, and the confirming covenant

So far, Abram has been tested chiefly in the realm of security (a burning issue to a homeless man), through stresses of anxiety and ambition. The pressure now builds up round a new centre, the promise of a son, a hope to be deferred through six more chapters and some twenty-five years. Even then the birth will precipitate a crisis of its own in chapter 21, and the supreme test of all in 22.

The New Testament finds this a momentous chapter in two respects: first in its declaration that Abram was justified by faith (6), a phrase at the heart of Paul's gospel in Romans 4 and Galatians 3; and secondly in its record of the covenant – for this, rather than Sinai's, was the fundamental covenant, and it spoke of grace and not law (Gal. 3:17–22). To honour this promise God would bring His people out of Egypt (Ex. 2:24), and His Son into the world (Lk. 1:72,73).

1-6. Abram's faith clarified. Most modern commentators allow no reference to chapter 14 (because of its evidently separate origin) in the words *After these things* (1). But the events of that chapter followed convincingly those of chapter 13, and Abram's fine renunciation in 14:20b–24 makes the promise of this verse doubly apt. God's interventions to cheer a hard-pressed servant are not uncommon in Scripture and Christian experience (*cf.* 32:1; Je. 45; Jn. 9:35; Acts 23:11).

The run of the Hebrew sentence, and Abram's response in 2a (which is jarringly out of key in AV, RV), indicate that RSV is right to translate the promise, *I am your shield;*[2] *your reward*

---

[1] See W. A. Irwin, *JBL*, LXXX, 1961, pp. 133ff.
[2] Or, possibly, 'benefactor': *cf.* M. Dahood, in *Bib.*, XLV, 1964, p. 282; also M. Kessler, in *VT*, XIV, 1964, pp. 494–497.

shall be very great. Trust, then, is to be in the person of God; hope, in the promise. It is noteworthy that the *vision* was given not primarily for its visual impact but to convey *the word*.

2, 3. The Hebrew of 2 is obscure,[1] but 3 explains the point of it, and it is well known that among the Hurrians[2] a childless man might adopt an heir to ensure his proper burial, or a borrower secure a loan by adopting the lender. The concrete details of name and place bring Abram's predicament vividly to life, and even if Eliezer is to be identified with the fine servant of chapter 24, he was still no son or 'seed' to inherit the promise. It is important to see that, though it is not fully formed, Abram's *faith*, not his unbelief, shines out in this answer. A lesser man would have basked in the comfort of verse 1: Abram is stung into expostulation, for he has set his heart on the original vision and call with its promise of descendants (12:1ff.). So verse 1 (RSV) is seen to have been a test, and his spirited response opens the way to the explicit pledge of verses 4 and 5 and the informed faith of verse 6.

4. The Old Testament can speak of a legal heir as a 'son' (*e.g.* Ru. 4:17), so the emphatic expression *out of thine own bowels* (AV, RV) now settled a legitimate doubt for Abram. A further question, whether this son could possibly be his through Sarai, would be the next challenge to his faith, worked out in the heart-searchings of chapters 16 and 17.

5. It only now emerges that the vision was at night; the actions of verses 9–11 will have followed next day.

God's sign, the starry sky, proved nothing; it was not that kind of sign. But it did serve as a 'visible word', a focus of the promise, somewhat as the sacraments do; for the experience was unforgettable. The stars are not in contrast with the 'dust'

---

[1] M. F. Unger, in *JBL*, LXXII, 1953, pp. 49f., suggesting that one occurrence of *ben* ('son of') has dropped out, reconstructs it 'And the son of my house is the son of Meseq'. He takes 'Damascus' and 'Eliezer' to be explanatory notes identifying the place (Meseq, short for Dammeseq (Damascus); *cf.* Salem short for Jerusalem, 14:18) and the person concerned. O. Eissfeldt, however, in *JSS*, V, 1960, p. 48, argues that *m-š-q* = cup, and Eliezer is 'possessor of the goblet (*i.e.* the 'essence and life') of my house'. In other words, he is the heir. But this strange expression is inadequately supported.

[2] *Cf.* on 12:13.

of 13:16 (some have equated the two with Abram's spiritual and physical sons respectively) but are another illustration of the same thing; *cf.* the parallelism of 22:17. The New Testament reveals that the promise is fulfilled, both before and after Christ, in the multitude of *believers* (*e.g.* Rom. 4:11,12; 9:7,8).

6. This great statement is quoted twice by Paul (Rom. 4:3; Gal. 3:6) and once by James (2:23) to confirm that justification has always been by faith (James adds that faith must show itself genuine, 2:18). This story and the argument of Romans 4 present faith not as a crowning merit but as readiness to accept what God promises. Note that Abram's trust was both personal (*in the Lord*, AV, RV) and propositional (the context is the specific *word of the Lord* in verses 4,5).

7–21. The promise clarified and covenanted. The emphasis moves to the other branch of the promise: the land to be inherited. Abram's '*how am I to know . . .*?' (8, RSV) reveals the strain he was under, for his faith was nothing facile: its spirit was that of 'Lord, I believe, help thou mine unbelief'; not that of Zacharias's retort in Luke 1:18, for it earned no rebuke, only reassurance. God's regular provision for such a need is 'signs' and 'seals' (*cf.* Rom. 4:3,11a) to confirm the spoken word. Here His full answer is a formal covenant (verse 18), executed in two stages. The first is in this chapter, an inauguration of a particularly vivid kind. The second stage, in chapter 17, was the giving of the covenant sign, circumcision. For good measure, as Hebrews 6:13,17 points out, there was finally an oath to reinforce it in 22:16ff.

9, 10. The covenant ritual resembles that of Jeremiah 34:18. In its full form, probably both parties would pass between the dismembered animals to invoke a like fate on themselves should they break their pledge. Here, however, Abram's part is only to set the scene and guard it from violation (11): see on verse 17.

11, 12. The setting is sombre in every detail, partly no doubt to emphasize that the covenant must be carried through in the teeth of opposition (11) and by means of great judgments (*cf.* 13,14). But the darkness, smoke and fire (12,17), like those of Sinai, chiefly proclaim the 'terror of the Lord', the impact of holiness on sin; *cf.* Isaiah 6:3–5. Even the New Covenant would be inaugurated in darkness and earthquake (Mt. 27:45,51).

13–16. This foretelling of bondage is doubly significant, both in showing it to be a deliberate discipline with a planned outcome (note the memorable words, *afterward . . . with great substance* (14); *cf.* Heb. 12:11), and in disclosing God's patience towards the inhabitants of Canaan. The clause *for the iniquity of the Amorite is not yet full* (16) throws significant light on Joshua's invasion (and, by inference, on other Old Testament wars), as an act of justice, not aggression. Until it was *right* to invade, God's people must wait, if it cost them centuries of hardship. This is one of the pivotal sayings of the Old Testament.

There is no conflict between the round figure *four hundred years* (13) and *the fourth generation* (16) since *generation* (*dôr*) could mean 'lifetime'.[1] In the patriarchal context a century is a conservative equivalent of this. Exodus 12:40 makes the period 430 years.

17. The smoke and fire (see on 11,12), like the 'fiery, cloudy pillar' of the Exodus, were evidently a theophany, a manifestation of God. In symbol, He alone makes the covenant: the accent is on His initiative and His giving, as verse 18 makes clear, in contrast with the bargain-like covenant of, say, 31:44. This emphasis persists throughout Scripture: see especially Hebrews 9:15ff., where the sense oscillates between 'covenant' and 'will'.[2]

18–21. Only in David's reign were the boundaries of verse 18 attained, and then as an empire rather than a homeland. The list of peoples, from the Kenites and Kenizzites, drawn early into the family of Israel, to the Jebusites vanquished by David with their citadel Jerusalem, indicates the diversity of groups inhabiting the land at this time, a diversity attested by con-

---

[1] *Cf.* W. F. Albright, *The Biblical Period from Abraham to Ezra*, p. 9; also *BASOR*, CLXIII, 1961, pp. 50f.

[2] See further: John Murray, *The Covenant of Grace* (Tyndale Press, 1954); J. A. Thompson, *The Ancient Near Eastern Treaties and the Old Testament* (Tyndale Press, 1964).

temporary sources. For further details, see *The New Bible Dictionary*; for the fulfilment of the promise see 2 Chronicles 8:7,8.

16:1–6. The birth of Ishmael

This chapter marks another stage in eliminating every means but miracle towards the promised birth. It is ironical that after the heights attained in the last two chapters, Abram should capitulate to domestic pressure, pliant under his wife's planning and scolding, and quick to wash his hands of the outcome. Meanwhile the Lord, 'with whom is no variableness', watches over the disregarded person and pattern, and 'works His sovereign will'.

1–3. Custom sanctioned this way of obtaining children[1] (although the present story and chapter 30 are proof of its unwisdom), and the fact that such sons were to count in Jacob's family as full members and heads of tribes must be borne in mind. Abram could reason that the promise of 15:4 could be fulfilled in this way, and the fact that ten years had now passed in Canaan (3) must have added to the pressure on him to act.

For all this, he had slipped from faith, to be guided by reason and *the voice of Sarai* (2), not of the Lord (*cf.* Mt. 16:22f.). The New Testament likens Hagar's son, 'born after the flesh', to the products of self-effort in religion (Gal. 4:22ff.), ever incompatible with those of the spirit (Gal. 4:29).

2. *Obtain children* is literally 'be built' (*cf.* Pr. 24:3).

4–6. Each of the three characters displays the untruth that is part of sin, in false pride (4), false blame (5), false neutrality (6); but Sarai's mask soon slipped (6b), to show the hatred behind the talk of justice.

16:7–16. Hagar and the angel

7–9. Hagar was making for her native Egypt (the wilderness

[1] For an equivalent see E. A. Speiser in *AASOR*, X, 1930, pp. 31ff., and in his commentary, p. 130. The practice is attested also in places as far apart as Ur and Cappadocia. For the latter, see J. Lewy, *HUCA*, XXVII, 1956, pp. 6ff.

of Shur was on its north-east frontier), and had possibly
travelled some days to have reached the vicinity of Kadesh (14).
But her lot was cast with Abram now, and God's exacting
goodness held her to it (9,15).

10–12. Similarly His comfort for her affliction (11) was
bracing rather than soothing, drawing her mind to things
ahead, away from past injuries. The name *Ishmael* ('God hear(s)';
see on 17:19) would always recall this encounter and oracle.
To her mind, lacking the questing faith of Abram, the promise might well offer all she could wish, though it said nothing
of blessing for the world or of a promised land. Enough that
Ishmael would multiply, and be at nobody's beck and call.
To some degree this son of Abram would be a shadow, almost
a parody, of his father, his twelve princes notable in their
times (17:20; 25:13) but not in the history of salvation; his
restless existence no pilgrimage but an end in itself; his non-
conformism a habit of mind, not a light to the nations.

In the last phrase of verse 12 there is a *double entendre* characteristic of such oracles of destiny (see footnote at 3:15), for it can
have equally a local and a hostile sense (lit. 'to, or against, the
face of'), and both were to be true of these cousins of Israel,
from whom the Arabs of today claim descent. The saying is
echoed at 25:18.

13, 14. The angel of the Lord is now disclosed to have been
the Lord Himself[1] (*cf.* 18:1ff.; Ex. 3:2,4; Jdg. 6:12,14; *etc.*),
and Hagar's words reflect her awe at the fact. It is God as
seen, even more than as seeing, that is the theme of the two
verses, which play on the root *rā'â*, 'to see'. Hagar's words run
literally: 'Thou art a God of sight' (*rŏ'î*, 'appearance'; *i.e.*
'a visible God'; *cf.* 1 Sa. 16:12, of David's 'looks'), followed by
'Have I here seen after (or, seen the back of)[2] my see-er?'
(*rō'î*, *i.e.* 'the one who sees me'; *cf.* Jb. 7:8).

In RSV's '*Have I really seen God and remained alive after seeing
him?*' every word after 'seen' represents an alteration or in-

---

[1] See Introduction, pp. 33f.
[2] *Cf.* 'thou shalt see my back' (Ex. 33:23); the expression is almost
identical. Here perhaps it could be freely rendered 'Have I caught a
glimpse of . . . ?'

sertion in the Hebrew, though it expresses similar emotions to those of the received text. Such was Jacob's reaction at Peniel (32:30); the fact of holiness was already well understood.

Beer-lahai-roi means literally 'the well of the living-one, my see-er'. So the name commemorated the abiding rather than the transient element in the experience.

15, 16. The epilogue emphasizes Abram's responsibility for Ishmael, which Hagar's return made explicit; a responsibility further acknowledged in the next chapter.

17:1-27. The covenant reaffirmed and sealed

The two stages of covenant-making, in chapters 15 and 17, not only tested Abram's faith by the long delay but brought out two sides of the one transaction. The earlier chapter fixed the basic pattern of grace and answering faith; nothing was asked of Abram but to believe and 'know of a surety'. Now emerge the implications, in depth and extension: in depth, for faith must show itself in utter dedication (1); in extension, for the whole company must be sealed, one by one, down the generations (10ff.). Together then the two chapters set out the personal and the corporate participation; the inward faith and the outward seal (*cf.* Rom. 4:9,11); imputed righteousness and expressed devotion (15:6; 17:1).

1-3. The prelude. This opening is no bargain: these are the conditions in which God can *give*, rather than get, all that He desires (indeed verse 2 begins, literally, 'that I may give (or grant) . . .'), for He wills no distant or half-hearted[1] relationship.

A special name for each party (1,5) marks the occasion, as later on an unfolding of the name of Yahweh would commemorate the burning bush encounter (Ex. 3:14; 6:3). *God Almighty* is the translation of El Shaddai (*'ēl šadday*) as understood by the LXX. A traditional analysis of the name is 'God (*'ēl*) who (*ša-*) is sufficient (*day*)'; more recently Shaddai has been equated with 'mountain'[2] (*cf.* the common Old Testament

---

[1] For the meaning of *perfect* (RSV *blameless*) see on 6:9.
[2] W. F. Albright in *JBL*, LIV, 1935, pp. 180–193, and in *FSAC²*, p. 244;

term 'rock' for God); but there is no universal agreement. A better guide is the study of its use, and this confirms the familiar emphasis on might, particularly over against the frailty of man (it is a favourite divine title in Job). In Genesis it tends to be matched to situations where God's servants are hard-pressed and needing reassurance.[1]

Abram's prostration before God (3; *cf.* verse 17), unlike Adam's arrogance, acknowledged the master-servant footing of the covenant. It rooted the matter in the truth; in such soil the relationship could grow to its full stature of friendship (Jas. 2:23).

4–8. The promises ('As for me ...'). The RV preserves the structure by its *As for me ...* (*'anî*, 4), *And as for thee ...* (*we'attâ*, 9). Materially, the promise of land is unchanged, but *nations* and *kings* come into view, and Genesis will tell of their emergence, including Midianites (25:2), Ishmaelites (25:12) and kings of Edom and of Israel (36:31). Beyond these, however, the New Testament could see the Christian multitude in the 'many nations' (Rom. 4:16,17). The name *Abraham* suggests a fusion of the original two elements *'Ab* (father) *rām* (high) with part of a third: *ha'môn* (multitude).

Spiritually, the essence of the covenant is personal, like the 'I will' of a marriage: so the pledge *I will be their God* (8b; *cf.* 7b) far outweighs the particular benefits. This *is* the covenant.

9–14. The stipulations ('And as for thee ...'). The striking feature of the stipulations is their lack of detail. To be *committed* was all. Circumcision was God's brand; the moral implications could be left unwritten (until Sinai), for one was pledged to a Master, only secondarily to a way of life.

---

but Speiser, p. 124, points out weaknesses in the equation. E. C. B. MacLaurin in *AN*, III, 1961–2, pp. 99–118, argues for a derivation from a root *dd*, with causative *š*, which would yield a sense 'who evokes love' or 'who establishes in dominion'.

[1] See Gn. 17:1; 28:3; 35:11; 43:14; 48:3; 49:25. *Cf.*, more fully, J. A. Motyer, *The Revelation of the Divine Name*, pp. 29–31.

Circumcision itself was widespread in the Near East; the Philistines from the west were thought outlandish for not practising it. The new feature was its new meaning, to mark the threshold not of manhood (as among modern Arabs) but of the covenant; hence its early administration (12). It implied commitment to God's people (14b) and to God (Je. 4:4); it also came to symbolize the discarding of heathen ways (Jos. 5:9) and of one's natural selfwill (Dt. 10:16; *cf.* Col. 2:11,12). Notice that the covenant was open to Gentiles (12b,13), but they must wholly belong to the community (*cf.* Ex. 12:45).

15-22. Sarah named for her part. It appears that Sarai and Sarah are only older and newer forms of the same word 'princess'; but the re-naming was a landmark and brought her specifically into the promise in her own right (verses 16,19).

17, 18. Abraham's laughter, to judge by God's reply and by Romans 4:19ff., was a first, incredulous reaction; real enough, as is shown by his gentle attempt to steer God into a more reasonable path (18), but open to correction. On such genuine struggles of faith God is never hard (see on 15:8) – and Abraham's doubt was wonderfully tempered by faith and love in the prayer for Ishmael.

19, 21. The name *Isaac*, like Ishmael, Jacob, Judah, Joseph, is of a pattern common at the time, expressing in most cases a prayer such as 'May God hear' (Ishmael), 'May He protect' (Jacob), *etc.* If Isaac analogously meant 'May He smile (upon him)', to those who were in the secret it spoke of the laugh, the promise and the miracle that made his birth unique and the covenant predestined beyond all doubt. See also on 21:6.

20. God's absolute right of choice meets us everywhere in these chapters (*cf.* Rom. 9:9ff.), but He had other blessings than those reserved for Israel, and other eventual heirs of the covenant than those who historically transmitted it (*cf.* Rom. 9:24ff.). There was honour for Ishmael suited to his capacity (see on 16:10ff.). The tenses of verse 20, incidentally, have light to throw on prayer, response and fulfilment.

22. It is God who closes the conversation, as it was He who opened it, a fact that will be particularly marked and significant in the intercession passage of 18:16ff.

23-27. Abraham and his household circumcised.
Verses 26, 27 bring out the main emphasis of the paragraph, which is on the diversity of men, in age, status and spiritual experience, who were gathered into the one covenant. For Abraham it sealed an old transaction (Rom. 4:9-12); for others it was a sudden introduction (*that very day*, 26, RSV) into a bond with God and each other, whose implications must now be grasped and lived out. In the sense that Pentecost was the birthday of the church, this was the birthday of the church of the Old Testament.

18:1-15. The visitation of Abraham
The noon encounter in this chapter and the night scene at Sodom in the next are in every sense a contrast of light and darkness. The former, quietly intimate and full of promise, is crowned by the intercession in which Abraham's faith and love show a new breadth of concern. The second scene is all confusion and ruin, moral and physical, ending in a loveless squalor which is even uglier than the great overthrow of the cities.

In verses 1-15 nothing is added to the promise of 17:15ff. What is new is its setting, and the challenge to Sarah's faith – for she must be brought into believing participation. How necessary the challenge was, can be seen in verses 12-15; how successful, in Hebrews 11:11.

1, 2a. Christian commentators have been tempted to discern the three Persons of the Trinity here; but the passage differentiates clearly between the Lord and His two companions (see verse 22, and 19:1). *Cf.* on 16:13,14.

2b-8. The almost royal honours paid to a chance visitor – the fervent welcome however inconvenient the moment (it was the midday siesta, 1b), the assurance that his arrival is an honour (3), even a providence[1] (5b, AV), and the lavish meal

---

[1] While this is in character, AV's '*for therefore* are ye come' is made less

deprecated as *a morsel of bread* (5ff.) – are still characteristic
of bedouin hospitality, even to the host's insistence in some
cases on standing (8b) until his guests have finished.[1] The
reader can see how appropriate beyond all imagining was
this deference; the New Testament goes on to show that there
is more than coincidence here (*cf.* Heb. 13:2; Mt. 25:35).

9–15. *Sarah was listening*: RSV rightly keeps the participle,
a vivid touch. Her derision suggests that either Abraham had
not yet told her of the promise (17:16,19) or he had failed
to convince her. God's rebuke, where He had been gentle
with Abraham (17:17,19), rather points to the latter, *i.e.* that
Sarah was persisting in unbelief, not merely reacting in
astonishment. Her purely sensual comment (12b) adds to the
impression that her interest in the covenant and promise was
still shallow. Nevertheless it drew forth one of the great
sayings of Scripture (14), which later became the starting-
point of a searching colloquy on omnipotence (Je. 32:17ff.,
27ff.) and was taken up again in Zechariah 8:6 (Heb.).

18:16–33. Abraham pleads for Sodom

The initiative in this great intercession was with God, in the
sense that He broached the subject Himself (17), waited for
Abraham's plea (22, see comment), and chose the point at
which the matter should end (33). Below the surface, too,
Abraham's spirit of love and justice derived from God as
surely as it strove with Him. But it was his own: his resource
and tenacity show that the gift had rooted and grown; he
was no yes-man but a true partner.

17–19. The question *Shall I hide . . . ?* proves Abraham the
'friend' of God (Is. 41:8) by our Lord's own criterion (Jn.
15:15), and the expression *I have known him* (19, RV) re-
emphasizes it; it virtually means 'I have made him my
friend'.

Verse 19 shows particularly clearly how grace and law work

---

probable by the occurrence of the same Hebrew phrase in 19:8 where it
must mean simply 'for' or 'since'.

[1] See, *e.g.*, W. Thesiger, *Arabian Sands* (Longmans, 1959), *passim*; *The
Marsh Arabs* (Longmans, 1964), p. 8.

together, for it opens with grace (*I have known him*) directed towards the firm discipline of law (*command . . . way . . . justice and judgment*) through which eventually grace may reach its goal (*that the Lord may bring . . . what he has promised*, RSV). It is also a revealing comment on parental responsibility, in line with 17:11ff.; *cf.* 1 Timothy 3:4,5.

20, 21. *The cry of Sodom* (AV, RV) may mean the *outcry against* it (RSV), or simply the crying evil of the place. It recurs at 19:13. Stripped of its bold colouring this saying of the Lord declares His judgments well weighed and perfectly informed. It gives solid ground for Abraham's exclamation in 25c.

22. There is good cause to reverse the roles in the last sentence, reading 'but the Lord still stood before Abraham'; for the present text is listed by the Massoretes as a scribal correction (to avoid the fancied irreverence of the original). Either way, whether God waits for Abraham to speak, or waits while he speaks, the whole passage displays His approachability to such a servant. See also on 18:1.

23-33. It would be easy to say that this prayer comes near to haggling, but the right word is 'exploring': Abraham is feeling his way forward in a spirit of faith (superbly expressed in 25c, where he grasps the range and rightness of God's rule), of humility, in his whole mode of address, and of love, demonstrated in his concern for the whole city, not for his kinsmen alone.

This is Abraham's second intervention for Sodom (*cf.* 14:14): it anticipates the blessing the whole world was to enjoy through him (12:3), and something of the self-giving which must be its means. Moses would carry the latter still further, in will (Ex. 32:32), and the divine Servant in deed (Is. 53:12).

19:1-29. The visitation of Sodom

In the development of the story two of the themes in counterpoint with Abraham and the Promise – the theme of Lot, the righteous man without the pilgrim spirit, and of Sodom, the standing example of worldly promise, insecurity (chapter 14) and decay – are now heard out to their conclusion. By a master-stroke of narrative, Abraham, who will outlive all such time-servers, is shown standing at his place of intercession (27), a silent witness of the catastrophe he has striven to avert. It is a superb study of the two aspects of judgment: the cataclysmic, as the cities disappear in brimstone and fire, and the gradual, as Lot and his family reach the last stages of disintegration, breaking up in the very hands of their rescuers.

1. The *two angels* are clearly distinguished from the Lord Himself: see 13, and on 18:1. As for Lot, his place *in the gate* (*cf.* 34:20) proclaimed him a man of standing in Sodom, little as he relished its ways (2 Pet. 2:7,8). His public ineffectiveness must be balanced against the influential careers of Joseph and Daniel, whose high office was a vocation; the difference lay there.

2, 3. Lot's alarm in 3a reveals that he knew his Sodom; the events of that night were a true sample. *Unleavened bread*, which is quickly made, shows that this was no leisurely feast like that of chapter 18 (*cf.* Ex. 12:39); there is already a suggestion of haste, which increases towards the climax.

4, 5. At this early point in Scripture the sin of sodomy is branded as particularly heinous. The law was to make it a capital offence, grouped with incest and bestiality (Lv. 18:22; 20:13), and the New Testament is equally appalled at it (Rom. 1:26,27; 1 Cor. 6:9; 1 Tim. 1:10).

On an attempt to reinterpret the story see Additional Note, pp. 136f.

6–8. That a virtue can be inflated into a vice is glaringly plain here, for Lot's courage in going out to the mob proves his sincerity, and the similar offer in Judges 19:24 reveals the same scale of values. It suggests that in any age human conventions will be a most fallible guide.

9–11. Doing his best, Lot has jeopardized his daughters, enraged his townsmen, and finally required rescue by those he was trying to protect. The angels' visit has shattered the uneasy peace in which he has lived too long. The rare word for *blindness* probably indicates a dazzled state,[1] as of Saul on the Damascus Road. The same word recurs in 2 Kings 6:18, also in a context of angels.

[1] *Cf.* Speiser, *in loc.*; also in *JCS*, VI, 1952, pp. 81ff.

12–14. The family's solidarity in God's eyes (*cf.* 7:1; 9:1; 17:9; 18:19) and the members' freedom to defy it are both vivid realities here. No doubt Lot's failure to impress his future sons-in-law[1] reflects on his own character; but it equally reflects on theirs. The mob of Sodom had had no ears for any appeal (9); Lot's closest associates had none for any warning. This was the temper of the city: not even the desperate visit by night could be taken seriously.

On *the cry of them* (13, RV) see on 18:20.

15–23. The grip of 'this present evil world', even on those who love it with a bad conscience, is powerfully shown in this last-minute struggle. The warning to 'remember Lot's wife' (Lk. 17:32) gives us reason to see ourselves potentially in the lingering, quibbling Lot himself, wheedling a last concession as he is dragged to safety. Not even brimstone will make a pilgrim of him: he must have his little Sodom again if life is to be supportable (20c).

Against this stands the patient mercy of God, shepherding even the straggler to safety (note 22; *cf.* 2 Pet. 2:7–9; 1 Cor. 3:15). See also the further factor expressed in verse 29.

24–26. The natural ingredients of the destruction (see on 14:3,10) were abundant in this region of petroleum, bitumen, salt and sulphur; but its character was a judgment, not a random disaster. The overwhelming of Lot's wife as the molten materials of the explosion rained down on her is physically nothing remarkable; but in the context of judgment it captures in a single picture the fate of those who turn back (*cf.* Heb. 10:38,39; Lk. 17:31–33).

27–29. The scene as Abraham makes his way at dawn to the vantage-point, to be confronted by the appalling answer, not only rounds off the story panoramically, after its concentration on a single household, but shows the judgment against its true background of God's longsuffering and man's intercession. The same background is affirmed for Lot's salvation in the terse summary, *God remembered Abraham, and sent Lot out . . .* (29).

---

[1] RSV surely rightly renders the participle in verse 14 as 'who were to marry'.

19:30–38. Epilogue: Lot and his daughters

The restlessness of fear is classically illustrated by Lot's attitude to Zoar. Fear had driven him there (19ff.); fear blindly drove him out again. It had brushed aside the call and now the pledge of God (17,21).

Lot's *cave* (30) is a bitter sequel to the house (3) which had dwarfed his uncle's tent, and the little trio is pathetic after the teeming crowd of 13:5ff. The end of choosing to carve out his career was to lose even the custody of his body. His legacy, Moab and Ammon (37f.), was destined to provide the worst carnal seduction in the history of Israel (that of Baal-Peor, Nu. 25) and the cruellest religious perversion (that of Molech, Lv. 18:21). So much stemmed from a self-regarding choice (13:10ff.) and persistence in it.

Additional Note on the sin of Sodom

In an influential book, *Homosexuality and the Western Christian Tradition* (Longmans, 1955), D. Sherwin Bailey denies that the verb 'know' in Genesis 19:5 and in Judges 19:22 has a sexual connotation. He bases his denial on (a) *statistics* (finding only fifteen examples of 'know' in a sexual sense in the Old Testament, against over nine hundred in its primary sense): (b) *psychology* (observing that intercourse as a path to personal knowledge 'depends upon sexual differentiation and complementation, and not merely upon physical sexual experience as such');[1] (c) *conjecture* (since both Lot and the host in Judges 19 were *gērîm*, sojourners, 'is it not possible that Lot . . . had exceeded the rights of a *gēr* . . . by receiving . . . two "foreigners" . . . whose credentials, it seems, had not been examined?').[2]

Lot's protest, on this view, was against the discourtesy of demanding such credentials. Sodom's general wickedness (which is described as 'pride, fulness of bread, and prosperous ease' in Ezk. 16:49, RV)[3] was sufficiently proved to the angels

[1] *Op. cit.*, p. 3.
[2] *Ibid.*, p. 4.
[3] But note the climax in next verse: 'and committed abomination before me'.

by this 'lawless commotion . . . and . . . boorish display of inhospitality'.[1]

To this we may reply: (a) *Statistics* are no substitute for contextual evidence (otherwise the rarer sense of a word would *never* seem probable), and in both these passages the demand to 'know' the guests is met by an offer in which the same word 'know' is used in its sexual sense (Gn. 19:8; Jdg. 19:25). Even apart from this verbal conjunction it would be grotesquely inconsequent that Lot should reply to a demand for credentials by an offer of daughters. (b) *Psychology* can suggest how 'to know' *acquired* its secondary sense; but in fact the use of the word is completely flexible. No-one suggests that in Judges 19:25 the men of Gibeah were gaining 'knowledge' of their victim in the sense of personal relationship, yet 'know' is the word used of them. (c) *Conjecture* here has the marks of special pleading, for it substitutes a trivial reason ('commotion . . . inhospitality') for a serious one, for the angels' decision. Apart from this, it is silenced by Jude 7, a pronouncement which Dr. Bailey has to discount as belonging to a late stage of interpretation.

It has been necessary to discuss the point as fully as this because the doubt created by Dr. Bailey has travelled more widely than the reasons he produces for it. Not one of these reasons, it may be suggested, stands any serious scrutiny.

20:1-18. Abraham deceives Abimelech

After his spiritual exertions Abraham's relapse into faithless scheming, as at other moments of anticlimax (see on 12:10ff. and on chapter 16), carries its own warning. But the episode is chiefly one of suspense: on the brink of Isaac's birth-story here is the very Promise put in jeopardy, traded away for personal safety. If it is ever to be fulfilled, it will owe very little to man. Morally as well as physically, it will clearly have to be achieved by the grace of God.

Critical scholars reckon the story a duplicate of 12:10ff., ultimately on the ground that a man does not repeat a lapse of

[1] *Ibid,*, p. 5.

this kind. But it is easier to be consistent in theory than under fear of death; in any case verse 13 shows that Abraham had made this precaution his policy. See Introduction, II*b*.3, pp. 21f., and comments on 26:1–11.

1. The term for *the South* is *the Negeb* (RSV); see on 12:9. The first half of the verse tells of the general area of Abraham's movements; the last sentence leads on into the ensuing story set in a place a little to the north, towards Gaza.

2. *Abimelech* ('the king (God) is my father') was probably a royal title; there is a later Abimelech in chapter 26, and king Achish has this name in the heading to Psalm 34. On his taking Sarah, at her age, see on 12:14.

3–6. The moral terms *righteous, integrity, sinning, etc.*, are clearly used here in a narrow sense, which throws some incidental light on the emphatic claims of innocence in certain Psalms.

7. In heathen religion the holiness of *a prophet* was nearer magic than morality (*cf.* Nu. 22:6); so the reader can see better than Abimelech how far short of his title Abraham had just fallen in speaking to deceive, and can compare the shame of this enforced intercession with the glory of the prayer for Sodom. He can also note how God stands by His servants, retrieving Abraham from his folly so soon after retrieving Lot.

8–13. Abimelech's three questions in 9,10 make it clear that Abraham had only asked himself 'What will this do for me?', stifling the reflections 'What will it do to them?' 'What do they deserve?' and 'What are the facts?' (*What sawest thou?*, 10, AV, RV). The end of 9c could be rendered simply ' . . . things that are not done':[1] he had affronted the most elementary laws of hospitality.

Abraham's reply confessed to a pattern of mistaken choice which is in essence every man's with its fallibility in the realms of facts (11), values (the casuistry of 12) and motives (the cowardice of 13). The confession is marred by an attempt to shift the blame, Adam-like, in 13, which reads literally ' . . . when (the) gods caused me to wander. . . '[2] It is the

---

[1] *Cf.* 34:7.
[2] The verb never occurs in a good sense. *Cf., e.g.,* Is. 3:12; Je. 23:13,32.

language and wry attitude of the pagan; one man of the world might be speaking to another.

On the *sister . . . wife* relationship, see on 12:13. On the significance of *at every place* (13) in relation to Abraham's earlier lapse, see the opening remarks to this chapter.

14-18. Abimelech's lavish gifts showed his respect for the power wielded by Abraham, whose intercession he still needed (see 17,18), and must determine the sense of the difficult 16. The contempt expressed in AV is therefore wrong; it should be read as in RV: *it is . . . a covering of the eyes . . .*, *i.e.* 'it will preclude all criticism' (RSV, *it is your vindication . . .*). The final verb, usually meaning *reproved* (AV), can mean 'proved', as in Job 13:15, and even 'approved' (Gn. 24:14), hence RV, RSV, *righted*. In offering the compensation Abimelech owned his error (though the term *thy brother* re-emphasized his innocence), and in accepting it Abraham acknowledged the matter as settled.

II. ISAAC AND THE FURTHER TESTS OF FAITH
(chapters 21–26)

21:1-7. The birth of Isaac

So ends the suspense maintained since chapter 12 and heightened by the last episode. The matter-of-fact style and the emphasis on what God has *said . . . spoken . . . spoken* (1,2) express the quiet precision of His control.

6. Follow RSV: *God has made laughter for me*: so the name, potentially a reproach (18:15), now conveys only joy (*cf.* the name Jezreel in Ho. 1:4; 2:22, RV, RSVmg).

Sarah, throughout, is no visionary: she has faith (Heb. 11:11), but her bent is domestic and physical — no doubt providentially, for Isaac had the ordinary needs of a child, who must be enjoyed for himself as well as for his destiny.

21:8-21. The expulsion of Ishmael

The discord, trivial as it seemed at first glance (11), came from a fundamental rift which time would disclose and the New Testament expound as the incompatibility of the natural and the spiritual (Ps. 83:5,6; Gal. 4:29 and context). Sarah spoke more truly than she knew; but the sequel shows how different was God's spirit towards the outcasts from hers – a fact to be remembered in discussions of His sovereign will. At the close (20,21) the natural affinities of the pair are emerging, to confirm the wisdom of the parting.

The story is the complement of chapter 16, where all the parties had acted on impulse and had been recalled to live together another fourteen years or more (*cf.* 17:25). Now, with the two sons born and circumcised, God's time has ripened; *cf.* another slow maturing in 15:16.

9. rsv's *playing* (implying that Sarah was insanely jealous) is unfair: it should be translated *mocking* (av, rv). This is the intensive form of Isaac's name-verb 'to laugh', its malicious sense here demanded by the context and by Galatians 4:29 ('persecuted'). rsv itself renders it 'jesting' (19:14) and 'to insult' (39:14,17).

10. *Cast out this bondwoman . . .* is cited in Galatians 4:30 as an inspired demand. In her anger Sarah had her eyes opened to the true colours and proportions of the clash.

12. The words *In Isaac shall thy seed be called* (av, rv) put God's choice beyond all doubt, bringing into the open both the fact of election, as Paul shows in Romans 9:7–9, and, for Abraham, the irreplaceability of Isaac. On this anvil there was no escape from the hammer-blow of the next chapter, and Hebrews 11:18,19 shows that Abraham's faith was brought to perfection by this very means.

14, 15. With the *early* start compare 22:3; it seems safe to infer a habit of facing a hard task resolutely. The supply of water, pitiable in face of a desert, was as much as could be taken, for the waterskin had to be shouldered. Modern commentators, isolating this story from the chronology of 17:25, tend to insist that Ishmael too was carried (on the strength of the word *cast*, 15, and a rearranged word-order in 14b, where the syntax is harsh).[1] But quite apart from 17:25 the story requires an Ishmael too big for carrying (for Isaac himself would be about three at his weaning), and the word

[1] But Speiser is aware of the fresh difficulties this raises.

cast suits the exhausted action of one who had half supported, half dragged her son towards the shade of the bush.

16-21. Hagar's was a cry without hope (RSV tamely follows LXX in tidying her out of the picture; see RSVmg): it was the lad's voice, not hers, that brought help, and his name is almost spelt out in the Hebrew of *God heard* (*cf.* 16:11). The episode tellingly portrays man's plight and God's grace: on the one hand, diminishing supplies, scant refuge and final despair; on the other, the abundance of the well (once it was revealed), the promise of life and posterity, and (20) the presence of God.

21:22-34. The pact with Abimelech

The scene is some twenty-five miles from Gerar (see on 20:1), where disputes could soon arise over pasturing rights. The incident brings out the uncertainties and trials of the life Abraham had accepted; but Beersheba would remain both his and Isaac's chief base, at the southern tip of the promised land. Jacob, on the other hand, was to know more of the far north and the centre.

Here, in contrast to chapter 20, Abraham found that God was the shield He had promised to be (22), and he proved the value of frankness (25) and clarity (30).

22. Since *Abimelech and Phicol* reappear in 26:1,26 in very similar dealings with Isaac, the two stories are often regarded as duplicates. But see on verse 25, and on 26:26.

God is with thee: the same fact would be noticed about Isaac (26:28), Jacob (30:27) and Joseph (39:3).

23. Abimelech had some right (but see verse 25) to speak of *kindness* or dealing *loyally* (RSV) after the encounter of chapter 20. The term (*ḥeseḏ*) is also part of covenant language, and the whole verse speaks very much as Jonathan spoke to David in 1 Samuel 20:14,15.

25. The Hebrew verb suggests that Abraham had to make his complaint several times; perhaps Abimelech was adept at evasive tactics. The glimpse of a running rivalry over the wells makes the reopening of the whole matter with Isaac in chapter 26 highly predictable.

27-30. Since covenants were usually sealed with blood (*cf.* on 15:9ff.), the animals of verse 27 may have been given for this purpose, leaving the *seven ewe lambs* as a goodwill gift. In accepting them on Abraham's terms (30) Abimelech committed himself to Abraham's statement.

31. *Beer-sheba* means 'well of seven' (*cf.* 30, and on 26:33). The fact that 'to swear' is from a similar root would not pass unnoticed, but the opening *Wherefore* points back to 30, and the word *because* should probably be translated 'when'.[1]

32. The *Philistines* arrived in Palestine in force in the early twelfth century; Abimelech's group will have been early forerunners, perhaps in the course of trade.[2]

33. The *tree* (RV, RSV) and the divine name *'ēl 'ôlām, the Everlasting God*, have both been taken to prove that Abraham worshipped the local god in the local manner. But there is no hint that the tree was anything but commemorative; and as for the divine name, Speiser points out that it would be 'a logical epithet of a Deity called upon to support a formal treaty . . . expected to be valid for all time'.[3] The name is one of a series that includes El Elyon (14:18), El Roi (16:13), El Shaddai (17:1), El-elohe-Israel (33:20), El-Beth-el (35:7), each an aspect of God's self-disclosure. See Introduction IV*a*, p. 33.

22: 1-19. The offering of Isaac

Both father and son stand revealed with special clarity at this supreme moment. From Abraham the harrowing demand evokes only love and faith, certain as he is that the 'foolishness of God' is unexplored wisdom.[4] So he is enabled, in the surrender of his son, to mirror God's still greater love, while his faith gives him a first glimpse of resurrection: see on 5. The

[1] See W. J. Martin, *NBD*, art. 'Beersheba'.
[2] See *NBD*, art. 'Philistines'; also D. J. Wiseman, *Illustrations from Biblical Archaeology*, p. 53.
[3] *Genesis*, p. 159.
[4] 'The troublesome fact, the apparent absurdity . . . is precisely the one we must not ignore. Ten to one, it's in that covert the fox is lurking' (C. S. Lewis, *Letters to Malcolm* (Bles, 1964), p. 83).

test, instead of breaking him, brings him to the summit of his lifelong walk with God.

Isaac too comes briefly into his own – not by what he does but by what he suffers. Here, it seems, is his role, undistinguished though he may be in himself. Others will do exploits; it is left to this quiet victim, in a single episode, to demonstrate God's pattern for the chosen 'seed': to be a servant sacrificed.

1. AV's *tempt* is better expressed by *prove* or *test* (*cf.* RV, RSV). Abraham's trust was to be weighed in the balance against common sense, human affection, and lifelong ambition; in act against everything earthly.

2. Each of the opening phrases heightens the tension another degree.

Moriah reappears only in 2 Chronicles 3:1, where it is identified as the place where God halted the plague of Jerusalem and where Solomon built the Temple. In New Testament terms, this is the vicinity of Calvary.

3. On Abraham's early start, see on 21:14.

4. The note of time, *the third day*, incidentally agrees with the placing of Moriah noted above, but chiefly speaks of the protracted test and sustained obedience.

5. The assurance that Isaac as well as Abraham would *come again* from the sacrifice was no empty phrase: it was Abraham's full conviction, on the ground that 'in Isaac shall thy seed be called' (21:12). Hebrews 11:17–19 reveals that he was expecting Isaac to be resurrected; henceforth he would regard him as given back from the dead. For an extension of this attitude, see Paul's reflections on life through death in 2 Corinthians, especially 5:14ff.

6. The loading of *the wood* on to Isaac brings inevitably to mind the detail in John 19:17: 'he went out, bearing his own cross'. But *the fire and the knife* are in the father's hands. Victim and offerer walking *both of them together* (the poignant refrain returns in verse 8) foreshadow, however, the greater partnership expressed in Isaiah 53:7,10.

8. Abraham's *God will provide* was to be immortalized in the name of the place: see verse 14. It might almost be called his lifelong motto; many have lived by it since. His complete certainty of God, together with complete openness as to detail, makes this a model reply to an agonizing question. God's method was His own affair; it would take them both by surprise.

9, 10. Von Rad points out the slowing down of the narrative towards the fateful moment; in 10 'even the single movements' are captured. It is consummate story-telling throughout.

11, 12. The exact moment of intervention wrings the last drop of meaning from the experience. On the human side, the ultimate sacrifice is faced and willed; on the divine side, not a vestige of harm is permitted, and not a nuance of devotion is unnoticed (as the phrase *thy son, thine only son*, echoed from 2 and re-echoed in 16, makes clear). It is the answer, vividly conclusive yet anything but facile, to the question of Micah 6:6,7.

13. For the second time (*cf.* 21:19) God's provision is found to have been ready and waiting. Note that in this sacrifice at least, the victim was a substitute (*instead of his son*); and what is explicit here the later ritual of Leviticus 1:4 seems well fitted to express.

14. *Jehovah-jireh* is, apart from the name for God, the expression Abraham had used in 8. *Provide* is a secondary meaning of the simple verb 'to see' (*cf.* our 'see to it'), as in 1 Samuel 16:1c. Both senses probably coexist in the little saying of 14b (which deserves to be better known), *i.e.* 'In the mount . . . it will come clear'.

15–18. To obey is to find new assurance, as Abraham had discovered in 13:14ff.; note too the new promise in 17c. The best comment on God's oath is in Hebrews 6:16-18.

22:20–24. The twelve children of Nahor

This family news, reaching Abraham after the reiteration of the promise, may well have suggested or confirmed the thought which produced the decision of 24:4.

The significant names are Bethuel and Rebekah; the rest are of interest chiefly as evidence of records carefully kept, and of Israel's consciousness of distant kinships.

Uz is the name of a land in Job 1:1 and Jeremiah 25:20; it may or may not be connected with Nahor's son.

23:1-20. The family burial-place

'These all died in faith': the importance of the chapter lies in this. By leaving their bones in Canaan the patriarchs gave their last witness to the promise, as Joseph's dying words made clear (50:25). 'While they themselves were silent . . . , the sepulchre cried aloud, that death formed no obstacle to their entering on the possession of it' (Calvin).

2. The older name for Hebron (possibly renamed on its rebuilding, *cf.* Nu. 13:22) sounds like 'city of four', but in reality commemorates a hero of the Anakim (Jos. 14:15). Speiser points out that *'arba'* ('four') could well be a foreign personal name Hebraized; he notes the prominence of the non-Semitic 'sons of Heth' here.

Abraham came (AV, RV): rather, *went in* (RSV).

3. In Hebron the *Hittites* (RSV) were far from their northern compatriots; presumably they settled there in the course of trade. It is often suggested that these 'children of Heth' (AV, RV) were Hurrians, not Hittites; but Ephron (10) was clearly one of them, and the Hebrew words Heth and Hittite belong together.

4-9. *A stranger* (*gēr*) was a resident alien with some footing in the community but restricted rights. In Israel, for example, the *gēr* would be granted no land of his own, and in this chapter the keen question under the elaborate courtesies was whether Abraham was to gain a permanent foothold or not. The flattery in 6 was an inducement to remain a landless dependent. Abraham's rejoinder, naming an individual, made skilful use of the fact that while a group tends to resent an intruder the owner of an asset may welcome a customer.

10-16. Ephron knew the strength of his position. The gesture of 11 would be a conventional fiction,[1] and it may be

---

[1] M. R. Lehmann, however, points out in *BASOR*, CXXIX, 1953, pp. 15ff., that in Hittite law to buy a man's whole property was to incur his feudal obligations; hence Ephron might be manoeuvring here towards selling him the whole, rather than the part he requested in verse 9. But as

suspected that his real price was heavy.[1] Abraham, with no choice, had the wisdom to accept it gracefully.

17-20. The details of the property and the mention of witnesses indicate that this was a fully secured contract. The reference to *the trees* (17) is characteristic of Hittite land transactions, which were careful to specify them.[2] The whole chapter seems to reflect the Hittite laws current in patriarchal times, though it must be added that these were not unique; various Babylonian parallels to them can be adduced.[3]

24:1-67. The chosen bride for Isaac

To the very end, God's will for Isaac continued to make demands on Abraham's faith. With old age and wealth to anchor him to the past or present, he now looked on steadfastly to the next stage of the promise and acted with decision. The story, told with unobtrusive artistry, gives living form to the charge 'In all thy ways acknowledge him, and he shall direct thy paths' (Pr. 3:6). At this distance from the event, we can see how decisively the courageous obedience of a few individuals over a family matter was to shape the course of history.

1. The word *stricken* (AV, RV) is a free rendering; the Hebrew merely implies *advanced* (RSV).

2. This chief steward is one of the most attractive minor characters of the Bible, with his quiet good sense, his piety (26f.,52) and faith, his devotion to his employer (12b,14b,27) and his firmness in seeing the matter through (33,56). If he is the Eliezer of 15:2,3, his loyalty is all the finer in serving the heir who has displaced him, almost as a John the Baptist to his Master (*cf.* Jn. 3:29,30).

---

we cannot know whether this field was Ephron's only possession, the point remains conjectural.

[1] Jeremiah paid only seventeen shekels for a field (Je. 32:9), and David fifty for a threshing floor and oxen (2 Sa. 24:24). On the other hand David paid 600 gold shekels for the whole temple site (1 Ch. 21:25), and Omri bought the virgin hill of Samaria for 2 talents (6,000 shekels) of silver (1 Ki. 16: 24). Without details of these properties or current prices no certainty is possible.

[2] *Cf.* Lehmann, *art. cit.*, p. 18.

[3] *Cf.* G. M. Tucker, in *JBL*, LXXXV, 1966, pp. 77–84.

The privacy of the *thigh* and its association with begetting (46:26, Heb.) made the oath particularly solemn. Jacob's dying charge to Joseph was similarly reinforced (47:29).

3, 4. The charge to marry only within God's people was to be maintained throughout the Old Testament and the New. *Cf.* Deuteronomy 7:3,4; I Kings 11:4; Ezra 9 – the voices of law, experience and contrition; *cf.* Paul's reminder, 'only in the Lord' (1 Cor. 7:39).

5–8. In this exchange Abraham is characteristically the man of faith. Unable to foresee the outcome, he holds fast to two things: first, that God will not, and secondly, that man must not, go back on the main enterprise. See the tenses of 7, and the repeated charge of 6 and 8b. The point is taken up in Hebrews 11:15.

10. *Camels* were domesticated before patriarchal times,[1] but not used for large-scale nomadism or military purposes until about 1200 BC.

The city of Nahor could mean either the place of that name, near Haran, or more probably merely the city where Abraham's brother lived.

12. The phrase *God of my master* does not dissociate the speaker from God, but stresses the covenant with Abraham (*cf.* the covenant term *ḥeseḏ*, kindness, AV, RV, *steadfast love*, RSV), to which the household was pledged by circumcision (17:13), and pleads Abraham's cause.

14. Characteristically, the servant asks for nothing spectacular or arbitrary; the test with its arduousness will bring to light the very qualities God prizes.

15–21. In a few strokes, with some most telling details (the movements with the pitcher, the running, the man's tense silence), the scene lives for us, and Rebekah stands revealed.

22. We learn from verse 47 (and the Samaritan text adds here) that the servant now put these ornaments on Rebekah, gracefully combining honour with thanks.

26, 27. Success, which inflates the natural man, humbles the man of God. This servant's first thought is for the Lord, his second for his employer (27b), and his final one, with

[1] See the evidence cited in *NBD*, p. 182.

unaffected delight, for himself: 'he led me – *me* – straight[1] to the house. . . .'.

29, 30. The general excitement shows in the quick movements of each in turn, from verse 17 onwards. Verse 29 hastens the story on, leaving verse 30 to mention that the jewels had not passed unnoticed, a fact which will lose none of its flavour for the reader on his further acquaintance with Laban.

31, 32. With Laban's excellent hospitality contrast the grudging reception accorded to Jesus in Luke 7:44ff.

33. This break with the leisurely tempo of polite custom gave uncommon urgency to his words (a similar purposefulness was impressed on our Lord's men in Lk. 10:4; *cf.* 2 Tim. 4:2).

34–51. From the simplicity of 34 to the frank question of 49 the words of this good ambassador owe their power to their transparency. There is no flattery, no pressure; and if the material aspect of 35,36 is eloquent, the sequence of oath, promise and providence recounted in 37–48 makes the call of God the dominant note. So it elicits a response at the same level in 50,51: ' . . . *the Lord has spoken.*'[2]

52. For the third time, the servant prays. It is a point of interest that he had stood, watchful for the answer, to make his request (12,13a, *cf.* RSV); it was the answers that progressively prostrated him (26, 'his head'; 52, 'to the earth').

53. The gifts to the family may have been the formal bride price (*cf.* 29:18), clinching the matter.

54–56. On the servant's refusal to linger, see on 33.

57, 58. The bride's consent is, at least in theory, an important counterpoise to the family's initiative. Speiser points out that contemporary Hurrian marriage contracts specified it.

59. This *nurse*, Deborah, had suckled Rebekah, so the

---

[1] 'Straight' is Speiser's rendering of 'in the way': *cf.* verse 48. AV's 'I being in the way' is a less likely meaning of the phrase.

[2] With Laban, Rebekah's brother, taking the lead, Bethuel her father might be supposed to have died, but for his appearance in this verse. Presumably he was too old to do more than be roused to give consent, unless it was a local custom that the head of the family abstained from the preliminary negotiations.

Hebrew term implies, and was to be a faithful retainer to the next two generations, dying at last at Beth-el in Jacob's household (35:8).

60. The family of Rebekah little knew that their conventional blessing echoed God's pregnant words to Abraham (22:17).

62. The place-name is evocative; perhaps especially so to Isaac in his loneliness (67b). Here God had met the friendless Hagar and spoken of a nation coming to birth (16:14). On *the South* (AV, RV), see on 12:9.

63. The verb translated *meditate* (*sûaḥ*) is found as yet only here, so its meaning is uncertain. But as LXX understood it so, and a similar form *śîaḥ*[1] can mean this, the translation is eminently reasonable.

65. *My master*: some have taken this to mean that news had come of Abraham's death; but this conflicts with 25:7,20. It could mean that Abraham had set up Isaac on his own (36), in view of his impending marriage (and possibly Abraham's own remarriage, 25:1), allotting him his chief servant. But the expression could be used of Isaac as heir, and the disappearance of Abraham from the story may be no more than the narrator's way of transferring attention to the two who are now the story's growing-point.

The *veil* was a badge of betrothal and marriage: it could be drawn across the face, as in 38:14,15 and probably here, but was used altogether more freely than in modern Islam.

67. Read simply *into the tent* (RSV): the words 'his mother Sarah' (*cf.* AV, RV) stand unrelated to it in the Hebrew, and have apparently drifted here from the end of the verse.

25:1–34. The peoples arising from Abraham

The death of Abraham is given its setting in the catalogue of families that sprang from him; such is the onward thrust of Genesis. Among these, true to pattern, those that were to play little part in the history of salvation make their bow first, to leave the chief actors in possession.

1–4. The sons of Keturah. From the Hebrew construction

[1] *Cf., e.g.,* the interchangeable forms *śûm, śîm, etc.*

this marriage appears at first sight to have followed the events just recounted: but see the footnote to 12:1. Abraham's vitality points to a much earlier date (*cf.* 24:1), even though he was to live another thirty-five years after Isaac's marriage (7,20); while the term 'concubine' for Keturah in 1 Chronicles 1:32, and probably in verse 6 here, suggests that Sarah was alive when Abraham took Keturah.

Midian is the best known of these Arab tribes, but some of the names recur in the Old Testament and also, apparently, in South Arabian inscriptions. *Asshurim* (or -*ām*) is not to be confused with its namesake the Assyrians.

5-11. Abraham's will, death and burial. In verses 5,6 we see how the promise, 'In Isaac shall thy seed be called', dictated Abraham's actions to the last.

On *the concubines*, presumably Hagar and Keturah, see note on verses 1-4. It is hard to resist a comparison between verses 5,6 and the rebuke given to some of Isaac's successors in Luke 15:31,32. In God's plan, these sons were sent away that there might be a true home, in the end, to return to: see Isaiah 60:6ff.

8. The expression *gathered to his people*, which could hardly refer to the family sepulchre where only Sarah was buried as yet, must point, however indistinctly, to the continued existence of the dead. *Cf.*, *e.g.*, Job's words, 'Then had I been at rest, with kings and counsellors . . .' (Jb. 3:13,14). See also on 47:30.

9. The reunion of Isaac and Ishmael was to be paralleled in that of Jacob and Esau, at Isaac's death (35:29).

11. If Isaac could never be an Abraham, nor escape his debt to him, God had His particular blessing for him none the less.

Beer-lahai-roi: *cf.* 16:14; 24:62.

12-18. The sons of Ishmael. On this, see comment on 16:10-12.

19-34. The twin sons of Isaac: the rivalry of Jacob and Esau. The story hastens on to the new generation before pausing for Isaac himself, whose affairs can wait to the next chapter: such is the importance of the succession.

The life of Jacob, which spans almost the whole remainder of the book, is deftly summarized in Hosea 12:3 (4, MT):

> *In the womb he took his brother by the heel,*
> *and in his manhood he strove with God* (RSV).

If we insert between these two lines the parenthesis of Hosea 12:12 (13, MT) –

> *Jacob fled . . . , did service for a wife, and . . . herded sheep*

– then in the principal nouns we trace his successive concerns: 'his brother . . . a wife . . . God'; and in the actions, his rough path to maturity: 'he took-by-the-heel . . . fled . . . served . . . shepherded . . . strove . . . prevailed'. Indeed the two verbs of Hosea 12:3 (4, MT) enshrine in their Hebrew form his two names, recording the beginning and end of his pilgrimage from Jacob (*ʿāqaḇ*, 'took by the heel') to Israel (*śārâ*, 'strove').

21. Verse 26, with 20, shows a waiting time of some twenty years. God's way of prefacing an exceptional work with exceptional difficulties was often to take this form: such men as Joseph, Samson and Samuel came into the world only after sorrow and prayer.

22. Rebekah's cry is a fragment, literally 'If so, *why* (am) I – ?', to which the Syriac adds 'alive' (*cf.* RV, RSV), which is hardly convincing. The context of answered prayer (21) and further enquiry (22b) rather suggests her disquiet that God's frown had so suddenly replaced His smile. AV is nearer the mark than RV, RSV.

23. *Separated* (AV, RV), *divided* (RSV): *i.e.* incompatible.

The elder shall serve the younger: the existence of this oracle throws important light on the intrigues of chapter 27, where see comments. It also expresses God's sovereign choice, as Paul makes clear in Romans 9:11,12.

25. *Red* (*ʾaḏmônî*): if this prepared the way for his nickname Edom, it was the cry of verse 30 that decided it. *Esau* (*ʿēśāw*) only faintly resembles *śēʿār*, 'hairy'.

26. *Jacob*, an existing name found elsewhere, means 'May he be at the heels' – *i.e.* 'May God be your rearguard' (*cf.* on 17:19). But it also lends itself to a hostile sense, of dogging another's steps, or overreaching, as Esau bitterly observed in 27:36. Through his own action Jacob devalued the name into a synonym for treachery; it is taken up in the Hebrew of Jeremiah 9:4 (3, MT) 'every brother will utterly supplant'. But the tenacity which was his bane secured blessing in the end (32:26). See also on 49:18.

27–34. The two characters are utter opposites, as the two nations will eventually be. *Plain* or (RSV) *quiet* represents the Hebrew *tām* which has a suggestion of 'sound' or 'solid', the level-headed quality that made Jacob, at his best, toughly dependable, and at his worst a formidably cool opponent.

The *birthright* was the status of firstborn: it meant the headship of the family and, in later Israel at least, a double share of the estate (Dt. 21:17). Evidence from Nuzi shows that among contemporary Hurrians it was transferable, and in one such contract a brother pays three sheep for part of an inheritance[1] – comment enough on Jacob's bargain.

If Jacob is ruthless here, Esau is feckless: the versions have toned down his spluttering: 'Let me gulp some of the red stuff, this red stuff . . .' Embracing the present and the tangible at any cost, going through with the choice (33) and walking away unconcerned (34) – incidentally far from dead, in spite of 32a – he earned the epithet of Hebrews 12:16: a 'profane person'.

The chapter does not comment 'So Jacob supplanted his brother', but 'So Esau despised his birthright'; and Hebrews 12 shares its standpoint, presenting flippant Esau as the antithesis of the pilgrims of Hebrews 11.

26:1–11. Isaac deceives Abimelech

This is the third episode of its kind, and the only one that involves Isaac. Against the suggestion that a single incident has been multiplied into three, see the opening comments on chapter 20, and note further that 1a distinguishes the present story explicitly from the first in the series. The general similarities should not blind us to the divergent details of the

---

[1] *BA*, III, 1940, p. 5.

three (*e.g.* Rebekah, unlike Sarah, is not taken from her husband, nor is there any miracle here); but while these could be attributed to the changes and chances of story-telling it is very hard to account for Abimelech's agitation in verses 10,11 except as the outcome of an actual precedent known to him, *i.e.* the sharp warning in 20:7. The present story, then, alludes to the first incident (1a) and presupposes the second; the repeated lapses emphasize (like Peter's three denials) the chronic weakness of God's chosen material.

1. On *the former famine* (RSV), see remarks above. On *Abimelech* see on verse 26; and on the *Philistines*, 21:32.

2-4. Blessing had come to Isaac in bereavement (25:11); now God again meets him in adversity. The promise was searching: to refuse the immediate plenty of Egypt for mostly unseen (3a) and distant blessings (3b,4) demanded the kind of faith praised in Hebrews 11:9,10 and proved him a true son of his father – even though, like Abraham, he was to mar his obedience at once.

5. The heaped-up terms (*cf.*, *e.g.*, Dt. 11:1) suggest the complete servant, responsible and biddable. They also dispel any idea that law and promise are in necessary conflict (*cf.* Jas. 2:22; Gal. 3:21).

7. Typically human, Isaac mixes faith (see on 2–4) and fear, an incompatible combination which can give a special quality of meanness to the sins of the religious; and nowhere more so than here.

8. The force of *a long time* is that Isaac's fears have proved groundless; yet he persists in them. In the word *sporting* (*fondling*, RSV) the *leit-motiv* of his life recurs: it is his name-verb (17:17,19; 18:12; 21:6,9) transposed by the context into yet another key.

10, 11. On Abimelech's scruples see the opening comments to the chapter.

26:12-22. Isaac's fluctuating fortunes

12-14. The Lord's blessing (12) fulfilled the promise of 3a which Isaac had chosen against the attractions of Egypt (2). But he must remain a pilgrim, and wealth must therefore be allowed to bring its own irritants (14b), as it would do, one day, to Jacob (31:1-3).

15ff. *The wells* now dominate the story to the end, for Isaac's living riches, far from cushioning him against reality, threw him back on his basic resources all the harder.

Verse 15 prepares us to measure the blow that fell in 16, for Isaac would now be caught between a hostile city and a waterless countryside. His labour on the lost wells, the contesting of his early gains (20, 21), the timely reliefs and encouragements (22-24; *cf.* Acts 18:9,10) and the eventual reward of his tenacity (26-33) make a story which still speaks to the man of God engaged in the same struggle (Heb. 11:39, 40) and enhances his respect for this one who was called not so much to pioneer as to consolidate.

26:23-33. The covenant at Beer-sheba

24. On God's reassurance, see the paragraph above.

25. The altars built by the patriarchs were a response, rather than an initiative: for the most part they gratefully record God's coming and speaking to His servants (*cf.* 12:7; 13:17,18; 35:7).

26. The covenant revived an earlier one with Abraham (21:22ff.), which certainly needed renewal, and the present scene closely resembles its predecessor. The reappearance of the names Abimelech and Phicol after this long interval may mean that they were official names (*cf.* 'Pharaoh', *etc.*; see on 20:2) or recurring family names.[1]

27-31. By his initial frankness (27) and subsequent restraint (in passing over the effrontery of 29a; *cf.* Pr. 17:27) Isaac was able to make peace with honour. The *feast* (30) was an accepted

---

[1] Naming sons after grandfathers ('papponymy') was customary at various times. In a nearly contemporary example from Egypt the royal house and a provincial governing family retained this pattern side by side for four generations, so that Ammenemes I appointed Khnumhotep I, and his grandson Ammenemes II appointed Khnumhotep II. Alternating with them, Sesostris I and II appointed Nakht I and II, and certain negotiations were repeated as well. Yet these are not literary doublets. See G. Posener, *Littérature et Politique dans l'Egypte de la XIIe dynastie* (Champion, 1956), pp. 50ff.; P. E. Newberry, *Beni Hasan I* (Kegan Paul, 1893), pp. 57ff.; II, p. 16. (For these examples I am indebted to Mr. K. A. Kitchen.) See also *BA*, XXVI, 1963, p. 121.

way of cementing a covenant: see, *e.g.*, 31:54, and at a higher level Exodus 24:8,11; Matthew 26:26–29.

32, 33. The word *Shibah* (*šiḇ'â*, seven) is a variant of *sheba;* see on 21:31. Whether this was Abraham's well, now reopened (21:30,31; *cf.* 26:18), or a second one (*cf.* Jos. 19:2?), the name Beer-sheba now commemorated two separate pledges.

26:34, 35. Esau's Hittite wives

There is more in this notice than meets the eye, for it underlines Isaac's folly in still favouring Esau for the family headship (*cf.* 35 with 24:3), and it prepares the ground for Jacob's despatch in 27:46ff. to his cousins at Paddan-aram.

III. JACOB AND THE EMERGENCE OF ISRAEL
(chapters 27–36)

27:1–46. Jacob seizes the blessing

For a survey of Jacob's career, see on 25:19ff. We shall misjudge the situation if we overlook the evidence of Hebrews 12:16,17 that in selling the birthright (25:31ff.) Esau had traded away the firstborn's blessing. This makes all four participants in the present scene almost equally at fault. *Isaac,* whether he knew of the sale or not, knew God's birthoracle of 25:23, yet set himself to use God's power to thwart it (see verse 29). This is the outlook of magic, not religion. *Esau,* in agreeing to the plan, broke his own oath of 25:33. *Rebekah* and *Jacob,* with a just cause, made no approach to God or man, no gesture of faith or love, and reaped the appropriate fruit of hatred. (Long afterwards Jacob would learn, as he blessed Ephraim and Manasseh, with what simplicity God could order such affairs: see comments introducing chapter 48).

These rival stratagems only succeeded in doing 'whatsoever (God's) hand and . . . counsel foreordained' (*cf.* Acts 4:28). As a crowning touch, at a moment when Isaac was in no mood to care whom Jacob might marry, Jacob found himself thrust out of the nest he had feathered, to seek refuge and a wife among the very kinsmen to whom Abraham had turned in obedience to the vision (24:3ff.).

1ff. All five senses play a conspicuous part, largely by their fallibility, in this classic attempt to handle spiritual responsibilities by the light of nature. Ironically, even the sense of taste on which Isaac prided himself gave him the wrong answer. Rebekah had not the slightest doubt that she could reproduce Esau's gastronomic masterpiece – had she often smarted under this? – in a fraction of Esau's time. But the real scandal is Isaac's frivolity: his palate had long since governed his heart (25:28) and silenced his tongue (for he was powerless to rebuke the sin that was Esau's downfall); he now proposed to make it his arbiter between peoples and nations (29). Unfitness for office shows in every act of this sightless man rejecting the evidence of his ears for that of his hands, following the promptings of his palate and seeking inspiration through – of all things – his nose (27). Yet God put these very factors to work for Him.

12. RSV rightly replaces AV, RV's *a deceiver* with *mocking*; the verb is rare, but 2 Chronicles 36:16 establishes the meaning.

27–29. God takes and redirects Isaac's gropings and ambitions – which contain a core of faith (Heb. 11:20) – so as to answer them beyond anything he can ask or think. The hunter's garments, redolent of the country, evoke the promise of the land, enhanced now to a vision of plenty (in terms to be amplified in, *e.g.*, Dt. 11:11–15), not of mere living-space. His fierce pride in Esau demands an empire for him, against the decree of 25:23 – and Psalms 72 and 87 will show in different ways how *Jacob's* king and city will enjoy it. Finally the protective curse and blessing are made to speak of what will hinge on the attitude of *every one* (29b) to the true Israel.

33. Isaac's *yea, and he shall be blessed* expresses more than mere belief that the spoken word is self-fulfilling: he knows he has been fighting against God, as Esau has, and he accepts defeat.

34. On Esau's *bitter cry* the last word is spoken in Hebrews 12:16,17.

39, 40. Esau's blessing opens with an echo of Jacob's; clearly a mournful echo, for the words *of the fatness* . . . (RV) can equally mean *away from the fatness* . . . (RSV), as the context now demands. *Cf.* the *double entendre* in 40:13,19, and see footnote 3 at 3:15.

So Isaac pronounces over Esau the appropriate destiny of the 'profane person': the freedom to live unblessed (39) and untamed (40).

41-46. Rebekah's quick grasp of situations and characters shows itself again, first in her recognition that she must lose Jacob to save him, and then in her persuasive handling of both son and father. In Jacob she aroused enough alarm (42), hope (43–45) and compunction (45c) to uproot him, home-lover as he was. Yet he must not go as a fugitive, but with his father's backing and to the shelter of her family – and Isaac must preferably suggest the idea himself. For this, her broaching the subject of Jacob's marriage was a masterstroke: it played equally on Isaac's self-interest and his principles. The prospect of a third Hittite daughter-in-law and a distracted wife would have unmanned even an Abraham. Rebekah's diplomatic victory was complete; but she would never see her son again.

28:1-9. Jacob is sent to Mesopotamia

The second phase of Jacob's life now opens (see on 25:19–34), and providentially, through Rebekah's diplomacy (see above), he could now leave home with an aim before him and a father's blessing behind him – itself an implicit warning to Esau not to interfere. While Esau took the point, his attempt to do the approved thing was, like most religious efforts of the natural man,[1] superficial and ill-judged. To take a third wife, even though an Ishmaelite was better than a Hittite, was hardly the way back to blessing.

2. *Paddan-aram, i.e.* the plain of Aram, was the district near Haran in N.W. Mesopotamia where Abraham's brother Nahor had settled. It was Rebekah's homeland.

3. The title *God Almighty*, El Shaddai, was specially associated with the covenant with Abraham (17:1), which Isaac was concerned to emphasize, as the next verse shows. Jacob in his loneliness could be assured that he was far from isolated, and the unusual phrase *a company of peoples* (RV, RSV) adds a

[1] *Cf.* 1 Cor. 2:14.

new richness to the promises made to Abraham and Isaac. In the word *company*, from the root 'to assemble', the Old Testament term for the church or congregation makes its first appearance, bringing with it the idea of coherence as well as multiplicity. It is associated with Jacob again in 35:11; 48:4.

5. *Syrian* (AV, RV) is better rendered *Aramean* (RSV), which retains the allusion to Paddan-aram. Arameans would later establish a kingdom at Damascus, but at this time they were mainly found much farther north.

28:10-22. Jacob's dream and vow

This is a supreme display of divine grace, unsought and unstinted. Unsought, for Jacob was no pilgrim or returning prodigal, yet God came out to meet him, angelic retinue and all, taking him wholly by surprise. Unstinted, for there was no word of reproach or demand, only a stream of assurances flowing from the central 'I am the Lord', to spread from the past (13a) to the distant future, from the spot where Jacob lay (13b) to the four corners of the earth (14) and from his person to all mankind (14b). It was also immediately apposite, meeting his solitary, homeless and precarious condition by assuring him of the covenant with his forbears, allotting him a landed inheritance, and promising him safe conduct.

Jacob's reply is often condemned as mere bargaining; yet it was as thorough a response as he knew how to make. It expressed profound awe (16,17), a preoccupation first of all with the One who had been encountered, not with the things that were promised. From this it issued in homage and in the vow to pledge himself in covenant. The vow was no more a bargain than any other vow (the 'if' clause is inherent in the form); it would be fairer to say that Jacob was taking the promise of 15 and translating the general into the particular. Further, he rightly saw his tithe (22b) not as a gift but as a giving back.

12. 'Stairway' would be a better term than *ladder*, in view of the stream of messengers ascending and descending (the word is akin to the 'mount' thrown up against a walled city,

2 Sa. 20:15, *etc.*).[1] On the angelic patrolling of the earth, *cf.* Zechariah 1:10ff.; Job 1:6ff.

Jesus took this figure of a means of access between heaven and earth, as a vivid foretaste of Himself as the Way (Jn. 1:51).

13. The fact that *the Lord stood*, whether 'above it' or (mg) 'beside him', marks this as no minor occasion: God and all heaven are intent on it. There may even be a contrast between the angels on God's errands to the earth at large, and the Lord dealing in person with Jacob (*cf.* Dt. 32:8,9, RSV). Certainly this call and its outcome rank in Scripture far above the rise and fall of empires.

14. On the expression *be blessed*, see on 12:1–3.

17. *The gate of heaven* invites fruitful comparison with the story of Babel, especially in view of the latter's name: see on 11:9.

18. *Pillar* and *oil* are regular symbols of memorial (*cf.* Dt. 27:2ff.; Is. 19:19) and consecration (Lv. 8:10,11; *cf.* the Messiah or Christ, the 'anointed'). The pillars that were later forbidden were tokens of Baal (Dt. 12:3) and objects of worship (Mi. 5:13).

19. *Beth-el* means 'House of God': *cf.* verses 17,22.

22. The gift of *the tenth* was voluntary before it was commanded. It was to become a fetish with the Pharisees (Mt. 23:23); but the principle of proportionate giving is upheld, though unspecified, in the New Testament (1 Cor. 16:2).

29:1–30. Jacob and the daughters of Laban

In Laban Jacob met his match and his means of discipline. Twenty years (31:41) of drudgery and friction were to weather his character; and the reader can reflect that presumably Jacob is not the only person to have needed a Laban in his life.

Through this man he also drank deeply of his own medicine of duplicity; yet even as the loser he displayed qualities that were lacking in Esau. The tenacity that showed at his birth and, supremely, at Peniel, enabled him to regard the defeat over

---

[1] A. R. Millard, in *ET*, LXXVIII, 1966, pp. 86f., draws attention to a cognate Akkadian word in the story of *Nergal and Ereshkigal*, where messengers of the gods traverse 'the long stairway (*simmiltu*) of heaven'.

Rachel as only a setback. By staying the course he was to win a greater prize than he yet knew.

1–14. The incident at the well was especially timely in that it introduced the newcomer to Laban as a benefactor instead of a suppliant – no small asset in dealing with such a man. It also portrays Jacob to us, characteristically full of thrust and enterprise: the shepherds' acquiescent outlook (with its watchwords (8) 'We cannot . . .' and, in effect, 'We always . . .') is not for him. Further, he knows how to present his actions to the best advantage, capping the feat of strength with one of service, and this in turn with the dramatic announcement. It is a superb entry.[1]

17. *Tender* (AV, RV) probably means *weak* (RSV), either in vision or (as von Rad suggests) in colour.

18. *Seven years* was a handsome offer: Jacob was clearly not risking a refusal – a fact which Laban would not fail to note and exploit, as Jacob had exploited Esau's eagerness (25:32).

19. Laban's reply managed to give the appearance without the actual substance of consent. He was covered.

20. One might have expected the seven years to seem tantalizingly long; the point is that as a *price* for such a bride they seemed a trifle.

21. Jacob's wording, mentioning no name, played into Laban's hands; but Laban would in any case have had no difficulty in prompting the form of the request.

24. The abrupt mention of the gift of a maid to the bride (*cf.* 29) is another of the details illuminated by the Nuzi tablets.[2]

25. The words, *behold, it was Leah,* are the very embodiment of anticlimax, and this moment a miniature of man's disillusion, experienced from Eden onwards.

Yet the story reveals that God, not Laban, had the last word. The deceiver Jacob was deceived, and the despised Leah

---

[1] The well-side encounters in Gn. 24 and Ex. 2 invite comparison with this. Eliezer, with his straightforward piety, prayed and was answered. Moses, champion of the downtrodden, gained a home through the very chivalry that had cost him one; and Jacob did likewise through a proper use, now, of his competitiveness.

[2] See comment and footnote on 16:1–3.

was exalted to become the mother of, among others, the priestly and kingly tribes of Levi and Judah.

26. Laban's bland reply was doubtless true, if a little belated (*cf.* 18,19); it was useless to argue, and Jacob characteristically set himself to retrieve what he could.

27. The *week* was the wedding week (*cf.* Jdg. 14:17); it was followed by marriage to Rachel, and the seven years' extra service was subsequent, as the sequence within verse 30 indicates.

28. It was later forbidden to marry two sisters in each other's lifetime (Lv. 18:18). The present story helps to show why; it is also an example of honest reporting, not reading back the law into an earlier time.

29:31 – 30:24. Jacob's children, from Reuben to Joseph

In his family relations Jacob continued to sow bitter seed. His coolness to his unwanted wife was understandable, but 29:31ff. shows what God as well as Leah thought of it, and there are few things more pathetic than the naming of her first three sons. Some fruits of the miseries and intrigues of this period emerge in the last chapters of the book, and the tribes were to go through history labelled with reminders of their stormy origins. On the human plane the story demonstrates the craving of human beings for love and recognition, and the price of thwarting it; on the divine level it shows once again the grace of God choosing difficult and unpromising material.

31. The meaning of *hated* in this kind of context (*cf.* Dt. 21:15ff.) is shown by verse 30; a near equivalent would be 'unloved'.

32ff. The special meaning Leah attached to *Reuben* matches the pattern already discussed at 4:1. The name was probably one in current use ('Look, a son'); on a single strand from it she now threads her thoughts and longings.

So with the rest of the names. Mostly, as here, a verb begins the train of thought, and some of the arabesques are freer than others. All of them reflect the immediate domestic tensions and triumphs; later, in the Blessing of Jacob (chapter 49), the names and their associated incidents will give rise to forward-looking oracles for the twelve tribes.

30:3. The expression *upon my knees* is similarly used in 50:23 to mean 'children counted as my own'. *Cf.* comment on 16:1–3.

8. *Mighty wrestlings* are literally 'wrestlings of God'.

11. *Gad*, which can mean *troop* (AV), is also a word for *fortune* (*cf.* LXX, RV, RSV), and in spite of 49:19 this is the likelier meaning, especially in view of verse 13. In Isaiah 65:11 Fortune has become a god, as did the equivalent terms Tyche and Fortuna in Greek and Latin.[1]

14. *Mandrakes* were thought to induce fertility, as their amorous Hebrew name suggests; hence Rachel's eagerness for them. The outcome was ironical, the mandrakes doing nothing for Rachel, while Leah gained another son by parting with them. It is a further example, in this family, of trading in things that should be above trade, and resorting in trouble only half-heartedly to God. But the name *Issachar*, with its wry reminder of the strange bargain, was overlaid with a happier meaning by Leah in verse 18; *cf.* on 21:6. Later still it would acquire yet other associations: see on 49:15.

20. Two Hebrew roots, *z-b-d* and *z-b-l*, are played upon in the two halves of this verse, and it now appears that they are linked by meaning as well as sound, in the light of the Akkadian *zubullû*, 'bridegroom's gift'. Speiser, who draws attention to this root, translates the second clause 'This time my husband will bring me presents . . .'. Since AV, RV had to insert 'with', to make sense of *dwell*, and RSV's *honour* is precariously derived, this suggestion has much to commend it.

21. *Dinah* will reappear in chapter 34.

23, 24. There is some assonance between *'āsap* (*has taken away*, lit. 'gathered up') and *yōsēp* (*may . . . add*). The prayer enshrined in the name is a good example of faith pressing on for more than God has yet given.

30:25–43. Jacob outdoes Laban

If Laban seemed oddly unsuspecting over his son-in-law's

---

[1] To conjecture from this that the tribe thought itself descended from the god (*cf.*, *e.g.*, Oesterley and Robinson, *Hebrew Religion*[2] (S.P.C.K., 1937), p. 100) is quite unwarranted. Even if Fortune were found deified as early as this (of which there is no evidence), the name need still have no theological bias; *cf.* the term *'aštārōt* (ashtaroth) in sheep-breeding (Dt. 7:13, *etc.*, Heb.), or our own use of the word jovial, the name Diana, *etc.*

proposal, it was surely because he had seen through it and formed the swift counterplan of 35c,36. To put three days between the two flocks, and his own sons in charge of the piebalds, tipped the balance neatly in his favour. Any protest would have given Jacob away.

Jacob's winning riposte owed more to God than he may have realized, in spite of his proper acknowledgment in 31:9. In displaying the striped rods at breeding time he acted on the common belief that a vivid sight during pregnancy or conception would leave its mark on the embryo; but this is apparently quite unfounded.[1] No doubt some of his success came from selective breeding (40–42), but by itself this would have worked very slowly, as Laban reckoned it would. Clearly God intervened (see 31:9–12) to fulfil the hopes Jacob placed in the rods, using them as He used the arrows of Joash or the bones of Elisha, as the means (or the occasions) of working miraculously. It would not be the last time that His part in a success would be much greater than it seemed to the observer.

27. AV, RV are surely right in supplying some such word as *tarry*: Laban is feeling his way towards his proposal in the next verse, rather than being gratuitously obsequious as in RSV. For his expression *I have divined* (RV, rather than AV's *I have learned by experience*), see 44:5,15. Laban may have literally looked for omens, or have been speaking figuratively. The Old Testament use of the verb suggests the former.

32. In the first half of the verse the words *every speckled and spotted sheep* (RSV, *cf.* AV, RV) seem to have crept into the text from the second half. They are absent here from LXX, and Laban's action in verse 35 would confirm that Jacob's share was the black sheep and the particoloured goats – in each case the rarer kind.

37. *Pilled* (AV): *i.e.*, *peeled* (RV, RSV).

38, 39. RSV inserts the words *since* and *so*, but the Hebrew is content to state the bare sequence, as in AV, RV, not pro-

---

[1] *Cf.* D. M. Blair, *A Doctor Looks at the Bible*[2] (I.V.F., 1959), p. 5. In support of such beliefs Delitzsch quoted breeding customs of his own day, and S. R. Driver and J. Skinner, among others, followed him. But such customs tend to be credited with results due to other factors. See also note on 30:38,39.

nouncing on cause and effect. Verse 39 is *post hoc*, not explicitly *propter hoc*.

43. Jacob built up this wealth over a period of six years (31:41).

31:1–21. Jacob's flight from Laban

Of the factors that now stirred the nest for Jacob, to impel him homewards, the most pressing was Laban's dangerous mood, nicely understated in verse 2, as the contract now chafed him whichever way he turned (7,8). But Jacob was called as well as driven. There was his vow to keep, at God's bidding in the new dream; there was also his brother to be faced, purely at the call of conscience – for he seems to have taken the hard course of 32:3ff. spontaneously. This high motivation must not be obscured by his stealth: no doubt he was too much of a tactician here, as anyone was tempted to be with Laban, but he was also a man obeying a divine summons.

1. If Jacob was getting the lion's share, his critics conveniently ignored the immense growth of the total (30:30) and the fourteen underpaid years. It was fair enough.

The root idea of *glory* (AV, RV) in Hebrew is weight, therefore substance or *wealth* (RSV) is appropriate; but the choice of word suggests that his kinsmen took umbrage at his style of living (*cf.* 30:43).

2, 3. The sequence, *Jacob beheld . . . and the Lord said*, is worth noting as an example of divine guidance. The outward facts alerted him to the inward voice; they were not a sufficient guide in themselves. Note too that what the Lord said agreed with His earlier promise of 28:15. Jacob gives a fuller account of the vision in verses 11–13 below.

4. From this and verse 19 it emerges that Laban had now abandoned his too clever exchange of flocks (*cf.* 30:35,36), no doubt in making one of his revised agreements.

5ff. As Jacob wanted to take a willing and a pilgrim family with him, his speech attempted more than self-defence: it pointed to the hand of God in his success and now to the call of God in his proposal; and it duly evoked a response of faith, shown in the reply of verse 16 (*cf.* on 24:34–51).

7. *Ten* is often a round number: we should probably have said 'a dozen' or 'time after time'.

8, 9. Put this way, the proof of God's favour looks incontestable; and indeed it was as decisive a factor as Jacob implied. This is the gist of the dream (*cf.* verse 12); see also comment on 30:25-43.

11. *The angel of God* is once again a term for God Himself: *cf.* verse 13, and Introduction, p. 33.

13. The Hebrew construction (unless some words have fallen out, as LXX suggests) makes the phrase mean 'The God at Beth-el'.

14, 15. Laban's capitalizing of his daughters had not escaped their notice. In losing their goodwill he was paying part of the hidden price of all covetousness (*cf.* Hab. 2:6-8).

16. See comment on 5ff., above.

19. In stealing the *teraphim* (RV; *images*, AV) or *household gods* (RSV), Rachel may well have had a partly religious motive (*cf.* 35:2,4), but the fact that possession of them could strengthen one's claim to the inheritance (as the Nuzi tablets disclose)[1] gives the most likely clue to her action. It chimes in with her words of 14-16, and she can be imagined telling herself that she was taking no more than her due. Once more in this story the very act that hard-headed self-interest suggested led to the edge of disaster.

21. Follow RSV: . . . *and crossed the Euphrates, and set his face toward the hill country of Gilead.*

31:22-42. Pursuit and confrontation

The hand of God is again decisive. On the human level Laban might well have won every business deal (see on 30:25-43) and the present physical encounter as well (*cf.* verses 23,29a). It was only by divine prospering and protection (24) that Jacob brought anything, even his life, back from exile.

24. The warning dream recalls Abimelech's in 20:3ff. Each of the three patriarchs had to be ingloriously extricated from some adventure.

26-30. The temptation to strike every chord was too much

[1] *BA*, III, 1940, p. 5.

for Laban: the attitudes of hurt father and baffled avenger hardly went together, and by fulminating on what he would have done if God had not called him off he only conveyed reassurance to Jacob. But his final sarcasm (30) was superb.

32ff. Jacob's blissful ignorance makes the search unbearably tense, and his own counter-attack devastating.

38-40. The tale of hardships is an astringent corrective to romantic ideas of the biblical shepherd. This, and nothing idyllic, is the pastor's calling, reminiscent of the adversities of Paul in 2 Corinthians 11:26ff., or indeed of David, Amos or Jesus (Ps. 23:4,5; Am. 3:12; Jn. 10:11ff.).

41. *Ten times*: see on verse 7 above.

42. Albright has suggested 'the kinsman of Isaac' for *the fear of Isaac*, adducing support from related languages.[1] But the normal meaning, 'fear' (lit. 'trembling'), makes good sense, illuminated by the synonyms in, *e.g.*, Isaiah 8:13.[2]

31:43-55. The parting covenant with Laban

The covenant, limited though it was, made a far happier end to the twenty years' sparring than the jagged break left by Jacob's flight. God's ability to bring Laban to the point of proposing it was an object-lesson to Jacob – and remains so – in favour of faith against panic ('I was afraid', 31), and of open dealing against scheming, in handling a difficult relationship. Laban was unchanged; but this time Jacob was not leaving behind him 'a brother offended'.

45ff. Whether the cairn's role as witness was an idea borrowed from the witness clauses of treaties or not, it was natural to have a visible token (*cf.* Jos. 24:27) and boundary mark. Its two names in verse 47 are the Aramaic and Hebrew

---

[1] *FSAC*, p. 248n.

[2] A. Alt's theory (*Der Gott der Väter*, 1929, in *Kleine Schriften²* I (Beck, 1959), pp. 24ff.), that the God of Abraham, the Fear of Isaac and (49:24) the Mighty One of Jacob were originally three distinct deities is precariously erected on a gratuitous theory that the three patriarchs were unrelated and unknown to each other. But a host of examples shows that the Old and New Testaments delight in multiplying names for the one God (*cf.*, *e.g.*, Ps. 18:2; Rev. 15:3), while as for the patriarchs' father-son relationship, this is the crux of the middle chapters of Genesis, where all hinges on the promise of a son to Abraham and the election of the younger son of Isaac.

for 'heap of witness'; its further name *Mizpah* (49), 'watch-tower', leads on to the thought of the divine witness and guarantor, which again may be a feature suggested by standard treaty forms. This impression is strengthened by the Hebrew of verse 53 which reads as though in Laban's mind a god on each side was invoked, as in political covenants.[1] (On the expression *the fear of . . . Isaac* (53) see on verse 42, above.)

54. The covenant feast, being sacrificial, was intended to create more than a merely social bond between the parties, who would regard themselves as bound together in the table-fellowship of their divine host. See also on 26:30.

32:1–32. Vision, foreboding and wrestling
'In his manhood he strove with God' (see on 25:19–34). In Jacob's pilgrimage, the way to the heights now led through a valley of humiliation which he made no attempt to skirt. Geographically, the call to Beth-el would take him nowhere near Esau, ensconced in the far south at Mount Seir; spirit-ually, he could reach Beth-el no other way. God had promised him the land (28:13, 14), and its borders must march one day with Esau's; besides, to meet God he must 'first be reconciled' with his brother. The sequence of chapters 32, 33, culminating in 35:1–15, acts out powerfully the principles of Matthew 5:23–25a.

1, 2. The vision of angels. *On his way* – the phrase is significant: the reassurance was given as he went forward (*cf.* Lk. 17:14; Jn. 4:51), and what came to meet him out of the unknown was God's host (*cf.* Is. 64:5), a reminder and new foretaste of Beth-el. The force of the name *Mahanaim*, 'double camp', is that Jacob's own company, as he could now see, was matched by another. It was a heartening beginning to his ordeal, in which very soon his own company would be split up for fear of a massacre (8).

3–21. Esau's imminent approach. *Thy servant . . . , my lord* (4,5): it was the language of courtesy (*cf.* 30:27), but it

---

[1] *Judge* is a plural verb in verse 53, and the preceding phrase can be read 'the gods of their father': *cf.* Jos. 24:2.

struck the proper note of awaiting Esau's pleasure, without wheedling and with simplicity.

6ff. Nothing could be more ominous than Esau's silence and his rapid approach in force. Jacob's reaction is characteristically energetic: he plans, 7,8 – prays, 9–12 – plans, 13–21 – prays, 22–32 – plans, 33:1–3. It is over-facile to condemn his elaborate moves as faithless, for Scripture approves of strategy when it is a tool rather than a substitute for God (*cf.* Jos. 8:1c,2c; Ne. 4:9ff.). Jacob's prayers show where his confidence lay.

9–12. This moving plea is a model of its kind. It rests securely on the foundation of covenant, command and promise (9), and shows the true spirit of worship in its wonder at God's mercy (10), seen as beyond all deserving or predicting (even the dividing of his company is viewed now in this positive light). The urgent request, kept back till this point, reveals a new gap in Jacob's armour by its last phrase, *the mother with the children* (11): he is no longer self-sufficient; even his past is not his own affair. But the acknowledged fear of verse 11 is at once exposed to the remembered promise, which now flanks the prayer on both sides (12; *cf.* 9b) and brings the distant future into the reckoning. The short-term threat already looks less overwhelming.

20. Jacob's sacrificial terms unconsciously illustrate the gulf between man's thinking and God's. The pagan approaches his deity as Jacob now approached Esau (*cf.* 33:10), reckoning that 'a man's gift maketh room for him' (Pr. 18:16). But in the Old Testament, a man's gift is first God's gift to him, before ever it is his to God (Lv. 17:11). As Jacob would soon discover, grace, not negotiation, is the only solvent of guilt.

22–32. The wrestling at Peniel. The great encounter with God came when Jacob knew himself to be exposed to a situation wholly beyond him. The threat of it had already driven him to prayer (9–12), and both his renewed desire to be alone (see on verse 23, below), and the form that the night struggle took, indicate a hunger now for God Himself; a hunger awakened by the crisis but not determined by it.

The identity of Jacob's assailant emerges only gradually,

and Jacob is quick to seize every clue to it. Behind the human limitations (24,25a) there is an awesome reserve of power (25b), and behind the reluctance to be overtaken by the day there could be the elusiveness of some night phantom or else the holiness of God, whose face must not be seen. Jacob's answering plea for a blessing showed that he glimpsed the truth, and the further exchanges dispelled all doubt, both by what was said (28b) and by what was withheld (29). To Jacob, as to Manoah in Judges 13:18, the withholding of God's name was not absolute: it warned against intrusion but left the door open on God's side to reveal Himself: *cf.* the disclosure to Moses in Exodus 33:18 – 34:7, with a similar balance between reserve and revelation.

The conflict brought to a head the battling and groping of a lifetime, and Jacob's desperate embrace vividly expressed his ambivalent attitude to God, of love and enmity, defiance and dependence. It was against Him, not Esau or Laban, that he had been pitting his strength, as he now discovered; yet the initiative had been God's, as it was this night, to chasten his pride and challenge his tenacity. 'With the cunning thou dost wrestle' (Ps. 18:26; *cf.* AVmg). The crippling and the naming show that God's ends were still the same: He would have all of Jacob's will to win, to attain and obtain, yet purged of self-sufficiency and redirected to the proper object of man's love, God Himself.

It was defeat and victory in one. Hosea again[1] illuminates it: 'He strove with the angel and prevailed' – this is the language of strength; 'he wept and sought his favour' – the language of weakness. After the maiming, combativeness had turned to a dogged dependence, and Jacob emerged broken, named and blessed. His limping would be a lasting proof of the reality of the struggle: it had been no dream, and there was sharp judgment in it. The new name would attest his new standing: it was both a mark of grace, wiping out an old reproach (27:36), and an accolade to live up to. The blessing, this time, was untarnished, both in the taking and in the giving: it was his own, uncontrived and unmediated.

[1] Ho. 12:4, RSV; *cf.* note on Gn. 25:19–34.

22. The *Jabbok* (modern Zerqa) flows westward through Gilead, in a deep cleft of the mountains, to the Jordan.

23, 24a. Jacob's motive in sending his family ahead was not to shield himself, as 33:3 makes plain. Whether or not he felt his need to be *left alone* before the crisis, God saw it, and saw to it.

24b, 25. When God appears as *a man* in the Old Testament He is usually called the Angel of the Lord, a title interchangeable with 'God' or 'the Lord' (28,30; *cf.* Ho. 12:3,4). See Introduction, p. 33.

26. *The day is breaking*: see the second paragraph introducing verses 22–32, above.

27. Knowledge of a man's *name* gives an ill-wisher some power over him, according to magical religions; but the Bible regards the name as potentially a pointer to his character. To declare one's name could sometimes be an act of self-disclosure (see verse 29, and, for Jacob, 27:36; *cf.* Mk. 5:9).

28. *Israel* is a verbal name, like Jacob (see on 25:26). In itself it would convey the meaning 'May God strive (for him)', but like other names in Genesis it takes on a new colouring from its occasion, and commemorates Jacob's side of the struggle and his character thus revealed. The key verb, 'strive' (possibly 'persevere'), is found only here and in Hosea 12:4,5, and its meaning is not certain; but there is no support now for deriving it from the noun 'a prince' as in AV (where the whole phrase *as a prince hast thou power* represents this single word).

30, 31. *Peniel* or *Penuel* means 'face of God'. A town of this name, in this vicinity, appears in Judges 8:8; 1 Kings 12:25.

The story implies that the vision of God was only dim, even though it was *face to face*. For Jacob's protection God withdrew with the dawn (26), and at sunrise Jacob was alone (31).

32. The ban on eating this part of an animal does not reappear in the Old Testament, but is found in Rabbinic Judaism (*e.g. Pesaḥim* 22a,83b). Together with the two names Israel and Peniel it made a third lasting reminder of this decisive night.

33:1-17. The meeting with Esau

True to biblical pattern, Jacob's vision was no escape from reality: his language shows that he saw the two encounters, with his Lord and his brother, as two levels of a single event: *cf.* 10b with 32:30.

The meeting is a classic of reconciliation. The stream of gifts and the demure family processions, almost comically over-organized (as it turned out), give some idea of the load on Jacob's conscience and the sheer grace of Esau's reply. Guilt and forgiveness are so eloquent in every movement of the mutual approach (3,4), that our Lord could find no better model for the prodigal's father at this point than Esau (*cf.* 4 with Lk. 15:20).

Yet the very warmth of the welcome brought a new danger of false partnership and consequent diversion. Although Jacob managed, somewhat dubiously, to extricate himself, the next incident shows that it was a particularly live issue for him so soon after his bondage to Laban.

8. *All this company* (RV, RSV) refers to the droves of animals, 32:13ff.

10. On Jacob's cultic language, see the opening comment on the chapter; also on 32:20.

11. The two Hebrew terms for *present* (homage-offering) (10) and *gift* (*blessing*, AV) express the humility and the goodwill with which they were offered. In accepting them, Esau for his part was showing goodwill by clinching the reconciliation: *cf.* Judges 13:23a.

13. *With me* (AV, RV) is literally 'upon me': hence RSV's *a care to me*. *Cf.* on 48:7.

14. *Until I come . . . to Seir* – but in fact Jacob turned north, as soon as he was alone, to Succoth (16,17). Few of us could cast the first stone at him for failing to combine grace and truth in refusing an embarrassing invitation. It is also possible, as Delitzsch suggests, that he intended to visit Seir one day, and deceived Esau 'by deceiving himself'. None the less, some of the deviousness of the old Jacob comes out, for he could have said plainly that he was under oath to go to Beth-el.

17. *Succoth* was a backward step, spiritually as well as geographically (see on verse 14): it is difficult to reconcile the call to Beth-el with the prolonged stay involved in building cattle sheds (whence the name, Succoth) and a house, east of the Jordan. The implied ages of Jacob's daughter and his elder sons in the next incident, at Shechem, show that several years were indeed spent in one or both of these places, since Dinah was evidently a child of about seven when the family left Paddan-aram (*cf.* 30:19–25; 31:41).

33:18 – 34:31. Massacre at Shechem

Shechem offered Jacob the attractions of a compromise. His summons was to Beth-el; but Shechem, about a day's journey short of it, stood attractively at the crossroads of trade. He was called to be a stranger and pilgrim; but while buying his own plot of land there (33:19) he could argue that it was within his promised borders. It was disobedience none the less, and his pious act of rearing an altar and claiming his new name of Israel (20) could not disguise the fact.

Chapter 34 shows the cost of it, paid in rape, treachery and massacre, a chain of evil that proceeded logically enough from the unequal partnership with the Canaanite community. There would still be echoes of it in the days of the Judges (*cf.* Jdg. 9:28). Its very fierceness, as it turned out, saved Jacob, in his mood of appeasement (5,30), from re-enacting the story of Lot: only fear for his life opened his ears again to God's call to Beth-el.

Modern critical studies tend to assume that this story, with 49:5–7, is only a personalized version of some attempt by the *tribes* of Simeon and Levi to settle at Shechem. Nothing in the story itself, however, necessitates this: it is vivid and coherent, and serious difficultie⸱ arise when it is tribalized; in particular there is no room left for Jacob or for the central character Dinah (unless she is brought in as a personification of the mixed marriage problem, which is far-fetched). This drastic reinterpretation arises in fact not from the text but from the prior opinion that Jacob did not have sons and a daughter bearing these names.

33:18. The word *šālēm* could mean *in peace* (RV; *cf.* 34:21),

but more probably *safely* (RSV). AV's *to Shalem, a city of Shechem,*
is also possible; S. R. Driver pointed out that there is still a
village called Salim four miles east of (*i.e.* 'before') Shechem.

19. The name *Hamor*, meaning 'ass', tempts Albright[1] to the
conjecture that *the sons of Hamor* is an expression for a group
bound together in treaty by the sacrifice of an ass, by analogy
with a custom attested at Mari. Certainly sacredness of this
animal may account for the name; but Hamor is an individual
both here and in Judges 9:28.

20. The title *El-elohe-Israel*, 'God (is) the God of Israel',
recalled Jacob's vow of 28:21 ('then shall the Lord be my God')
and at the same time claimed his own new name.

34:1. On the considerable lapse of time since Peniel see on
33:17. By halting his own pilgrimage Jacob was endangering
others more vulnerable than himself.

2, 3. The acquisitive verbs of verse 2 (see also on verse 7,
end) and the more generous ones of verse 3 faithfully reflect
this kind of love. Its finer side might mitigate the evil it
unleashed; it could not erase it.

5. Jacob's silence begins to look too diplomatic as the chapter
proceeds; his outburst in verse 30 suggests more concern for
peace than for honour. If he could swallow his scruples, as
his sons could not, he knew that status (9,10) and wealth
(12) were his.

7. *Folly* is too weak a term for *nᵉbālâ*, which always implies
some outrageous act or attitude, as in, *e.g.*, Joshua 7:15;
Judges 20:6; *cf.* Psalm 14:1. In 2 Samuel 13:12 it is coupled,
as here, with *ought not to be done* (or simply, 'is not done'), a
phrase that expresses the corporate conscience (*cf.* 20:9). The
term *in Israel* (*cf.* Dt. 22:21; Je. 29:23) suggests that the clan
knew its difference from the city; perhaps already in embryo,
the church from the world.

The terms already used of Shechem's treatment of Dinah
('humbled', 'defiled', 2,5), together with those of this verse,
give the stark biblical view of unchastity. Whether it was rape
or fornication is not clear: the second verb of verse 2 means
basically 'took' (AV, RV), possibly implying 'seized' (RSV), but

[1] *FSAC*, p. 279.

not certainly so. In either case it was not a casual liaison but one with a view to marriage, for Dinah remained in Shechem's house (17b,26). As 2:24 has already shown, however, marriage cannot truly be 'anticipated', in the nature of things.

13ff. The stipulation of circumcision was all the more plausible because the rite, outside Israel, was sometimes an initiation into marriageable status; *cf.* on 17:9–14.

20. *The gate* was the normal place of public business: *cf.* 23:18 and see Ruth 4:1ff.

25. Crudely performed, circumcision could be quite incapacitating, particularly after two or three days.[1] The massacre was no superhuman feat, even if Simeon and Levi acted alone (the remaining brothers seem to have joined them only for the looting and rounding up, 27ff.). Apart from Reuben, a man of impulse who lacked their cold ferocity and resolution (for better and worse: *cf.* 37:21; 42:37; 49:4a), these were the eldest full brothers of Dinah.

30, 31. The appeaser and the avengers, mutually exasperated, and swayed respectively by fear and fury, were perhaps equidistant from true justice. They exemplify two perennial but sterile reactions to evil.

35:1–15. To Beth-el again

Beth-el occupies something of the same focal place in Jacob's career that the birth of Isaac occupied for Abraham, testing his fluctuating obedience and his hold on the promise, for more than twenty years. His return there marks an end and a beginning: a time of parting, in the death of the old retainer Deborah and of the beloved Rachel; and a point of transition, as the promise was reaffirmed, and the family completed by the birth of Benjamin. Jacob was to live on, but the centre of gravity would now shift to his sons.

1. For the background to this command see 28:20–22; 31:13.

2–4. Any impression that patriarchal worship was free and easy is dispelled by these demands, which already have the makings of the Sinai law in their call for a single loyalty, ceremonial purity and the renunciation of magic (the *earrings*

[1] *Cf.*, *e.g.*, W. Thesiger, *The Marsh Arabs*, p. 102.

were evidently charms; *cf.* perhaps Ho. 2:13). At the same spot, possibly prompted by Jacob's example, Joshua was one day to issue a very similar call to Israel (Jos. 24:23ff.).

5. Whether the Hebrew phrase, literally 'a terror of God', merely expresses a superlative (RV) or defines the source of the fear (AV, RSV; *cf.*, *e.g.*, 2 Ch. 14:14), the protection is clearly divine, and clearly undeserved; *cf.* on 31:24.

7. The name *El-bethel*, 'The God of Beth-el', has suggested to some that Jacob conceived of God as tied to the locality or resident in the stone. While pagan analogies can be found for this, it is the Israelite and Christian analogies, of places where God has intervened, and of experiences commemorated in a phrase (*cf.* the hymn 'O God of Beth-el'), which agree with Jacob's known theology (*cf.* his prayer in 32:9ff.).

8. On *Deborah*, and her long service to the family, see on 24:59. *Allon-bacuth* means 'Oak of weeping'; *cf.* Bochim (Jdg. 2:5) from the same root.

10. With this reaffirming of the new name (and the persistence, even so, of the old one) *cf.* 'Simon . . . Peter' in both John 1:42 and Matthew 16:17,18.

11. On *God Almighty*, see on 17:1. The terms of the blessing, with the mention of *kings*, are like those of 17:6,7 to Abraham, while the *company of nations* is a prospect held out particularly to Jacob: see on 28:3.

14, 15. The actions of 28:18,19, almost exactly reproduced, now have the added content of fulfilment, as had, *e.g.*, Moses' second visit to mount Horeb-Sinai (Ex. 3:12; 19:3,4). 'New perils past, new sins forgiven' separate the two occasions, to make the second inwardly richer than the first. God's repetitions, if this is a sample, are turns of a spiral rather than a wheel.

35:16–20. The death of Rachel

16. *Ephrath*, or Bethlehem (19), is some twelve miles south of Rachel's burying-place, which 1 Samuel 10:2 locates at the Benjamite border. Some difficulty has been felt over the distance between the two places, but this verse and 48:7 both emphasize that Ephrath, for which Jacob was evidently making, was still some way ahead.

18. In the Old Testament the soul is not conceived of as a separate entity from the body, with an existence of its own (as in Greek thought), but rather as the life, which is here slipping away. *Cf.* on 2:7, end.

It was a fine gesture of faith to re-name the 'son of my sorrow' 'son of the right hand', the positive aspect of so dark an experience. The name, as usual, was an existing one, known to us from the Mari documents as that of a tribe, meaning there 'son of the south'.[1] Possibly Jacob's southward journey helped to suggest it, but 'right hand' is to be taken in its normal sense, accompanied by its propitious overtones of honour (Ps. 110:1), skill (Ps. 137:5) and soundness (Ec. 10:2).

20. The *pillar*, set up so soon after that of verse 14, witnessed to the transience and pain which are one side of existence, while its fellow commemorated the goodness and mercy which are the other side. Rachel's pillar, with such a background, has poignancy, but not the dull despair of Absalom's (2 Sa. 18:18).

35:21–22a. Reuben's unchastity
The laconic report leaves the shock of this breach in the family to be imagined; it is partnered by the scathing judgment of 49:3,4.

35:22b–26. The twelve sons of Jacob
The point of this summary is that the promise or prayer expressed in the name of Jacob's eleventh son (30:24) is now fulfilled in the birth of Benjamin, and the family stands complete. Throughout the Old Testament and the New, twelve will be the number symbolizing the whole 'Israel of God'. *Cf.* Revelation 21:12,14, the twelve tribes and the twelve apostles.

35:27–29. The death of Isaac
The reunion of Jacob and Esau at their father's deathbed closes the long story of their generation: others will now dominate the scene.

On Isaac's age, see on 12:14. On the phrase *gathered to his people*, see on 25:8.

---

[1] To us, east is mentally on our right; to those who took their bearings by facing east, the right denoted the south, as in Hebrew.

36:1-43. The descendants of Esau

The brotherhood of Esau and Jacob, living on in the nations of Edom and Israel, is never forgotten in the Old Testament. The present chapter, with its painstaking detail, is a witness to this sense of kinship, which will later come to the surface in contexts of diplomacy, law and national feeling (see, respectively, Nu. 20:14; Dt. 23:7; Ob. 10-12).

After the usual pattern in Genesis, where a new stage of the story is to be introduced, the record of the collateral branch of the family is first completed, before the main thread of events is picked up again. This chapter clears the ground for the final section of the book.

1-8. Esau and his immediate family. For the name *Edom* (1), see 25:30.

2, 3. On *Hittite*, see on 23:3; on *Hivite*, see on verse 20, below. The names of Esau's wives are evidently taken from a family record independent of 26:34 and 28:9. The present list agrees with the latter over two of the families into which Esau married (Elon's and Ishmael's), but Basemath appears now in one, now in the other, and the remaining names do not coincide. The simplest explanation is that the lists have suffered in transmission;[1] but there may also have been some alternative names (like Esau's own nickname Edom); further, Esau may have had not three wives but four, for there is no apparent point of contact between Judith (26:34) and Oholibamah. (The latter name, meaning 'tent of the high place', may have suggested to Ezekiel his allegorical names Oholah and Oholibah, in Ezk. 23:4ff.)

Anah (2) was evidently the son (RSV, after the LXX, *etc.*), not the daughter, of Zibeon: see verse 24.

6-8. This summary shows only the clinching factor that confirmed Esau's choice of mount Seir; the foregoing ten chapters fill in the story.

9-14. Esau's sons and grandsons. The conjunction of

[1] *E.g.*, the Samaritan text has Mahalath (*cf.* 28:9) for Basemath in 36:3,4,10,13,17.

the names *Eliphaz* and *Teman* in verse 11 points to Edom as the probable setting of the book of Job, where an 'Eliphaz the Temanite' is prominent. Teman recurs several times in the Old Testament as a tribe and town of Edom, and *Amalek* (12) was to be one of Israel's bitterest enemies – if this Amalek is connected with the tribe of that name.

15-19. Chiefs descended from Esau. *Chief* (RSV) is a better title than *duke* (AV, RV) for an *'allûp̄*, the head of a 'thousand' or clan.

20-30. Chiefs of the Horites. Deuteronomy 2:12 records that Esau's group dispossessed the Horites, as Israel dispossessed the Canaanites; but Esau married into a leading family, that of Anah son of Zibeon (*cf.* 2 with 24,25). Anah's family is called Hivite in verse 2, but Horite here, which indicates either that the terms overlap, or that Hivite may be, here and elsewhere, a copyist's error for Horite. The term Horites usually seems to denote the Hurrians, a non-Semitic people widely dispersed in the Ancient Near East; the Semitic names in these verses however suggest that the Horites of mount Seir were of different stock.[1] The word could mean cave-dwellers, possibly miners.[2]

24. In this intriguing note there is the ring of a family tradition. But *hot springs* (the Vulgate's translation) may or may not be the meaning of *yēmīm*, found only here. LXX makes no attempt to translate it; conjectures include 'vipers' (K-B) and, assuming a transposition of consonants, 'water' (*mayim*) (Speiser).

31-39. Kings of Edom. From the allusion to kingship in Israel (31), negative though it is, the most natural inference is that this statement or section was written in the monarchy. For the bearing of this on the date of Genesis, see Introduction, pp. 15f.

---

[1] Speiser, pp. 282f.
[2] So G. Dossin, cited by D. J. Wiseman in *NBD*, *s.v.* 'Horites'.

None of these kings is the son of his predecessor. This probably points to succession by election, although Albright suggests that kingship was transmitted through the 'distaff' side,[1] in view of the recording of three female generations in verse 39. Some scholars have conjectured that the short-lived dynasties of Northern Israel owed some of their instability to this example of non-dynastic kingship in a neighbour-state. But the indignation of King Saul over Jonathan's acquiescent attitude to David, and the fact that Saul's son Ish-bosheth partially succeeded him, weakling though he was (2 Sa.2:8-10; 3:8), indicate that kingship in Israel was counted as hereditary from the first.

40-43. A final list of chiefs. The emphasis in this section falls on the spheres of ownership and influence held by the leading Edomite families (*after their places*, 40; *according to their habitations*, 43), rather than on their relationship to one another as in the earlier part of the chapter.

IV. JOSEPH AND THE MIGRATION TO EGYPT (chapters 37-50)

It was God's intention, already revealed to Abraham (15:13-16), to bring the chosen family under foreign domination until 'the iniquity of the Amorites' should be full, and Canaan ripe for possession. So the train of events to lead Israel into Egypt is set in motion through the rivalries and predicaments of the twelve brothers, under the hand of God. The story is a *locus classicus* of providence. It also exhibits, as Stephen was to show, a human pattern that runs through the Old Testament to culminate at Calvary: the rejection of God's chosen deliverers, through the envy and unbelief of their kith and kin – yet a rejection which is finally made to play its own part in bringing about the deliverance.

The book of Genesis reaches an appropriate close at the end of Joseph's career, with the promise to Abraham clearly in process of fulfilment yet pointing on to a new intervention,

[1] *ARI*,[3] p. 206, n. 58.

and with Abraham's descendants rapidly increasing to the limits of what can be called a family. This 'book of families' ended, the sons of Israel will be found at the next stage of their history no longer even a clan, but 'a nation, great, mighty and populous'.

37:1-11. Joseph alienates his family

Like Isaac and Jacob before him, Joseph is introduced as a specially chosen member of his family. This divine election is one of the themes of Genesis (*cf.* Rom. 9:11ff.), and God's design is seen to be no more thwarted by the indiscretion of its allies (here Israel and Joseph) than by the malice of its opponents. The account of the dreams, coming at the outset, makes God, not Joseph, the 'hero' of the story: it is not a tale of human success but of divine sovereignty.

1. After the parenthetical chapter on Esau and the Edomites, verse 1 takes up the thread from chapter 35, leading to the section-heading in 2a (on which see comment at 2:4a).

2. The phrase *he was a lad with* . . . (RV, RSV) probably uses *lad* in its sense of servant or helper (so, *e.g.*, Delitzsch, Speiser), since his age has already been mentioned. The note then contributes something to the sense: *i.e.* he was with his ten elder brothers, but assigned particularly to the four who were sons of the secondary wives. Joseph's *evil report* of his brothers must not be judged by the criterion of group solidarity. The narrative, as usual, makes no comment; it leaves it at least presumable that Joseph's first duty was to his father: *cf.* the obligation to testify in Leviticus 5:1.

3. Israel had learnt nothing from his early experience of favouritism. It would bear an even heavier crop of hatred and deceit than it had yielded in his own youth. Whether the mark of favour was *a coat of many colours* (AV, RV), *a long robe with sleeves*, or a ceremonial robe with ornaments,[1] it was ostentatious and provocative. A garment so named in 2 Samuel 13:18 was royal apparel.

4ff. Not only was new fuel making the blaze continually

---

[1] So Speiser, *in loc.*, from an item in a cuneiform text listed in *JNES*, 8, 1949, p. 177.

hotter against Joseph in the four stages of 2,4,8 and 11, but the
fire was also spreading. In 2b only four of the brothers seem to
have been involved; in 4 it was the whole group: in 10 the
father's rebuke, moderate though it was, completed the boy's
isolation, leaving him apparently at odds with his entire
world. But see 11b, a fact hidden from Joseph.

10. On the expression, *thy mother*, the only convenient
designation of Leah, see on 37:35 ('daughters'); *cf.* Luke 2:48
('thy father'). It is unrealistic to make it imply that Rachel
was still alive.

11. The two attitudes in this verse are those that always
divide people in their reactions to news from God. The
brothers' scepticism was emotional and hasty; the father's
open mind was the product of some humility. Israel had
learnt by now, as his sons had not, to allow for God's hand in
affairs, and for His right of choice among men.

37:12-24. Joseph at his brothers' mercy
The scene of the conspiracy, a day's journey on from Shechem,
was suitably remote from Hebron. Everything, from the ill-
conceived errand to the chance meeting with the stranger,
combined to deliver Joseph into his brothers' hands. Yet it
would turn out that God had been as watchful in His hidden-
ness as in any miracle. The two extremes of His methods meet
in fact at Dothan, for it was here, where Joseph cried in vain
(42:21), that Elisha would find himself visibly encircled by
God's chariots (2 Ki. 6:13-17).

17. Archaeologists have drawn attention to the known
antiquity of *Dothan* and the other towns mentioned in these
records, and to the sparse population of the countryside which
made it possible in patriarchal times (but less so in later
centuries) for nomadic shepherds to roam the central hills
of Palestine.[1]

19. RVmg's 'master of dreams' over-translates a common
Hebrew way of denoting a characteristic (*e.g.*, greedy,
Pr. 23:2; wrathful, Na. 1:2, *etc.*). *This dreamer* is exactly right.

21, 22. Verse 21 summarizes what 22 describes (precisely

[1] *Cf.* J. Bright, *A History of Israel* (S.C.M., 1960), p. 74.

as 5 summarizes 6, as Delitzsch points out). If Reuben's intention only half succeeded, it was still true that he delivered Joseph.

Reuben had every cause, in addition to his natural temperament (*cf.* note on 34:25ff., end), to hesitate over the plot. *Blood*, especially a brother's (4:10; 9:5b), was sacrosanct, and he as eldest of the family would be chiefly answerable for it. Also he was already out of his father's favour (35:22). What he did with Joseph could either ruin him or reinstate him.

Quite without textual support, most modern commentators[1] propose altering 'Reuben' to 'Judah' in 21, 'in view of the rest of the analysis', as Bennett puts it, *i.e.* in order to supply a variant to 22, which otherwise agrees with this verse. This remarkable expedient is discussed in the Additional Note, p. 185.

24. The absence of *water* called for comment because these pits were cisterns.

37:25–36. Joseph sold into Egypt

25. The meal is a final touch of callousness. *Cf.*, in different contexts, Proverbs 30:20; Matthew 27:35ff.

On the *Ishmaelites*, see on verse 28. Their route past Dothan from Gilead was part of the immemorial way between Damascus and the coast road to the south, and their spices were a staple trade with Egypt. For Gilead's *balm*, *cf.* Jeremiah 8:22.

26, 27. *Judah* will later develop some fine qualities (43:9; 44:33); at present nothing higher than self-interest, and in 27b a certain compunction, can be taken for granted. *Profit* is no metaphor here: it is a harshly monetary word like 'loot' or 'rake-off'. The force of the phrase *and conceal his blood* (26) is 'even if we conceal . . . ', and the concealment is perhaps thought of as twofold: from man and, by avoiding actual bloodshed, from God.

28. The alternation of the names *Ishmaelites* and *Midianites* in verses 25, 27, 28, 36 and chapter 39:1 would suggest that they were synonymous or overlapping terms, even if no other

[1] Speiser is an exception.

evidence confirmed it. It is in fact settled by Judges 8:24, which says of the Midianites 'they had golden earrings, because they were Ishmaelites'. It appears from this that 'Ishmaelite' was an inclusive term for Israel's nomadic cousins (Ishmael was the senior offshoot from Abraham), somewhat as 'Arab' embraces numerous tribes in our way of speaking, and can alternate with one of their names without awkwardness.[1] The alternation may be partly for variety and partly to record both the main point (that Joseph was sold to a people outside the covenant) and the concrete detail.

In its context the statement *they drew* . . . must refer to those who had just planned to do this thing. Only if this verse is artificially isolated from its predecessor do the Midianites become the subject. On this, see the Additional Note, p. 185.

With the *twenty pieces of silver*, *cf.* Leviticus 27:5. It was the current slave price in the early second millennium.[2]

29. Reuben's absence, so far from constituting a difficulty in the story, as some have suggested, is wholly in keeping with real life, where there is always coming and going (particularly with flocks of sheep to supervise). Obviously his plan for a rescue envisaged opportunities to detach himself from the group without arousing comment.

31. It is a masterly touch of narrative to leave Reuben's agitation answered only by the grim activity over Joseph's cloak. And there was irony in the choice of a goat (*cf.* 27:9) for the deception.

32. The coldness of the expression *thy son*'s, disdaining the personal name, is recaptured in the dialogue of Luke 15:30ff.: 'this thy son . . . ' (with the gentle correction there, 'this thy brother . . . ').

35. The plural, *daughters*, presumably includes daughters-in-law (*cf.* Ru. 1:11, to which von Rad draws attention). The disconcerting refusal of the father to be reconciled to his

[1] *Cf.* the following: 'I asked if we should find Arabs at Jabrin, and Muhammad said "We are bound to find Murra there" . . . I sincerely hoped we should find Arabs at Jabrin' (W. Thesiger, *Arabian Sands*, p. 232). For an Egyptian example (*c.* 1850 BC) of three designations in a few lines *cf.* K. A. Kitchen *NBD*, p. 657b.

[2] *Cf.* K. A. Kitchen, *NBD*, p. 1196.

loss illuminates the Gospel sayings about the attitude of
another Father to brotherly valuations (Mt. 18:6,10; *cf.* Pr.
24:11,12).

On Jacob's words *cf.* on 25:8 and 42:38.

36. The Hebrew text here has Medanites, not *Midianites*.
This may be a textual slip,[1] but since 25:2 shows the close
kinship of the two, the company could well have included
elements of both.

On the name *Potiphar*, recognizably Egyptian, see the brief
discussion in *NBD*. *Officer* is strictly 'eunuch', but the term
became a general synonym for 'courtier'. The translation
captain of the guard is debatable but probably right. The
alternative is 'chief butcher', supported by etymology (from
the verb 'to slaughter', as in 43:16; *cf.* 1 Sa. 9:23f., 'the cook'),
also by LXX and by the use of a similar title in Egyptian for
a kind of major-domo.[2] *Captain of the guard*, however, accords
with Potiphar's command of the prison (40:3f.) and is clearly
correct in 2 Kings 25:8.

Additional Note to chapter 37

It is widely held that the entire Joseph story was handed
down in different forms in the south of Israel (J) and the north
(E), the two traditions being woven together in Genesis by
a redactor of perhaps the eighth century BC and unravelled
by the literary critics of the nineteenth century AD. Since the
prestige of the theory tends to protect it from criticism, its
standard form (for the abduction and prison episodes) is
set out below, and some comments offered.

The J version is said to tell in 37:21 how Judah (not Reuben
as stated) restrains his brothers from murdering Joseph and
suggests selling him to some approaching Ishmaelites (there is
no pit episode), who re-sell him to an unnamed Egyptian
(39:1a,bβ). Through the malice of his master's wife, Joseph
is thrown into the common gaol (39:20, deleting the reference

---

[1] All the ancient versions have 'Midianites'.
[2] J. Vergote, *Joseph en Égypte* (Louvain, 1959), pp. 31-35.

to 'the king's prisoners'), where he rises to a position of trust, and meets the royal butler and baker (40:1,3b).

In E the sequence opens with Reuben persuading the brothers to consign Joseph to a pit (37:22), from which however he is stolen away by Midianites as the brothers eat their meal. The Midianites sell him to Potiphar, a high official (37:36), where he is made to wait on the royal butler and baker held prisoner in Potiphar's house (40:2,3a,4ff.). There has been no seduction episode, and Joseph is only a slave, not himself a prisoner (for 40:3b,15b are counted as intrusions from J).

a. The most glaring feature of this is the liberty it takes with the text. Reuben is deleted from 37:21 (J) and Judah substituted,[1] only in order to differ from verse 22 (E). Potiphar's name and rank are disallowed in 39:1 (J), only because it agrees with 37:36 (E). The reference to the king's prisoners is removed from 39:20 (J), only lest it should support 40:2ff. (E). The statements that Joseph was a prisoner, in 40:3b,15b; 41:14 are disallowed to E, only because they corroborate J's 39:20. Further (to anticipate), the statement that Joseph was sold and not merely stolen, in 45:4,5, will also be deleted, lest that E passage should fail to conflict with J.

Any theory that must do this to its data is confessing its own failure.

b. It assumes a quite inflexible narrative technique. Reuben's dismay at finding the pit empty (37:29) – from which the reader suddenly learns of his temporary absence – is thought a discrepancy, not because his absence was inconceivable but because it was unreported. This is to impose an unduly plodding approach on any author. It is a quibble, again, to treat Joseph's word 'stolen', in 40:15, as contrary to the buying and selling *motif*, as if the sale had been an honest one. Indeed, Deuteronomy 24:7 makes it clear (if it needs saying at all) that kidnapping with a view to sale is stealing of a particularly heinous kind.

c. It underestimates the complexity of real events. To return

---

[1] But Speiser dissents from this (*Genesis*, p. 291).

to Reuben, a fiction writer may keep ten brothers and their flocks compactly together between one incident and the next, with no straying sheep or calls of nature to detach one or another from the group. By contrast, there is the untidiness of actuality in the circumstance that Reuben had somehow missed the transaction with the traders. It is truth, not fiction, that has these loose ends. Again, the presence of more than one cause of the envy against Joseph, so far from being 'another safe clue' to a double narrative,[1] is a most natural phenomenon – as von Rad, almost alone of the moderns, points out.[2]

d. It assumes that where a thing is said twice it is said by two writers. This is an uneconomical hypothesis. *E.g.*, in 37:5ff., the summary statement of 37:5 and the details of 6–8 first relate the new event to what has gone before, and then unfold it. This is an intelligible and even admirable method: it needs no apparatus of two authors and an editor to account for it. The same may be said in relation to verses 13,14; to verses 18,19f.; to verses 21,22; and so on. It is an expansion of the familiar form: 'he answered and said', 'he lifted up his eyes and looked', *etc.* Yet this school of thought seldom pauses to consider so simple a possibility.

e. Underlying all the foregoing is the unspoken assumption that a harmonizing approach to Scripture is somehow dishonest. So the simple answer to the Ishmaelite-Midianite problem given in Judges 8:24 is passed over almost invariably in silence, and where the text of Genesis explicitly supports the unity of the story it is the text, not the theory, that is amended, as the references in section *a.* and the further examples in the Additional Note to chapter 42 make clear. This may spring from a quixotic desire to face the worst, but it is scarcely an adequate attitude. A theory which insists on altering its primary datum the text, repeatedly, drastically and without the support of a single ancient version, may be well intentioned; it can hardly be true.

[1] Skinner, p. 443.
[2] But von Rad then attributes this to the 'preliterary growth of the material', not to the actual shape of events (*Genesis*, p. 354).

38:1-30. Judah and his family succession

As a piece of family history this chapter is important in settling the seniority within the tribe of Judah, and it contributes to the royal genealogy in Matthew 1:3; Luke 3:33. As a rude interruption of the Joseph story it serves other purposes as well. It creates suspense for the reader, with Joseph's future in the balance; it puts the faith and chastity of Joseph, soon to be described, in a context which sets off their rarity; and it fills out the portrait of the effective leader among the ten brothers. There is no good reason for the assertion, more often made than supported, that the actors in this story are personifications of clans. The narrative (like that of chapter 34) has a coherence and a precision of detail which argue strongly for the actuality of its persons and events.

The sins and stratagems of these individuals, however, are of family import, and the story can only be appreciated in these terms. The future hangs on their choices: the plot revolves round Tamar's right to be the mother of Judah's heir, and her successive frustrations and eventual victory are its dominant concern. On a higher plane the book of Ruth treats a variant of this theme; and both times the Davidic, Messianic lineage was involved, all unknown, in the issue.

1-11. Judah's lineage in jeopardy. In verses 1,2 there is a haphazardness in Judah's steps towards marriage, similar to Samson's (Jdg. 14:1ff.), and his Canaanite wife is left unnamed, like the latter's Philistine one: she is still known merely as Shua's daughter at the end of her story (12). Adullam, later to be famous for David's cave, was in the territory south or south-west of Jerusalem allotted after the conquest to Judah's tribe (*cf.* 2 Ch. 11:5,7).

7. The unspecified wickedness of Er, like the specific sin of Onan (*cf.* 9,10) is recorded for its contribution to the succession crisis. At the same time, it emphasizes the steep moral decline in the chosen family, which only the outstanding piety of Joseph would arrest for a while. This tendency to an immediate plunge from grace, whenever faith is no longer an active force, is evident more than once in Genesis; but the pattern is most explicitly worked out in the book of Judges.

8–10. The fact that a single Hebrew word suffices for the phrase *perform the duty of a brother-in-law* (RSV) would confirm that this was a standard practice, even if there were no record of the law in Deuteronomy 25:5ff. Each of the three Old Testament references to this regulation (*cf.* Ru. 4:5f.) shows that it could be most unwelcome, chiefly through the very fact that the donor himself set great store on family inheritance – but his own. The enormity of Onan's sin is in its studied outrage against the family, against his brother's widow and against his own body. The standard English versions fail to make clear that this was his persistent practice. *When* (9) should be translated 'whenever'.

11. Judah's insincerity would eventually come out, as postponement followed postponement (14b,26), for he had clearly decided that Tamar was ill-omened, and had no intention of hazarding his last remaining son – or of facing Tamar's wrath by saying so.

12–26. Tamar's stratagem. Tamar was wholly concerned with her right as matriarch of Judah's eldest line. The last phrase of verse 24, 'let her be burnt', shows the risk she accepted; Judah's admission in verse 26 recognizes the injustice which her desperate step defeated. She shows something of the indomitable spirit of an Esther, a Jael or a Rizpah; but the text, true to its practice, makes no comment on the morality of her act. Indirectly, however, its setting, within the story of Joseph, brings it into telling contrast with the faith that could be displayed, and vindicated, in far worse straits than hers.

12ff. Sheep-shearing was a festive time (*cf.* 1 Sa. 25:4,11,36), when sexual temptation would be sharpened by the Canaanite cult, which encouraged ritual fornication as fertility magic. The word for *harlot* in verses 21,22 suggests that Tamar posed as a cult-prostitute, perhaps to make doubly sure of her victim.[1] The *veil* of verse 14 seems to confirm this, since (if Assyrian

[1] M. C. Astour, *JBL*, LXXXV, 1966, pp. 185–196. See esp. pp. 192f.; elsewhere the argument tends to part company with the data.

law is any guide) no prostitute except a (married) cultic one might wear it.[1]

Such was the world into which Judah had married. The prophets (*e.g.* Ho. 4:14) report its corrupting power over Israel for generations to come.

18. The *cord* (RV, RSV) makes it clear that the *signet* was not a ring but a seal (probably cylindrical) hung round the neck, which was part of the dress of any man of substance. The *staff*, often carved, was equally distinctive of its owner: *cf.* verse 25.

24. We need not suspect conscious hypocrisy in Judah's outburst, so much as the deeper dishonesty of having one standard for men and another for women. Hosea 4:14 (RSV), cited above, is one of the earliest explicit attacks on this.

27–30. The twin sons of Tamar. The pre-natal struggle, not unlike that of Jacob and Esau (25:22–26), brings a violent chapter to a fitting end, and appropriately launches the tribe of Judah on its career. The scarlet thread is the kind of detail which a family remembers and transmits; but Perez ('breaking out') is reckoned the firstborn in the genealogies, and it was his line that led to David (*cf.* Ru. 4:18ff.) and so to Christ.

39:1–23. Joseph under test

The symmetry of this chapter, in which the serene opening (1–6) is matched, point for point, at a new level at the close (19–23) despite all that intervenes, perfectly expresses God's quiet control and the man of faith's quiet victory. The good seed is buried deeper, still to push upward; the servant, faithful in a little, trains for authority in much.

On the Egyptian *Tale of the Two Brothers*, see the Additional Note to this chapter, p. 192.

1–6. Joseph as trusted slave. In verse 1, the opening clause is more strictly 'Now Joseph had been . . .'; it resumes the story after the digression of chapter 38.

For Potiphar's name and titles, see on 37:36; and on the

[1] Verse 15, however, uses the common word for harlot, and Speiser may be right in suggesting that it was Judah's friend who introduced the religious term, 'in order to place the affair on a higher social level'.

evidence of this verse for the unity of the narrative, see Additional Note to chapter 37, p. 185.

2. RSV is best, with *he became a successful man*; the key word recurs in verse 3, which could be rendered '. . . made . . . successful'. The slightly complacent ring of the expression in English is no part of it: it is the word used for, *e.g.*, the outcome of Eliezer's mission in 24:21,40, and of the Servant's suffering in Isaiah 53:10; it speaks of achievement rather than status.

3-6. The way verse 3 picks up verse 2 and carries it a step further (from success, to success observed) is followed again in verses 4 and 5, where the servant's promotion becomes the master's blessing; and the whole progression is crowned by verse 6, its final pinnacle preparing the reader for the attack which it almost invites.

7-18. Joseph's temptation. Joseph's reasons for refusal (8,9) were those that another man might have given for yielding, so neutral is the force of circumstances. His freedom from supervision and his rapid promotion, which have corrupted other stewards (*cf.* Is. 22:15–25; Lk. 16:1ff.), and his realization that one realm only (9) was barred to him (which others, from Eve onwards, have construed as a frustration) were all arguments to him for loyalty. By giving the proposition its right name of *wickedness* (9) he made truth his ally, and by relating all to God (9c) he rooted his loyalty to his master deep enough to hold.

10. The constant pressure, *day after day* (RSV), was profoundly searching: it was this that would find out Samson twice in his career (Jdg. 14:17; 16:16). *Cf.* by contrast the persistence in another kind of pressure enjoined in Hebrews 3:13. Further, the attack had flexibility: if Joseph could not be stormed he might be coaxed, for a refusal to be so much as *with her* (10c) could look quite unreasonable. In declining to be drawn he shows the realistic wisdom of, *e.g.*, Proverbs 5:8 ('Remove thy way far from her . . .') and of the Lord's Prayer; *cf.* Hezekiah's advice to his citizens in 2 Kings 18:36.

11, 12. Resisted to the end, the temptation could run its full course and display all its strategy: the first approach, flattering and startling (7); the long attrition, for ever re-opening the closed question (10); now the final ambush, where all is lost or won in a moment (12). Joseph's flight, unlike a coward's, saved his honour at the cost of his prospects; the New Testament recommends it (2 Tim. 2:22; 2 Pet. 1:4).

14. The note of scorn here and in verse 17 in speaking of *a Hebrew* chimes in with the social overtones of the name, as far as they are known. See on 10:24. By the side-thrust at her husband in the aggrieved *See, he has brought among us . . .* (RSV), Potiphar's wife gave colour to her pose as victim, and pressure on her husband to act.

19-23. Joseph as trusted prisoner. On the symmetry of these verses with verses 1-6, see the opening comments to the chapter. Joseph's humiliation, severe enough before, is re-enacted at a deeper level, yet not too deep for God.

19, 20. Death was the only penalty Joseph could reasonably expect. His reprieve presumably owed much to the respect he had won; and Potiphar's mingled wrath and restraint may reflect a faint misgiving about the full accuracy of the charge. But the unfolding story makes it obvious that God who had brought him here was preserving him for his task.

An unusual word, *sōhar*, found only in these chapters, is used for *prison*: the Hebrew root suggests a round structure and therefore perhaps a fortress, which is the term used by LXX. Prisoners are known to have been sent to such defence posts and put to forced labour. Alternatively the word may transliterate an Egyptian name, but no convincing identificacation has yet been made.[1]

This chapter agrees with chapter 40 in using this rare term for prison (40:3,5), in representing Joseph as a prisoner (*cf.* 40:3c,15) and in noting that *the king's prisoners* were also confined here. Those who set the two chapters against each other (see Additional Note, p. 185) do so in the teeth of this evidence, which is textually unchallenged apart from the Syriac's omission of *sōhar* in 40:3 (not 5).

21. For the Lord's presence and its effects, *cf.* verses 2-4a.

[1] See Vergote, pp. 25-28.

But the memory preserved in Psalm 105:18 corrects any idea that Joseph had a gentle reception: 'His feet they hurt with fetters; he was laid in chains of iron.'

22, 23. *Cf.* verses 4b–6, and 41:40,44: Joseph's outstanding abilities and integrity, crowned with the touch of God, were constant at every level: as prisoner and as governor he was simply the same man.

Additional Note to chapter 39

The Tale of the Two Brothers, an Egyptian fantasy known from a manuscript of the late thirteenth century BC, has often been compared with the story of this chapter and even credited with inspiring it. It opens with the attempted seduction of a youth by his brother's wife, who avenges her failure by accusing him of rape. The lad escapes death at his brother's hands by a spectacular miracle, and his further adventures, which include his transformation into a bull and into a pair of trees, are a farrago of magical wonders. Certainly the seduction, the refusal and the slander are points of distinct resemblance; but as J. M. Plumley remarks, 'it would require much greater similarity of detail . . . to justify the oft-made suggestion that the Egyptian story is the origin of the incident described in Genesis'.[1] Plumley points out further that the situation is not an altogether unique one, as the literature of other peoples makes plain.

40:1–23. The dreams of the butler and baker

1. *Offended* is misleading: the Hebrew has 'offended against'. *I.e.*, this verse shows that there were grounds for the displeasure of verse 2.

Chief *butler* (cupbearer) and *baker* were valued officials: *cf.* in a later day Nehemiah, who as cupbearer to Artaxerxes was a man of influence and much ability. See also on verses 11 and 17.

3. *Joseph was confined* (RSV): only by refusing this evidence

[1] *DOTT*, p. 168. The full text of the Tale is given in A. Erman, *The Literature of the Ancient Egyptians* (Methuen, 1927), pp. 150–161.

and that of verse 15 can it be maintained that this chapter portrays a Joseph who was not a prisoner. See Additional Note, p. 185.

4. It is not surprising that arrangements were made for these notable arrivals by *the captain of the guard* himself[1] (presumably still Potiphar, who would remember Joseph's reliability), not by his subordinate the 'keeper of the prison',[2] whose dealings with Joseph were described in 39:21ff. So Joseph, having at last gained higher ground, was at the bottom again, a servant of prisoners.[3] This, however, rather than his former promotion, was to prove the way forward.

6-8. Joseph's quick concern brings out another aspect of him besides efficiency and integrity; and his immediate reference to God rings true: it was the habit of his mind (*cf.* 39:9; 41:16,51,52; 45:8; *etc.*). On the dreamers' part, the conviction that the dreams had a meaning is equally in character: it was common belief in Egypt that they were predictive, and a body of writings grew up on the art of interpreting them.

11. As J. Vergote points out,[4] the dream-actions may symbolize rather than describe the cupbearer's duties, but they possibly throw light on the epithet 'clean of hands' which sometimes went with his title. His duties included opening and tasting the wine; *i.e.* he was responsible for the quality of what he presented.

13. For the expressive metaphor of lifting the head of one who is down, *cf.* 2 Kings 25:27 and, with another Hebrew verb, Psalms 3:3; 27:6. But see on verse 19.

15. On the significance of *stolen*, and *put me into the dungeon,* see Additional Note to chapter 37.

---

[1] For the cushioning effect of even the hint of money or position, *cf.* Acts 23:18,19; 24:23,26.

[2] On the grades of prison staff see K. A. Kitchen, 'A Recently Published Egyptian Papyrus and its bearing on the Joseph Story' in *Tyndale House Bulletin* No. 2 (Winter 1956-7), pp. 1, 2.

[3] It is curious that this new vicissitude, so characteristic of the abrupt reversals in an authoritarian régime, is commonly taken to be in conflict with 39:22f., despite the statement that it took place 'after these things' (40:1).

[4] *Op. cit.,* p. 36.

16. A Hebrew word *ḥōrî*, found only here, accounts for the variant translations. One Arabic root similar to it suggests whiteness (*i.e.*, of the baskets or their contents); another, favoured by Speiser, wickerwork.

17. J. Vergote[1] draws attention to the thirty-eight varieties of cake and fifty-seven of bread listed in the Erman-Grapow *Wörterbuch der ägyptischen Sprache*, which lend body to the phrase *all manner of bakemeats* (AV, RV) and give an idea of the professional standards of this department.

19. For the cryptic, ambiguous opening of this oracle of destiny, *cf.* 27:39,40 and note: it seems to have been an accepted style. The apparent cruelty of the phrase, however, as it appears in cold print, raising hopes only to dash them, may be illusory. There was nothing to prevent the sadness of the news from being immediately apparent in the speaker's manner and tone.

41:1–45. Pharaoh's dreams and Joseph's elevation to office

1, 2. RSV rightly specifies *the Nile*, as the Hebrew makes clear. We may notice in passing the Egyptian colouring of the dream, with the cows coming up out of the river (where, as Vergote points out, they like to stand almost submerged, at refuge from the heat and flies) for pasture in the *reed-grass* (RV, RSV) or papyrus-beds. The Hebrew *'āḥû*, for the latter, is a loan-word from Egypt;[2] it recurs in Job 8:11 (*cf.* LXX of Is. 19:7 and of Ecclus. 40:16).

6. *The east wind* is almost a technical term for the desert wind, whether its quarter is strictly east or not. This scorching blast, in Palestine the sirocco, and in Egypt the khamsîn, can be devastating to crops (*cf.* Ezk. 17:10; Ho. 13:15f.).[3]

8. *Magicians* is another Egyptian-based word, *ḥarṭummîm*:

---

[1] *Op. cit.*, p. 37.

[2] See Vergote, pp. 59–66. It seems unnecessary, and precarious, to try to establish more subtle connections with Egyptian thought by exploring the ideas connected with the cow. Actual cattle and corn, in the two dreams, register the conditions of plenty or famine vividly enough.

[3] *Cf.* D. Baly, *The Geography of the Bible* (Lutterworth, 1957), pp. 67–70;

it appears to be part of a composite title for those who were expert in handling the ritual books of priestcraft and magic.[1] They appear in Exodus 7:11 where spells were needed; here they would be consulting the considerable literature on dreams (*cf.* on 40:6–8).

13. The Hebrew way of putting things, reproduced in AV, RV, *me he restored . . . him he hanged*, is worth noting for its bearing on other biblical sayings in which a declaration may have the sound of a deed (*e.g.* Jn. 20:23: '. . . ye forgive . . . , . . . ye retain . . .').

14. The words *out of the dungeon* are yet another sign of the unity of the narrative; see Additional Note to chapter 37.

Joseph's shaving is a further detail of Egyptian as against Semitic etiquette (*e.g.* Je. 41:5).

15, 16. While Pharaoh naturally thought of expertise in the 'science' of dreams, Joseph almost explosively disavowed this whole approach (the exclamation, *It is not in me*, is a single word). With hasty brevity he points from himself to *God* (the position in the sentence makes it emphatic) as sole revealer, disposer and benefactor, his abruptness contrasting with the polished speech of Daniel to the same effect (Dn. 2:27–30). One can sense, perhaps, the agitation which has not yet subsided after the sudden turn of events.

19ff. The extra touch of description in verse 19b makes the recital more than a repetition, and only now do we learn the startling lack of change in the thin cattle (21), which will be interpreted in verse 31.

25ff. The reiteration of the phrase, *What God is about to do . . .*, in verse 28, and the emphasis in verse 32 on its certainty and imminence, are calls to action, not resignation – exactly as in the preaching of the prophets. The principle is discussed in Jeremiah 18:7–10. But see further, on 33ff.

33ff. It is important to note that the impending famine, unlike many of the disasters foretold in the Old Testament, is

---

G. A. Smith, *The Historical Geography of the Holy Land*[13] (Hodder and Stoughton, 1907), pp. 67–69.
[1] *Cf.* Vergote, pp. 66–73.

not a judgment. It is one of life's irregularities, and Joseph points out that a wise manager will insure against them, taking extra measures if he can see extra hazards. The principle of predictive prophecy holds good (see on 25ff., above): God looks for an active response. To a threat of judgment this will be repentance: to a friendly warning (*cf.* Je. 38:17ff.; Mt. 24:15ff.), realistic precautions.

38, 39. *The Spirit of God* would be a phrase coloured by polytheism for Pharaoh, who was not the last man in Scripture to speak more wisely than he knew (*cf.* Jn. 11:49–52). His words in the two verses show that Joseph's opening protest (16) had made its mark.

40. On the significance of *over my house*, see comment and footnote on 42. While the general sense of the second clause is clear, the expression translated *be ruled* or (RSV) *order themselves* has given difficulty. RVmg's second alternative, 'do homage', is nearest the Hebrew, which is literally 'kiss'. This agrees well with the metaphor either of a homage-kiss, which was a common enthronement custom, or of kissing the dust (prostrating oneself), which corresponds to an Egyptian idiom.[1] The term *'al pîkā* (lit. 'on your mouth') means 'on your command', as in 45:21.

42. Joseph's office as 'over the house' and second only to Pharaoh (40) is generally held to be that of vizier.[2] The *signet ring* carried the king's authority, although this was delegated to more than one high officer (see footnote), and the *fine linen* (an Egyptian word) was court dress. A *gold chain* (or collar) was a customary mark of royal appreciation from

[1] Vergote, p. 97. *Cf.*, for the homage kiss, Ps. 2:12; and for prostration, Ps. 72:9.
[2] This is disputed, however, by W. A. Ward, *JSS*, V, 1960, pp. 144–150, who argues that Joseph's pre-eminence was departmental, as Overseer of the Granaries of Upper and Lower Egypt, and steward of the crown lands, directly under the king. While he was, on this view, 'one of the most important officials of the Egyptian government' and among the *élite* of the nobility, he would not be the only holder of the royal seal or the only bearer of the title 'Father of God' (*i.e.* of Pharaoh) implied in 45:8. Against this view, see on verse 43. From another angle, J. M. A. Janssen, *Ex Oriente Lux*, XIV, 1955–6, pp. 66ff., notes the absence of Joseph's name from the viziers known to us; but J. Vergote points out that few such names survive from the Hyksos period (p. 105).

a very early period: it was commonly a reward for past
services, but it is shown also as a detail in a vizier's investiture
in the reign of Sethos I (*c.* 1300). The value of the latter in-
scription (a tomb painting)[1] for throwing light on Joseph's
story, however, is disputable, since the occasion was some four
hundred years later.

43. While Joseph's other honours could be read as marks of
a merely departmental primacy (see footnote to verse 42), the
second chariot clearly proclaims him the next after Pharaoh:
first citizen, or vizier, of the whole land. *Bow the knee* is confirmed as the most likely meaning of the command *'aḇrēḵ,*
which seems to be an adapted form of a Semitic root, known to
have been borrowed in Egyptian. It reflects an etiquette
depicted in Egyptian drawings. (For other suggestions see
NBD, p. 7, *s.v.* 'abrech', and reference there.)

45. The practice of giving foreigners an Egyptian name is
very well attested, but no agreement exists on the meaning of
Zaphenath-paneah. Egyptian-based interpretations have been
offered as diverse as 'God has spoken and he lives' (G.
Steindorff), 'He who knows things' (J. Vergote), and '(Joseph),
who is called 'Iṗ'ankh' (K. A. Kitchen).[2]

Asenath and *Potiphera* are recognizably Egyptian names,
meaning respectively 'She belongs (or, May she belong) to
Neith' (a goddess), and 'He whom Re has given'. Re was the
sun god, worshipped at *On*, a city which the Greeks later called
Heliopolis, city of the sun.

41:46-57. Joseph begins his administration

46. The note of Joseph's age punctuates a story which
began when he was seventeen (37:2) and will reach its climax
in another nine years' time (45:6), more than twenty years
after the first breach with his brothers. It is comparable with
the length of time for Abraham between promise and fulfilment
(12:4; 21:5), and for Jacob in the service of Laban (31:41).
Each of these delays was fruitful, but no two were alike in
form or purpose.

[1] Reproduced in *NBD*, article 'Joseph'.
[2] These are discussed in Vergote, pp. 141-146, and in *NBD*, p. 1353.

The note that Joseph *went throughout all the land of Egypt*, almost repeating 45c, emphasizes the personal energy of his administration; was this enhanced by the joy of release?

51, 52. These names, which are Hebrew, not Egyptian, tally with the two sides of Joseph's experience. With *Manasseh* there were still the mixed feelings that go with the closing of a chapter in life, voiced in the two phrases of 51b. With *Ephraim* there was a more buoyant sense of fulfilment, perhaps owing something to the phenomenal fruitfulness of the land at this moment (*cf.* verse 47), according to the promise.

55. There may be an intended echo of this story of the great provider, in John's record of the similar words ('Whatsoever he saith unto you, do it', Jn. 2:5) which made way for the miracle at Cana. What Joseph was to the men of his day (John may imply), this and more would Jesus be to the world.

56, 57. How severe a famine could be in Egypt, which is a thin fertile strip between deserts, is twice indicated by records of its inhabitants resorting to cannibalism.[1] But because Palestine was watered by rainfall and Egypt by the Nile, the harvest seldom failed simultaneously in both (*cf.* 12:10; 26:1,2). This time it was only the exertions of one man that averted a multiple disaster.

42:1–38. Joseph's brothers seek corn in Egypt

1–5. Jacob sends all but Benjamin. The touch of asperity in Jacob's words shows an undiminished firmness of grip, reminiscent of his brisk advice to the shepherds of Haran many years before (29:7); and his refusal to part with Benjamin reveals plainly enough what he had come to suspect. His firm decision and non-committal words (4b)[2] exactly reflect the state of his knowledge: about Joseph's fate not a fact had come to light; about the brothers' guilt little doubt remained. Under a father's eye their actual crimes might be covered up, but not their character.

5. On the use of the name *Israel* in this passage, see on 45:21.

[1] J. Vandier, *La Famine dans L'Égypte Ancienne* (Cairo, 1936), pp. 8f., 14f.

[2] Or thoughts (*cf.* RSV): the expression *he said* (AV, RV) can be used of words spoken or unspoken.

6-17. The first encounter with Joseph. At first sight the rough handling which now dominates the scene to the end of chapter 44 has the look of vengefulness. Nothing could be more natural, but nothing further from the truth. Behind the harsh pose there was warm affection (42:24, *etc.*), and after the ordeal overwhelming kindness. Even the threats were tempered with mercy (*cf.* 42:16-19; 44:9,10), and the shocks that were administered took the form of embarrassments rather than blows. A vindictive Joseph could have dismayed his brothers with worthless sackloads, or tantalized them at his feast as they had tantalized him (37:24,25); his enigmatic gifts were a kinder and more searching test. Just how well-judged was his policy can be seen in the growth of quite new attitudes in the brothers, as the alternating sun and frost broke them open to God.

6. *Governor* is a rather strong Hebrew word, emphasizing Joseph's complete mastery.

9. The memory of *the dreams* was more than a confirmation: the present scene fell short of their full promise, and perhaps moved Joseph to press for the presence of the whole family, which he now proceeded to do. *To see the nakedness of the land* (AV, RV) was a forceful way of saying 'to pry into all our private affairs'.

18-38. Simeon is left as hostage. The three days together in prison were ample proof of the governor's power; in the light of this, his concern for their families and his confessed motivation, *I fear God*, could not fail to be thought-provoking (18-20). The new decision may have been an actual change of mind; either way, it brings out the wholesome effect of godliness on government. The converse is shown in Psalm 14:1,4.

21. The victim's cries, *when he besought us*, or 'begged mercy of us', are not heard in chapter 37, but only here, ringing again in the ears that had been closed to them before. A taste of retribution (*distress . . . this distress*) was awaking feelings which a brother's and father's tears had left totally untouched.

24. The hostage was needed to ensure their return, and Simeon, eldest after Reuben, was the obvious choice.

25. Whether Joseph meant the money to be found at the first halt, or not till the homecoming (if the *provision for the way* was a separate package), the event proved more effective than either, with its initial shock repeated still more forcibly at home in the presence of Jacob.[1]

The sense of guilt, already aroused (21), made the group quick to see the hand of God in the governor's action. Consequently their question, *What is this that God has done to us?* (28), is, as far as it goes, a model of fruitful reaction to trouble (*cf.*, *e.g.*, the attitude of Ps. 60), while Jacob can see no farther than the trouble itself. His emphasis in verse 36 is understandably but instructively self-orientated: '*Me* have ye bereaved . . . : upon (or against) *me* is all this' (so runs the Hebrew), and he is locked in the suicidally defensive posture of verse 38 and of 43:1–10.

37. On the relation of Reuben's offer to that of Judah (43:8ff.), see Additional Note, below.

38. RSV's *Sheol*[2] is more accurate than *the grave* (AV, RV), and conveys more of the essence of this foreboding, which may have included the idea of finding no rest in death. The words left a deep impression: *cf.* 44:29,31,34.

Additional Note to chapter 42

The school of thought which finds two traditions behind the Joseph story[3] holds that from chapter 39 onwards they are no longer intertwined but alternating. The editor is thought to have followed the J tradition in 39, E in 40–42 (except the last verse), J in 43,44 (plus 42:38), and E again in 45–46:5, dropping in a phrase, however, from time to time, from one account to the other.

This analysis has to defy its usual linguistic criteria, since from chapter 40 to the end of Genesis the name Yahweh

[1] In 43:21 the brothers understandably compress the story for the steward, to whom the two stages of the discovery would be a digression.
[2] On this term, see *NBD*, *s.v.* 'Hell' 1; R. Martin-Achard, *From Death to Life*, pp. 36–47; A. Heidel, *The Gilgamesh Epic and Old Testament Parallels*, pp. 137–223.
[3] See Additional Note to chapter 37, p. 184.

appears only once (49:18), and the passages here ascribed to J use the E term Elohim (and indeed the P term (El) Shaddai in 43:14; 49:25). The names Jacob and Israel, another criterion, also cut across the analysis repeatedly in chapters 42–46.[1] The approach is therefore more subjective, starting from the conviction that the two traditions postulated for chapter 37 will have continued, leaving traces of themselves in duplicates and variants, while the editor will have done his best to blend them together.

Thus, if the broad analysis gives E the beginning of the Simeon incident, any references to it in J are ruled out of order, and J's consequent 'silence'[2] on the subject (see further, below) is treated as an important disagreement. Or, if Judah and his brothers tell Israel in 43:3ff. (*cf.* 44:19) that their family history was only elicited by cross-questioning, this is treated as incompatible with 42:7ff., where the information seems to be volunteered in reply to a charge of espionage. The elementary answer, that these passages give complementary extracts from the interview, is not even considered: it is assumed that we cannot know what *happened*, only what stories lay before the pentateuchal editor.[3] The same treatment is given to the corn-money episode. That only one man should notice his money when the sacks were broached on the journey is hardly a difficulty, and that the brothers should compress their account of the two stages of discovery (43:21) is no more than natural. But an issue is made of it. In J all the money must have come to light on the journey, and in E all at home; the one man's discovery must therefore be an opening fragment of J, robbed of its conclusion and inserted into E to mediate between the two incompatibles.[4]

[1] Passages given to E have Jacob eight times and Israel five times; those given to J have Israel three times and Jacob once.

[2] *Cf. e.g.*, von Rad, p. 377: 'ch. 43:1ff. . . . knows nothing at all of a detention of Simeon' – this, in spite of 43:14,23!

[3] 'The various patriarchal narratives . . . can no longer be regarded as trustworthy reports which come from these men's actual lives' (G. von Rad, *Old Testament Theology*, II (Oliver and Boyd, 1965), p. 424). *Cf.* Skinner, p. 473: 'The writers tax their inventiveness to the utmost in retarding the *dénouement* of the plot.'

[4] The allegedly J word for 'sack', *'amtaḥaṭ*, occurs in this 'fragment'

The two chief discrepancies, however, are detected in the parts played by Simeon, Reuben and Judah.

a. Simeon. As remarked above, Simeon is said to appear only in E (42:19,24ff.). In J's family conclave of 43:1–14, hunger rather than the hostage is allegedly under discussion, and Benjamin, not Simeon, is first in Israel's thoughts.

But this is artificial. The difficulty arises precisely because chapter 43 has been lifted from its context. In the unmutilated story the brothers had expected to return for Simeon at once, with Benjamin, but had been forbidden (42:33–38). Only the renewed pressure of famine had reopened the question (43:1ff.). This sequence is not only coherent: it exactly fits the twin realities of Jacob's fixation and the famine's persistence.

The difficulty is artificial in a further sense. According to 43:14 Simeon *was* mentioned in the discussion, and this chapter can only be said to 'know nothing of him' by silencing this witness (on no textual evidence) and then proceeding to silence the companion witness of verse 23. For, to the embarrassment of the theory, the end of Simeon's story is embedded in the wrong stratum. Imprisoned in E, he manages to be released in J (43:23) – he was always undisciplined – and once again a harmonizing gloss has to be diagnosed, to adjust the text to the theory.

b. Reuben and Judah. By the analysis, E is said to make Reuben (42:37) Benjamin's surety, while J gives the role to Judah (43:8–10); so the northern source E espouses the northern tribe, and the southern source the southerner. But Reuben, by this theory, does not only make the offer: he is *accepted*, by the silence of E, just as Judah is accepted in J. Instead of two stages, then, there are two rival stories.

If it is wondered what has become of Jacob's rebuff to Reuben (42:38), the answer is that the analysis amputates it,[1] grafting it on to the next chapter (after 43:2) so as to leave Reuben unanswered and by implication accepted. Once again

---

42:27,28. But so does the E word, *šaq*; so too the E word for God, Elohim. Linguistically the balance is even, and the presence of the two synonyms in one verse should discourage the attempt to set one against the other.

[1] Speiser, however, dissenting (*Genesis*, p. 323).

there is no linguistic basis for the displacement; and this time it has exactly reversed the meaning.

Here again, discord is created gratuitously out of harmonious material. It was true to situation and character that Jacob should refuse the ill-timed offer of Reuben, whom in any case he distrusted (42:37,38; *cf.* 49:4), but should accept that of Judah (43:8ff.) when famine had forced his hand. It was only common sense that a different son should make the second approach, and it is consistent that these two should be the ones to rise somewhat above the rest, as in chapter 37. To break up so compelling a sequence, the evidence would have to be overwhelming.

At no point is there this weight of evidence against the narrative's integrity. The reader may well ask himself which view of the text requires the less elaborate justification or accounts more convincingly for the power and vitality of the story.

43:1–34. The second visit to Egypt

1–14. Judah guarantees Benjamin's safety. Israel's querulously negative attitude is very true to life: his scolding was an escape from the decision he dreaded and a comfort to his self-esteem. But in clutching his advantage over those who had wronged him he was jeopardizing himself and them – including his beloved Benjamin, whom he must lose in order to save (*cf.* 27:41–46). It betrays his self-absorption that he still saw the threat to Benjamin primarily in terms of himself: 'Why did you treat me so ill . . .?' (6; *cf.* 42:36).

The breaking of the deadlock is doubly instructive: the cruel pressure of the famine (*cf.* Ho. 5:15) and the warmly personal initiative of Judah were each needed to reinforce the other. So Judah now succeeded where Reuben had failed (*cf.* 42:37f., and Additional Note to that chapter).

7. On this glimpse of the interview with Joseph, see Additional Note, p. 201.

11. The *present* (*minḥâ*) was an almost indispensable courtesy in approaching a person of rank (*cf.*, *e.g.*, 1 Sa. 16:20; 17:18).

14. *God Almighty* (*'ēl šadday*) was a title specially evocative of the covenant with Abraham (17:1) and therefore of God's settled purpose for this family.

On the implications of this name, and of the allusion to Simeon, for source-criticism, see Additional Note, pp. 201ff.

15–34. Joseph's eleven guests. There may be a hint of naïvety in the brothers' fear (18) that Egypt, like some petty clan, had designs on their asses. It highlights the contrast between the tent-dwellers and their novel surroundings.

23. The steward was not confessing to having 'planted' the money, only assuring them that it had been safely received, and suggesting that the money which they found must have been from heaven – which the reader knows to be true in a sense still hidden from them.

The detention of *Simeon*, prolonged though it was by the wrangling over Benjamin, had lasted less than two years (*cf.* 45:6). On this mention of his release, see Additional Note to chapter 42.

26, 28. The repeated obeisance is another moment of fulfilment: *cf.* 42:6,9.

32. As J. Vergote points out,[1] the prejudice against eating together was probably not social (as in 46:34) but cultic, since foreigners would technically defile the food. There is abundant evidence of this belief at a later period, in Egyptian attitudes to Greeks; it resembles the Jewish refusal to eat with Gentiles.

33. The mysterious accuracy of the seating order would have its part to play in Joseph's plan, by increasing the brothers' uneasy sense of exposure to divine intervention.

34. For this special courtesy *cf.* 1 Samuel 9:24, and, paradoxically, John 13:26,27.

44:1-17. The arrest of Benjamin

Joseph's strategy, already brilliantly successful in creating the situations and tensions he required, now produces its masterstroke. Like the judgment of Solomon, the sudden threat to Benjamin was a thrust to the heart: in a moment the brothers

---

[1] *Op. cit.*, pp. 188f.

stood revealed. When the steward converted their challenge of verse 9 into a chance of freedom at Benjamin's expense, all the conditions were present for another betrayal, at a far more compelling price – their liberty – than the twenty pieces of silver they had once shared out. The response, by its unanimity (13), frankness (16) and constancy (for the offer was repeated, 17), showed how well the chastening had done its work. Judah's plea to be imprisoned for Benjamin is among the finest and most moving of all petitions (see on verses 18–34, below).

1. As the sequel shows, the *money* this time would not be incriminating, except as an additional 'good' which they appeared to be repaying with 'evil' (4) by stealing the cup. It was clear by now, after 43:23 and the subsequent feast, that the governor was set on treating them as guests – a dangerous honour from a tyrant.

5. The fact that the cup was in use for drinking would point to the folly of expecting the theft to be unnoticed, and if it were also used for divining it would be doubly precious. But as Vergote points out,[1] the phrase *whereby he certainly divineth* could be translated 'about this he would certainly have divined'. It is a small difference, but it would give added point to verse 15, where the implication would be: 'Did you think you could be undetected?' It also meets the objection, such as it is, that divining by means of a cup is not otherwise clearly attested for the Egypt of this period.

Divining, whether by attaching meanings to the movements of liquids in a cup (and to other random configurations, *cf.* Ezk. 21:21) or by a kind of crystal-gazing, is fundamentally alien to Israel, to whom God revealed His will explicitly, as Balaam would reluctantly testify: '. . . Neither is there any divination with Israel: At the due time it shall be told to Israel what God is doing' (Nu. 23:23: *cf.* RVmg). Unless this was part of his pose, Joseph here took his colouring from Egypt, in a matter on which no law was as yet in being.

15. See on verse 5.

16. No doubt there was double meaning in the words *God*

---

[1] *Op. cit.*, pp. 172ff., developing a suggestion of A. van Hoonacker

has found out the guilt . . . (RSV), as the heart-searchings of 42:21,22,28 indicate.

44:18–34. Judah's intercession
This noble appeal does not rely only on pathos: it has the cumulative weight of factual reminder (19–23), graphic portraiture (20,24–29,30b) and a selfless concern proved to the hilt in the plea not for mercy but for leave to suffer vicariously (30–34). In its spirit it bears comparison with the intercession of Moses (Ex. 32:9–14, 31f.), though this indeed was made by the innocent for the guilty.

20. RSV's *young* (rather than *little*, AV, RV) does justice to the Hebrew and the context. Benjamin was at least in his twenties, more probably in his thirties, since Joseph was now about forty (*cf.* 37:2; 41:46,53). See also 46:21 and note.

29. See on 42:38.

30. The vivid figure of speech in the last phrase, where *his life* (his *nepeš*) means his very self, is used in 1 Samuel 18:1 of Jonathan's devotion to David.

45:1–15. Joseph makes himself known
The certainty that God's will, not man's, was the controlling reality in every event, shines out as Joseph's guiding light and the secret of his astonishing lack of rancour (see on verse 5). It was applied theology, God's truth releasing the will for constructive effort and the emotions for healing affection. In this passage strong feeling and sound spiritual argument complete the work of reconciliation which had called for surgical severity throughout the early stages. It had been a task for the whole man, patiently sustained by conviction and not mere impulse.

3. This question, after all that Judah had been saying, illustrates the fact that to *live*, in the Old Testament, tends to include the idea of enjoying health and well-being (as in verse 27, where 'revived' is lit. 'lived'; *cf.* also Lv. 18:5; Dt. 8:3; Pr. 14:30; Hab. 2:4; *etc.*).

4. On Joseph's allusion to being *sold* – so relevant to this

tense moment, yet so embarrassing to the critical analysis –
see Additional Note to chapter 37, p. 185.

5. The words, *you sold me . . . God sent me*, are one of the
classic statements of providential control. This biblical realism,
to see clearly the two aspects of every event – on the one hand
human mishandling (and the blind working of nature), on
the other the perfect will of God – and to fix attention on the
latter as alone being of any consequence, was to be supremely
exemplified in Gethsemane, where Jesus accepted His betrayal
as 'the cup which the Father has given me' (Jn. 18:11). *Cf.*
verse 8; 50:20; Psalm 76:10; Acts 2:23; 4:28; 13:27; Romans
8:28; Philippians 1:12.

6. On this note of time, see on 41:46.

7. Although the whole family would in fact survive, Joseph's
words *a remnant* and *a great deliverance* (AV, RV) emphasize the
peril it had escaped, one of the Old Testament's many crises
of judgment and salvation.

8. *Not you . . . but God* expresses the fact of Providence (see
on verse 5, above) in a typically sweeping biblical idiom. For
this idiom, *cf.* the 'not . . . but . . .' of John 6:27; 15:16; and
the alternative way of putting such contrasts, in Hosea 6:6b.

The phrase *a father to Pharaoh*, a recognized title of viziers
and high officials, J. Vergote interprets as virtually 'king's
adviser'.[1] See also footnote to 41:42.

9. Notice that *God* is the subject of Joseph's first sentence
to his father.

10. *Goshen* is a name which remains unattested, so far, in
Egyptian remains; but 47:11 gives us the name it bore in
later times, 'the land of Rameses'. This name, coupled with
the fact that the district was fertile (47:6) and *near* to Joseph
at court, suggests that it was in the eastern part of the Nile
delta, near Tanis, the seat of the Hyksos[2] kings of the seven-
teenth century and of the Ramessides of the thirteenth century,
the probable periods of Joseph and Moses respectively.

[1] *Op. cit.*, pp. 114f.
[2] The Hyksos ('Chiefs of Foreign Lands') were Semitic invaders who
dominated Egypt from about 1720 to 1580 BC. After their expulsion,
until the founding of the Nineteenth Dynasty, the Pharaohs ruled chiefly
from Thebes, some 400 miles to the south.

45:16–28. Pharaoh sends for Israel

This royal invitation, for Joseph's sake, to an Israel near the
end of hope, and to ten brothers burdened with guilt, can
hardly fail to remind the Christian of the divine 'come . . . and
I will give . . .' (*cf.* verse 18), couched in such terms of welcome
and challenge. But historically this is a turning-point of a
different kind, long foretold (15:13–16): the beginning of a
phase of isolation (where the family, thoroughly alien, could
multiply without losing its identity), and of eventual bondage
and deliverance which would produce a people that for ever
after knew itself redeemed as well as called.

21. The name *Israel* is, to critical scholars, an anomaly
in this section, which is attributed to a source (E) which should
speak only of Jacob (see Additional Note to chapter 42, p. 201).
The stock expression *sons of Israel* could account for it here,
but not in verse 28, and the weakness of the theory is particularly evident in 46:2.

23. On the antiquity of the word *māzôn* (*provision*, RSV),
which used to be considered a late Aramaism, see D. J.
Wiseman in *Tyndale House Bulletin*, 14, June 1964, p. 11.

24. Joseph's parting shot was realistic, for the ancient
crime was now bound to come to light before their father, and
mutual accusations were likely to proliferate (*cf.* 42:22).

46:1–7. God's blessing on the journey

1. The place and character of Jacob's worship indicate his
frame of mind, for *Beer-sheba* had been Isaac's chief centre.
In addressing God as *God of his father* he was acknowledging the
family calling, and implicitly seeking leave to move out of
Canaan. His attitude was very different from that of Abram
in 12:10ff.

2. See on 45:21.

3, 4. God's answer spoke to Jacob's concern (see above) and
added a new detail to the old promise made at Beth-el:
namely, that the growth to nationhood would take place in
Egypt (*there*, 3). So little is God tied to one locality. But the
promise of Canaan remained (*cf.* Rom. 11:29), and Egypt was

in the long run a step towards it – as foreshadowed to Abram in 15:13ff.

Notice in verse 4 the quick transition from the corporate sense of *thee* in the middle phrase, to the quite individual *thine* at the end. The thin boundary between the two may have a bearing on the interpretation of, *e.g.*, the Servant passages in Isaiah, as corporate and individual in different contexts.

The reference of the last phrase is probably to Joseph's closing of Israel's eyes for him at death – a contrast to the troubled end he had predicted for himself in 37:35.

46:8-27. Jacob's family of seventy
This list arranges the family into its Leah and Rachel groups: first the descendants of Leah and her handmaid Zilpah (thirty-three plus sixteen), then those of Rachel and Bilhah (fourteen plus seven). This gives a total of seventy, according to the sub-totals listed in verses 15,18,22,25. But Dinah (15) must be added, making seventy-one, and five names subtracted (Er and Onan, buried in Canaan, verse 12; Joseph, Manasseh and Ephraim, already in Egypt, verse 20), to arrive at the number of Jacob's progeny who actually travelled with him (*i.e.*, sixty-six, verse 26). Verse 27 then adds Joseph's two sons and, by implication, Joseph himself and Jacob, to give the total of 'all the souls of the house of Jacob' who had arrived in Egypt sooner or later in the story. The daughters-in-law, although members of the family, are not reckoned in these totals, which refer only to actual descendants of Jacob (verse 26).

9. *Hanoch* is the name better known as Enoch; for its meaning, see on 4:17.

12. Judah's family history is given in chapter 38.

21. That Benjamin could already have ten sons would agree with other indications of his age: see on 44:20. However, from Numbers 26:38-40 and 1 Chronicles 7:6ff.; 8:1ff. it appears that some of these names are of grandsons, presumably included by anticipation (*cf.* Heb. 7:10).

26, 27. On these two totals, see the opening comment to this paragraph.

46:28–34. Joseph and his father reunited

28. Judah's mission is most simply understood as that of escorting Joseph to his family in Goshen. To *show the way* (RV) would admittedly be an act of courtesy rather than necessity, unless indeed the family had agreed with Judah on a rendezvous. RSV substitutes *to appear before him in Goshen* (a slight change in the Hebrew, indicated by LXX), but as Joseph was not yet in Goshen this makes little sense.

30. In its way, this is an Old Testament *Nunc Dimittis*. Almost all of Jacob's recorded words since 37:35 are of death, and continue to be so, but after the turning-point of 45:28 the bitterness is largely replaced by a sense of fulfilment and hope.

34. The Egyptians' abhorrence of shepherds has sometimes been ascribed to their bitter memories of the Hyksos rulers, after their expulsion, as 'shepherd kings'. But this interpretation of their name seems to have been the misunderstanding of a later age, and Joseph's period probably fell within their régime, not after it.[1] A more likely explanation is that of J. Vergote,[2] that this is only the perennial antipathy of the town-dweller for the nomad or the gipsy. Joseph saw the importance of emphasizing this, to ensure that Pharaoh's good-will would be to the family's real benefit, not to their detriment by drawing them into an alien way of life at the capital.

47:1–12. Joseph's family before Pharaoh

It was through Joseph's wise advice in 46:33f. that his brothers knew what they wanted and made no secret of what they were; the interview is a good model of straightforward, peaceable dealings between a pilgrim people and the temporal power (*cf.* 1 Pet. 2:11–17).

As for Jacob, he is sovereign old age personified: unimpressed by rank (7b,10; *cf.* Heb. 7:7), diffuse and deliberate, taking an independent view of events, and making sombre comparisons with the past. It is a masterly little portrait.

11. *The land of Rameses* is the later name, current in Moses' day (*cf.* Ex. 1:11), for Goshen. For its probable location, see on 45:10.

[1] See footnote to 45:10.   [2] *Op. cit.*, pp. 188f.

47:13-27. Joseph's economic policy

It was axiomatic in the ancient world that one paid one's way so long as one had anything to part with – including, in the last resort, one's liberty. Israelite law accepted the principle, while modifying it with the right of redemption (Lv. 25:25ff.). Joseph's tactics were therefore remarkable chiefly for their thoroughness on the king's behalf. It has been suggested that he used commercial means, buying up the glut of grain with royal money in the good years;[1] but it is simpler to take it that he imposed a levy, as he initially recommended in 41:34, by authority.

19ff. Commenting on a later Pharaoh, A. H. Gardiner says, 'there is ample evidence that he considered himself the owner of all Egyptian property whatsoever'.[2] On Joseph's achievement K. A. Kitchen observes that 'Joseph's economic policy in Genesis 47:16–19 simply made Egypt in fact what it always was in theory: the land became Pharaoh's property and its inhabitants his tenants'.[3]

21. The Hebrew text, as in AV, RV (*he removed them to the cities*), perhaps suits a situation which called for a simplified pattern of distribution. On the other hand the remedy is so drastic that the alternative text (*he made slaves of them*, RSV) makes better sense in view of the people's own declaration in verses 19,25 (' we will be slaves') and of Joseph's distribution of seed to sow (23). RSV follows LXX and the Samaritan text.

22. It is worth pointing out[4] that this passage speaks of a priestly exemption only from the harvest tax, not from dues of other kinds.

47:28-31. Jacob names his burial-place

'The dying Israelite', as R. Martin-Achard has said, 'seems to be less concerned about the unknown world he is entering

---

[1] So Vergote, p. 192, in conformity with his theory that Joseph was no more than controller of crown property; but see on 41:43.
[2] *The Wilbour Papyrus. II. Commentary* (O.U.P., 1948), p. 202 (cited by Vergote, p. 191).
[3] *NBD*, p. 659a.
[4] *Cf.* Vergote, *loc. cit.*, Kitchen, *loc. cit.*

than about the future of God's people.'[1] This will be directly
evident in the next two chapters; here it is indirect, in Jacob's
sense of continuity: he must go where he belongs, and this is
neither the Egypt of Joseph nor the Mesopotamia of his
ancestors, but the land promised 'to Abraham and his seed
for ever'. *Cf.* the opening comments on chapters 23 and 48.

28. On the patriarchal life-span see on 12:14.

29. For the placing of the hand under the thigh, *cf.* 24:2.

30. Although the sequence should perhaps not be pressed,
RV gives the nearest idea of the Hebrew with its *when I sleep
with my fathers, thou shalt carry me . . .* ; it strengthens the
impression that the ancestral reunion was felt to be only
symbolized, not created, by burial in the family place. Jacob
would have joined them before his body was laid with theirs.
Cf. on 25:8.

31. The MT has *bed* (*miṭṭâ*), but the LXX (used in Heb. 11:21)
interpreted the same Hebrew consonants to represent *maṭṭeh*,
'staff'. While both versions have 'bed' at 48:2, the present
occasion tells of Jacob before his last illness (*cf.* 48:1), and
'staff' may well be the right meaning. It would be an appropriate object to mention, as the symbol of his pilgrimage
(*cf.* his grateful words in 32:10), worthy of the prominence
it receives in the New Testament passage.

48:1–22. Jacob blesses Ephraim and Manasseh

Out of Jacob's long career Hebrews 11:21 selects this as his
outstanding act of faith. It has the quality, praised in that
chapter, of reaching out towards the promise, even in face of
death, 'having seen it and greeted it from afar'. There is
gentle irony in the fact that this is just such a situation as
the one on which he had exercised his guile in his youth. Once
more the firstborn's blessing is destined for the younger
brother, but now there is no faithless scheming or bitter
aftertaste (*cf.* Pr. 10:22). It is an object-lesson in quiet
responsiveness and faith.

3. On the name *God Almighty*, see on 17:1; 43:14. *Luz* is
the old name for Beth-el (28:19).

[1] *From Death to Life*, p. 24.

5. This declaration of adoption (*cf.* 16b) left its lasting mark on the structure of Israel, in which Ephraim inherited the headship of the whole twelve, forfeited by Reuben (*cf.* 49:4). 1 Chronicles 5:1,2 states the position: '[Reuben's] birthright was given to the sons of Joseph . . . ; though Judah became strong among his brothers and a prince was from him, yet the birthright belonged to Joseph.'

7. The special place of Joseph in Israel's affections called to mind the beloved Rachel. It is a poignant backward glance in a context of hope; a sudden faltering which betrays itself in the effort with which the old man returns to the present in the next verse.

The expression *to my sorrow* (RSV) has the support of most commentators as the implication of (lit.) 'upon me': *i.e.*, 'as a burden to bear'; *cf.* on 33:13. But the reticence of the Hebrew, with its mere nuance of suffering, is perhaps better preserved by the understatement of AV, RV: simply, *by me.*

8, 9. The question, *Who are these?*, with the reply it elicited, made a fitting prologue to the blessing. *Cf.* the question and answer at the passover (Ex. 12:26f.) and, by contrast, the dialogue at Jacob's own blessing (Gn. 27:18f.).

10-12. This is still the affectionate preliminary to the blessing, confirming Jacob's acceptance of the youths as he takes them between his knees (12; *cf.* verse 5 and note on 30:3). Then Joseph withdraws them[1] and prostrates himself before presenting them for the blessing itself.

13f. On the quiet reversal of the blessings, see the opening comments to the chapter. Jacob had already named the younger before the elder in verse 5, and the ensuing history of Israel would show that God's hand was behind the hands now laid upon them.

15f. *Joseph*, in the opening phrase, is a collective term for the two sons, as in 1 Chronicles 5:2 (quoted in the comment on verse 5, above). It emphasizes that the blessing they are now to enjoy is for his sake, as his representatives.

---

[1] Possibly a symbolic act declaring them Jacob's own issue, as in the adoption rites of a later age. *Cf.* F. Büchsel in Kittel's *Theological Dictionary of the NT* (Eerdmans, 1964) I, p. 669.

The threefold invocation of God opens up many vistas, not by naming His attributes (though there is a place for this: *cf.* Ex. 34:6f.) but by recalling His dealings. He was the God in covenant with *my fathers*, a fact which had steadied Jacob's faith at many crises (*cf.* 28:13; 31:5,42; 32:9; 46:3). By New Testament times, not to say the present, Jacob's two generations would have lengthened impressively: *cf.* Luke 1:50. Turning to his own experience, to say that God had *fed* (AV, RV) or *led* him (RSV) was to acknowledge Him as shepherd: the verb anticipates Psalm 23, and Jacob knew its literal meaning intimately enough (see on 31:38–40). In the expression *the angel* (16) he calls to mind God's visible encounters with him[1] at turning-points of his life, above all at Peniel; and the word *redeemed* expresses the protection and reclamation which a man's *gō'ēl* or kinsman provided in times of trouble (*cf., e.g.,* Lv. 25:25,47ff.; Nu. 35:19 (Heb.); Jb. 19:25).

21. The word 'I' is emphatic here, in conscious opposition ,o the next clause: *cf.* the opening comment on the chapter.

22. This verse is obscure in meaning and allusion. The word translated *portion* in AV, RV is literally 'shoulder': possibly an expression taken from comparing people's heights (*cf.* 1 Sa. 10:23?), or more easily meaning a *mountain slope* (RSV). If the latter, it seems to play on the identical place-name Shechem, which was to fall in Manasseh's territory, at the centre of the area covered by the two Joseph-tribes (*cf.* Jn. 4:5). Speiser proposes the translation 'I give you, as the one above your brothers, Shechem . . . ', taking 'one' to refer to Joseph rather than Shechem; but the run of the sentence hardly suggests it.[2]

The end of the verse possibly refers to the massacre in chapter 34, seen as a token conquest; but it did not lead to the occupation of the city. The fact that Jacob disowned his sons' action (34:30) is less decisive: any spoils of victory

---

[1] 'The angel of God' or of 'the Lord' is a regular Old Testament expression for God manifest in human form. *Cf.* 31:11,13, and note on 16:13,14. See also Introduction, p. 33.
[2] He states that 'one' should be feminine if it referred to shoulder. But shoulder is masculine in Zp. 3:9, the only other occurrence to reveal its gender.

would be counted as his. But the allusion may be to some incident otherwise unrecorded.

49:1-28. The blessing of the twelve sons

This is the last (but for Joseph's dying oath, 50:25) of the great sayings of destiny, the blessings, curses, judgments and promises which punctuate the book of Genesis from the creation story onwards and give it its powerful forward thrust. To those who cannot accept prediction the oracles of this chapter are *vaticinia ex eventibus*, prophecies fabricated from the events they appear to foresee; and because the events are widely separated the speech then must be broken down into a string of sayings uttered over the centuries. But taken as the genuine vision of Jacob, its variable range presents no difficulty: there is no reason why the curtain should fall at the same point for all the tribes, every reason why it should not. As to the general period in view, it is mainly that of the settlement of the twelve in their tribal lands (a nearer sight of the promise that was the lodestar of the three patriarchs), though there is one glimpse (10) of a more distant consummation.

1. This verse, speaking of prediction, and verse 28 with its term 'blessing', sum up the nature of the oracle, which is potent as well as informative: *cf.* Isaac's affirmation in 27:33c,37.

RSV's *days to come* is preferable to *the last* or *the latter days* (AV, RV): the term can be quite general (*cf.* Dt. 31:29), as von Rad points out.

2. The Exordium. The names *Jacob* and *Israel* are used in poetic parallelism (*cf.* verses 7,24), as they will often be in, *e.g.*, Isaiah 40ff. Their different nuances are seldom stressed; it also makes the theory that different sources lie behind them look somewhat artificial.

3, 4. Reuben. The heaping of phrase on majestic phrase in verse 3, building up to an ignominious collapse, reflects the exalted hopes that were shattered at Reuben's fall (reported at 35:22). It would be hard to find a more withering contrast between a man and his calling, or a less flattering account of a '*grande passion*'. In the sudden shift at the end to the third person, *he went up* . . . (AV, RV), Jacob turns and exposes him to his brothers: it is a gesture of revulsion, not to be weakened by LXX's smoother construction in the second person (adopted by RSV).

Unstable (*paḥaz*) is from the root which describes the lawless mob of Judges 9:4 and the wanton prophets of Zephaniah 3:4: it suggests wildness as much as weakness (*cf.* Speiser, 'unruly')[1]. It is this aspect of *water*, so quickly becoming an undisciplined torrent, as in Proverbs 17:14, which is the point of the comparison. Reuben was a man of ungoverned impulse.

The tribe of Reuben was to fail in leadership. It earned a name for irresolution in Deborah's day (Jdg. 5:15b,16); later it seems to have been overshadowed by Gad and periodically overrun by Moab. Its only recorded moment of partial initiative was in the inglorious rebellion of Dathan and Abiram (Nu. 16:1).

It may be added, on a point of criticism, that the oracle makes good sense in its own terms, but becomes very hard to explain as a veiled allusion to a tribal incident.[2] To be sceptical of Reuben's personal existence is therefore not to solve problems but to create them.

5–7. Simeon and Levi. The Old Testament clearly distinguishes a massacre by divine sentence (*cf.* 15:16) from a mere vendetta (*cf.* Am. 1:1,6,9, *etc.*), and this oracle is a neglected witness to the fact. It is important also as a moral judgment on a story told earlier without comment (chapter 34): it makes it clear that the narrator's customary detachment is restraint and not indifference; 'the Judge of all the earth' sees, and cares.

5. This is more than a truism: these men are 'two of a pair', and their weapons are tools of anarchy (*cf.* 6:11), not justice.

---

[1] In Arabic a similar root means 'be boastful'; in Aramaic, 'be lascivious'. Lack of restraint seems to be the common element.

[2] *Cf.* von Rad, *in loc.*: 'If what is said in 4 about the ancestor contains some recollection of a severe crime committed by the tribe of Reuben, it is completely incomprehensible to us . . .'

The final word, not found elsewhere, somewhat resembles the Greek for 'sword'[1] (*cf.* RV, RSV), but there is no agreement on its meaning.

6. *My glory* (RV; *kᵉbōḏî*) is used in some of the Psalms in parallel with *my soul* or heart, as here. The root idea is of something weighty; the LXX version 'my liver' (*kᵉbēḏî*) could be right, since the vital organs are used figuratively of the life or emotions in many languages.

The name Levi ('joined', 29:34) may well have suggested the unholy alliance from which Jacob recoils in the words *be not . . . united*. But *united* is from another Hebrew root.

The poetry pinpoints two details from the massacre (the second of them unrecorded before):[2] the terms *man* and *ox* (RV) are vivid singulars for plurals. It might be rendered: "'Twas in their anger they killed men, and at their whim they crippled oxen.' It was the ruthlessness of spite, to be utterly disowned for its motive and, in 7a, its excess.

7. The eventual history of the two tribes is an instance of the openness of God's decrees, which have nothing of the fixity of fate (*cf.* Je. 18:7f.). Both tribes were scattered; but while Simeon disintegrated, to be sprinkled partly amongst Judah (*cf.* Jos. 19:2–9 with 15:26–32 and Ne. 11:25–28), partly amongst the northern tribes (2 Ch. 34:6), Levi was awarded an honourable dispersion as the priestly element in Israel (Ex. 32:26,29; Nu. 18:20,23; 35:2–8).

8–12. Judah. In length and eloquence this blessing is only matched by that on Joseph, which it far outdistances in its range of prophecy. It pivots on the 'until' clause of 10b. Up to that point the theme is the fierce dominance of the tribe among its fellows (8b, 9). Then with the advent of the promised one,

---

[1] Hebrew *mᵉkērâ*, *cf.* Greek *machaira*? The two forms could have a common ancestry, or the one be borrowed from the other (see Gordon, *Antiquity*, XXX, 1956, p. 23), since there were contacts between Semitic and Indo-European peoples in the Canaan of this period. But the resemblance may be fortuitous, and there are several Hebrew roots which could have yielded *mᵉkērâ*. E.g., Speiser hazards the meaning 'wares', from *mkr*, 'to sell, trade'.

[2] But 'ox' (*šôr*) may mean 'leading citizen', as B. Vawter points out in *CBQ*, XVII, 1955, p. 4, on the analogy of Keret III.iv.19.

who will rule the nations, the scene becomes an earthly paradise such as the prophets foretell in their Messianic poems. It is a miniature of the biblical scheme of history.

8. *Praise* is a play on Judah's name: see 29:35.

9. On Judah as the *lion*, *cf.* Balaam's oracle on Israel (Nu. 24:9). The word rendered *lioness* in RV, RSV, and *old lion* in AV, is simply a variant Hebrew term for lion. If Judah is 'the lion of the tribes', as H. B. Swete[1] comments on Revelation 5:5, '. . . the noblest son of the tribe of Judah is fitly styled the Lion of that tribe'; but the New Testament sees Him displaying a finer strength than the lion's. 'I saw a Lamb standing, as though it had been slain' (Rev. 5:6).

10. The verse as a whole predicts leadership for Judah (*cf.* Nu. 2:9; 10:14; Jdg. 1:1,2) up to the time denoted by the 'until' clause, and (to judge by the buoyant tone of the oracle) still more from that time onwards (*cf., e.g.*, the 'until' of 28:15).

On the precise meaning of this clause it is still unsafe to dogmatize. *Shiloh* (AV, RV) is not elsewhere a biblical title of the Messiah, nor has it any clear meaning as a word. The alternative construction, 'until he comes to Shiloh', corresponds to no Messianic event. But an early variant, revocalizing a shortened spelling of the consonants as *šellōh*, yields either 'till what is his comes' (*i.e.* 'till Judah's full heritage appears'; *cf.* LXX) or 'until he comes, to whom [it belongs]' (*cf.* RSV). The latter, elliptical though it is, seems to be taken up and interpreted by Ezekiel 21:26f. (MT 31f.) in words addressed to the last king of Judah: 'Remove the mitre, and take off the crown . . . *until he come whose right it is*: and I will give it to him.' Here is the best support for the Messianic content which Jewish and Christian exegesis has found in the saying from earliest times.[2]

[1] *The Apocalypse of St. John* (Macmillan, 1906), *in loc.*

[2] Among other interpretations, Speiser draws attention to a Midrashic vocalization of the existing consonants as *šay lōh*: 'until tribute comes to him', supported by Is. 18:7. The suggestion that Shiloh represents an Akkadian word *šēlu* or *šīlu*, ruler or counsellor (so Halévy, *Journal Asiatique*, 1910, pp. 383f., and, independently, G. R. Driver, *JTS*, XXIII, 1921–2, p. 70, and others), is attacked by W. L. Moran as a 'lexicographical myth', *šīlu* in fact meaning no more than 'hole' (*Bib.*, XXXIX, 1958, pp. 405–425).

11, 12. Every line of these verses speaks of exuberant, intoxicating abundance: it is the golden age of the Coming One,[1] whose universal rule was glimpsed in 10c. It is deliberately the language of excess: the reveller of 12a (whose 'redness of eyes' in real life is more coolly received in Pr. 23:29)[2] is startling enough, but verse 11 has already thrown care and thrift to the winds, with its talk of vines used as hitching-posts and wine as washing-water. In its own material terms it bids adieu to the pinched régime of thorns and sweat for 'the shout of them that triumph, the song of them that feast'. Jesus announced the age to come in just this imagery in His first 'sign' at Cana of Galilee.

13-15. Zebulun and Issachar. Zebulun's allotted land in Joshua 19:10-16 did not reach the coast, unlike the neighbouring Asher's (*cf.* Jdg. 5:17), nor did it closely approach Sidon. But it was near enough to both to be enriched by sea-borne trade (to 'suck the abundance of the seas', Dt. 33:19), and the prepositions in the verse could mean 'towards'. Another possibility, suggested by M. Noth,[3] is that in early days Zebulun, Dan and Asher (*cf.* Jdg. 5:17) paid for their settlement on territory dominated by Sidon, by providing *forced labour* (as Issachar did to an overlord further south, 15b) in the Sidonian ports.

In verse 14 AV's *two burdens*,[4] *i.e.*, panniers, is favoured by modern commentators, and suits the portrait of a tribe rather too willing to trade its liberty for the material things of life.

16-18. Dan. After the impressive opening, the anticlimax of verse 17 reveals the same gulf between calling and achieve-

---

[1] For quite another (but over-ingenious) reading of this oracle, as an allusively ironical comment on Judah's doings in Gn. 37 and 38, see E. M. Good, *JBL*, LXXXII, 1963, pp. 427-432.

[2] The blear-eyed drinker in Proverbs makes the translation 'darker than wine . . . whiter than milk' rather unlikely. It would in any case be a digression from the theme of plenty.

[3] *The History of Israel* (A. and C. Black, 1958), p. 79.

[4] At this word's other occurrence, Jdg. 5:16, the meaning 'sheepfolds' would seem easier; but possibly the picture there owes something to the present verse, and depicts a beast refusing to move with its load.

ment that was Reuben's disgrace in verses 3 and 4. Dan's name and call were to *judge*, vindicating the disconsolate as God had vindicated Rachel (30:6); but his choice, as a tribe, was violence and treachery, as in Judges 18. In the list of tribes which make up the Israel of Revelation 7:5-8, Dan finds no place.

Jacob's heartfelt aside in 18 is enigmatic: it could arise from a father's prayers, like Abraham's for Ishmael (17:18), or possibly from the sudden memory of his own treachery, long renounced, called up by the acts and the words (*heel(s)*, 17,19) associated with his own name. See on 25:26.

19. Gad. Four of the six Hebrew words of this verse consist of Gad's name and of word-plays on it. This may indicate that AV was right to translate it 'a troop' in 30:11; but puns can go by sound as well as sense (*cf.* the Hebrew of Is. 10:30: 'poor Anathoth'). Border raids were indeed to be his lot in Transjordan; the ninth-century Moabite Stone[1] records a sample of them. With his blessing, austere but bracing, *cf.* Julian of Norwich: 'He said not – " Thou shalt not be tempested, thou shalt not be travailed . . .": but he said: "Thou shalt not be overcome".'[2]

20. Asher. With a fertile plain and trade routes to the sea, Asher would 'dip his foot in oil' (Dt. 33:24) and produce a notable annual quota for the palace (*cf.* 1 Ki. 4:7). The contrast with the previous verse brings out the diversity that would enrich the fellowship of Israel, while the corresponding danger of disunity shows through in Judges 5:17.

21. Naphtali. This highland tribe was to win a name for itself under Barak by leading Israel to break loose from a crippling bondage (Jdg. 4 and 5). The *goodly words* of AV, RV are an abrupt transition, and apart from Barak's share in the

---

[1] See, *e.g.*, *DOTT*, p. 196.
[2] *Revelations of Divine Love*, ed. Grace Warrack (Methuen, 1949), p. 169, quoted by H. A. Williams in *Soundings* (C.U.P., 1962), p. 83.

song of Deborah (Jdg. 5:1) nothing of this kind is known to us in Naphtali. RSV's *comely fawns* is more probable, and involves no change of text: this free, mountain people, in other words, will breed true, and keep its character.

22-26. Joseph. There are obscurities of detail here, but an impressive eloquence. As translated in AV, RV, RSV, the thought moves from the present, the summer of Joseph's days, back to the stresses of the past, and behind both to God, whose array of titles forms the rich centrepiece of the oracle. Then His profusion of blessings is called down on Joseph, carrying the thought on into the future.

22. The well-watered, far-spreading fruit tree delightfully pictures Joseph's depth of character and width of influence, and the fact that it takes up his own metaphor, enshrined in the name Ephraim (41:52), supports the familiar translation of AV, RV, RSV. But the meaning is far from obvious in the Hebrew, which is full of ambiguities and grammatical anomalies.[1]

24. Both here and elsewhere (Is. 1:24; 49:26; 60:16; also, less obviously, Ps. 132:2,5) the word *'aḇîr*, *Mighty One*, is used of God as champion of His cause. On the special link with *Jacob*, see the second footnote at 31:42.

The phrase, *By the name (miššēm) of the Shepherd* (RSV), corresponds well with the expression *By the hands . . .* , just before, and entails no change in the consonantal text. The traditional pointing, *From thence (miššām) is the shepherd* (AV, RV), creates an abrupt aside and an impersonal reference to God,[2] for no apparent reason.

25. On the significance for Jacob of *the God of thy father*, see on 46:1. On the term *Almighty (šadday)* see on 17:1.

26. In the light of Deuteronomy 33:15, RSV is almost certainly right in reading (with LXX) *the eternal mountains*, in

---

[1] A case can be made for seeing metaphors from the animal world instead, as in Dt. 33:17. See the discussions of Speiser, *in loc.*, and B. Vawter in *CBQ*, XVII, 1955, pp. 7ff.

[2] For a parallel to 'thence', as meaning 'from God', Delitzsch cites 'there' in Ec. 3:17. But in Ec. the contrast with this earth (3:16) gives point to the expression.

place of MT's *my progenitors unto* (it is the difference between Hebrew *w* and the similar *r*), and in the translation *bounties* (lit. 'desirable thing(s)') rather than *the utmost bound* (AV, RV).

In a few magnificent words the Old Testament vision of God's 'earth with its store of wonders untold' is displayed. Even *the deep* (*tᵉhôm*; *cf.* 1:2), couching like a powerful beast (*cf.* verse 9), belongs to Him and to His servants. A foretaste of this blessing would come in the award to Ephraim and Manasseh of the pick of all Canaan, with presumably greater things to follow. If, in the event, the enjoyment of even this was insecure and brief, the reason can be found in Ephraim's pride (Jdg. 8:1; 12:1) and suicidal apostasy (Ho. 4:17; 5:3ff. and *passim*).

The final phrase, *separate from his brothers*, speaks of one singled out, not left out: the word is later used of the Nazirite, set apart for God.

27. Benjamin. It is striking that Moses was given the tender oracle to pronounce on Benjamin (Dt. 33:12), and doting Jacob the fierce one. Something of the dash and spirit of the tribe can be seen in Judges 5:14; Psalm 68:27; something of its violence in Judges 19–21.

49:29 – 50:3. The death of Jacob

On Jacob's fine attitude to his approaching death, see on 47:28–31.

31. Leah's death in Canaan is mentioned only here, though it was implied in her absence from the list of emigrants in 46:8ff.

33. The phrase, *yielded up the ghost* (AV, RV), translates a single Hebrew word, a synonym for 'died'; it has nothing in common with the expression 'gave up his spirit', used of our Lord's voluntary death (Jn. 19:30).

50:2. Since embalmers and physicians were members of distinct professions, Joseph's use of the latter has seemed anomalous to some writers. J. Vergote, however, points out that physicians were more than competent to perform the task, and that Joseph might well have wished to avoid the magico-religious rites of the professional embalmers.[1]

3. The embalming period was seldom less than a month, and when the art was at its height, from the 18th Dynasty onwards (*i.e.* a period beginning a century or two after Jacob's death), it normally took seventy days.[2] The mourning period for Jacob, as von Rad observes, was, significantly, very little short of the seventy-two days observed for a Pharaoh.

50:4-13. Jacob's burial

Once more the patriarchal sepulchre is prominent in the story as the one remaining stake in the promised land, and Jacob's family, with its attendant company of Gentiles rehearses, so to speak in miniature and in the minor, the ultimate home-coming of his sons, one day to be escorted to their inheritance 'from all the nations . . . upon horses, and in chariots' (Is. 66:20).

5. The word translated *digged* (AV, RV) or *hewed out* (RSV) could equally be rendered 'bought' (RVmg), from a root found in Deuteronomy 2:6; Hosea 3:2; and this seems preferable.

10. This site is unknown, but its position implies a detour round the Dead Sea to approach Hebron from the north-east instead of the south-west. Presumably there was political unrest at some point, which the cavalcade's arrival would have been in danger of aggravating. At the Exodus the direct route would again be impracticable (Ex. 13:17). But the mention of *the Canaanites* (11) indicates that the mourning took place on the west side of the Jordan: 'near' the river, not *beyond* it.[3] *I.e*, the party had now crossed into Canaan; it was a suitable moment for the pause.

Abel-mizraim contains a word-play, in that *'āḇēl* (*cf.* 37:35) can mean *mourning*, like the more common *'ēḇel*, but can also mean 'watercourse' or 'field'. *Mizraim* is Egypt.

---

[1] *Op. cit.*, pp. 197ff.   [2] *Ibid.*

[3] B. Gemser, in *VT*, II, 1952, pp. 349-355, shows that *b 'ēḇer hayyardēn* regularly means 'in the region of the Jordan' rather than 'beyond' it. He also points out that Jerome located Atad a little south of Jericho (at Beth-hagla: *cf.* Delitzsch, *in loc.*). This is Benjamite territory.

50:14-21. Joseph reassures his brothers

The manner of telling the story strongly suggests (*pace* von Rad) that the message in Jacob's name was fictitious. It was this, surely, together with the arm's-length approach (16), telling its own tale of fear and mistrust, that moved Joseph to tears.

Each sentence of his threefold reply is a pinnacle of Old Testament (and New Testament) faith. To leave all the righting of one's wrongs to God (19; *cf.* Rom. 12:19; 1 Thes. 5:15; 1 Pet. 4:19); to see His providence in man's malice (20; *cf.* on 45:5), and to repay evil not only with forgiveness but also with practical affection (21; *cf.* Lk. 6:27ff.), are attitudes which anticipate the adjective 'Christian' and even 'Christlike'. Note that in verse 21 the *I* is emphatic: Joseph was promising something more personal than philanthropy.

50:22-26. The death of Joseph

It is perhaps a crowning touch to Joseph's honour in Egypt that he was granted a life-span generally regarded there as ideally desirable.[1] However this may be, to see even one's grandchildren was a proverbial blessing (*cf.* Ps. 128:6; Pr. 17:6), and *Machir* was to found a vigorous clan in Manasseh (Jos. 17:1; Jdg. 5:14). On the expression *upon Joseph's knees* (23) see on 30:3.

The book of Genesis, like the Old Testament in microcosm, ends by pointing beyond its own story. Man had travelled far from Eden to *a coffin*, and the chosen family far from Canaan to *Egypt*, but Joseph's 'charge concerning his bones' was a gesture of faith (Heb. 11:22), which would not be disappointed (Ex. 13:19; Jos. 24:32). No funeral procession like Jacob's was to set out for Canaan: the matter could bide God's time and a better exodus. So the promise was signified as well as spoken, and would germinate one day in the mind of Moses (*cf.* Acts 7:23,25) to awaken him to his mission. Joseph's dying words epitomized the hope in which the Old Testament, and indeed the New (*cf.* Rev. 22:20), would fall into expectant silence: *God will surely visit you.*

---

[1] No less than twenty-seven references to such an age, from all periods, have been collected by J. M. A. Janssen (cited by Vergote, pp. 200f.).